beginner's mandarin chinese
elizabeth scurfield and
song lianyi

teach yourself
1938
2008
celebrate
with us

Launched in 1938, the **teach yourself** series
grew rapidly in response to the world's wartime
needs. Loved and trusted by over 50 million
readers, the series has continued to respond to
society's changing interests and passions and
now, 70 years on, includes over 500 titles,
from Arabic and Beekeeping to Yoga and Zulu.
What would you like to learn?

be where you want to be with **teach yourself**

For UK order enquiries: please contact Bookpoint Ltd, 130 Milton Park, Abingdon, Oxon, OX14 4SB. Telephone: +44 (0) 1235 827720. Fax: +44 (0) 1235 400454. Lines are open 09.00–17.00, Monday to Saturday, with a 24-hour message answering service. Details about our titles and how to order are available at www.teachyourself.co.uk

For USA order enquiries: please contact McGraw-Hill Customer Services, PO Box 545, Blacklick, OH 43004-0545, USA. Telephone: 1-800-722-4726. Fax: 1-614-755-5645.

For Canada order enquiries: please contact McGraw-Hill Ryerson Ltd, 300 Water St, Whitby, Ontario, L1N 9B6, Canada. Telephone: 905 430 5000. Fax: 905 430 5020.

Long renowned as the authoritative source for self-guided learning – with more than 50 million copies sold worldwide – the **teach yourself** series includes over 500 titles in the fields of languages, crafts, hobbies, business, computing and education.

British Library Cataloguing in Publication Data: a catalogue record for this title is available from the British Library.

Library of Congress Catalog Card Number: on file.

First published in UK 1996 by Hodder Education, 338 Euston Road, London, NW1 3BH.

First published in US 1996 by The McGraw-Hill Companies, Inc.

This edition published 2008.

The **teach yourself** name is a registered trade mark of Hodder Headline.

Typeset by Graphicraft Limited, Hong Kong.

Printed in Great Britain for Hodder Education, a division of Hodder Headline, an Hachette Livre UK Company, 338 Euston Road, London, NW1 3BH, by CPI Cox & Wyman, Reading, Berkshire, RG1 8EX.

The publisher has used its best endeavours to ensure that the URLs for external websites referred to in this book are correct and active at the time of going to press. However, the publisher and the author have no responsibility for the websites and can make no guarantee that a site will remain live or that the content will remain relevant, decent or appropriate.

Hodder Headline's policy is to use papers that are natural, renewable and recyclable products and made from wood grown in sustainable forests. The logging and manufacturing processes are expected to conform to the environmental regulations of the country of origin.

Impression number	10	9	8	7	6	5	4	3	2	
Year		2012		2011		2010		2009		

contents

Dedications

In memory of a much loved mother, Ella Jessie Scurfield, whose loving spirit and quiet courage will always be with me.

To Rong, my wife, whose support has been invaluable.

Acknowledgements

Our grateful thanks to all those who made this publication possible. In particular we wish to thank our two editors, Virginia Catmur and Rebecca Green, for all their encouragement and support.

About the authors

Elizabeth Scurfield graduated with a First Class Honours degree in Chinese from the School of Oriental and African Studies in London. She has over 30 years' experience of teaching Chinese to beginners successfully. She is former Chair of the Department of Modern Languages at the University of Westminster in London.

Song Lianyi grew up and was educated in Beijing. He has taught Chinese as a foreign language for more than 17 years. He is at present Lecturer in Chinese at the School of Oriental and African Studies, London. He completed his PhD in language teaching techniques at the Institute of Education, University of London.

about the course

Teach Yourself Beginner's Mandarin Chinese is the right course for you if you are a complete beginner or feel that you need to start back at the beginning again to rebuild your confidence. It is a self-study course which will help you to understand and speak Chinese sufficiently well to function effectively in basic everyday situations, both business and social. The course will also offer you an insight into Chinese culture and there is even an opportunity for you to find out something about the Chinese writing system if you want to.

Which Chinese will you be learning?

In one form or another, Chinese is the language most spoken in the world. It has many different spoken forms, but they are all written in almost exactly the same way, the difference being that the simplified script is used in the People's Republic of China and in Singapore and that full-form characters are used in Taiwan and Hong Kong (this may change in the future in the case of Hong Kong). The characters used in this book are always in the simplified script. For more information on the Chinese script, you can refer to *Teach Yourself Beginner's Chinese Script* and to *Teach Yourself Chinese*.

More than 70 per cent of Chinese people speak the northern dialect so the national language is based on this. More Chinese speakers can understand this national language than any other form of Chinese so it is what you will be learning in this book. In China it is called **Pǔtōnghuà** 'common speech', but it is sometimes referred to in the West as Modern Standard Chinese.

What is romanization?

Chinese cannot be written using a phonetic alphabet in the way that European languages can. It is written in characters. You will find out more about characters in Unit 11. Various ways have been devised for representing Chinese sounds alphabetically. The standard form in use today is known as pīnyīn (literally 'spell sound') and is what we have used in this book. In 1958 pīnyīn was adopted as the official system of romanization in the People's Republic of China. Please note that pīnyīn is not an accurate phonetic transliteration of Chinese sounds for English speakers.

How the course works

The book is divided into two main parts. Units 1 to 10 introduce you to the basic structures and grammatical points you'll need in everyday situations. These units should be taken in order as each builds on the previous ones.

Units 12 to 21 deal with everyday situations such as booking into a hotel, changing money, buying tickets, seeing a doctor, travelling and being entertained in a Chinese home. They give you the opportunity to put into practice and consolidate the language you have learnt in the first ten units. You can take these units in any order, although the vocabulary does build up from unit to unit.

A few words about the recording

This book can be successfully used on its own, but you are advised to obtain and use the accompanying recording if at all possible. This will help you to pronounce Chinese correctly and to acquire a more authentic accent. The recorded dialogues and exercises will also give you plenty of practice in understanding and responding to basic Chinese. The **Pronunciation guide** and the new words in the first few units plus items such as the days of the week, the months of the year and simple numbers are all recorded. This will help you to speak Chinese correctly in the important early stages of your study. Readers without the recording will find that there are some units which contain an exercise that cannot be done with the book alone, but a written alternative is always provided.

About Units 1–10

Each unit starts by telling you what you are going to learn in that unit. The **Before you start** section prepares you for the unit ahead. Then there is an easy exercise **Let's try** to get you speaking straight away.

Key words and phrases contain the most important words and phrases from the unit. Try to learn them by heart. They will be used in that unit and in later units. There are various tips throughout the book to help you learn new words.

Dialogue. Move on to the dialogues once you have read the new words a few times. The dialogues will show you how the new words are used and hopefully reinforce them. If you have the recording, listen to each dialogue once or twice without stopping or read through it without looking anything up. You don't have to understand every word to get the gist of it.

Now, using the pause button, break the dialogue into manageable chunks and try repeating each phrase out loud. This will help you gain a more authentic accent. If you don't have the recording, use a ruler or a book mark to cover part of the dialogue so you can concentrate on a small bit at a time. The most important thing in either case is to **speak out loud** because this will help you gain confidence in speaking Chinese.

Learning tips give you advice on everything from how to master vocabulary to how to improve your listening and reading skills and develop confidence in speaking.

Language notes. This section provides you with the nuts and bolts of the language. It goes over all the main grammar and structures for the units along with plenty of examples. Once you are confident about a particular grammar point, try making up your own examples.

Practice/Exercises. Each exercise in this section helps you practise one or more of the points introduced in the **Language notes** section. For some exercises you will need to listen to the recording. It is not essential to have the recording to complete this course and most of these listening exercises can also be completed without them. However, listening to the recording will make your learning easier and provide more variety.

Quick review, at the end of each unit, gives you the opportunity to test yourself on what you have learnt in that unit. In Unit 10 you are given the chance to test yourself on Units 1–10 with a **Halfway review** and to go back over anything you're not sure about. At the end of Unit 21 there is a **Final review**, you will be surprised at how much you have learnt.

i These sections are short notes in English which give you an insight into different aspects of Chinese culture and society and are usually linked to the situations being covered in that particular unit.

In each unit you will find at least one useful sign written in Chinese characters (**Hànzì**) so you can familiarize yourself with what they look like even though you haven't actually learnt any characters.

About Units 12–21

These units give you the opportunity to practise what you have learnt in meaningful and useful situations. The first page of each unit tells you what you are going to learn and under **Revise before you start** there is a check list of the structures you have already learnt which will reappear in that unit. This gives you the opportunity to look at some, or all, of these again and to go over them so you feel fully confident before beginning the unit. You will find that some structures come up time and time again so that you will not find it necessary to revise them after a while. You will also find a short text in Chinese (except for Unit 13 which is in English) about the topics in each unit followed by a comprehension exercise.

Cartoons and **proverbs.** You will find cartoons in some of the units which will give you an insight into Chinese humour and hopefully make you laugh! We have also included some proverbs (written in Chinese characters and in **pīnyīn**) which have some relevance to the topic and add some cross-cultural interest. These are short phrases which have their origins in classical Chinese.

Quick review (As in Units 1–10)

Key to the exercises. The answers to the **Practice/Exercises, Let's try, Quick review, Halfway review** and **Final review** can all be found at the back of the book. Do remember that variations are possible in some of the answers but we couldn't include them all.

Unit 11 – Let's look at Chinese characters!

Contrary to what most people believe, Chinese is not a difficult language to speak – particularly at beginner's level. Pronunciation and grammar are generally straightforward even if they require you to do a few things you're not used to. Even tones are not intrinsically difficult and can be fun, though they do involve a lot of time and practice.

Nobody can say, however, that learning to read and write Chinese characters is easy – fascinating yes, but not easy. That is why we have written this book in pīnyīn, so that the learner can get straight down to speaking Chinese without the barrier of an unknown form of writing.

Unit 11 is a special unit designed to give you the chance to find out something about the origin of Chinese characters and to have a taste of what's involved in reading and writing them. This unit is designed as a 'one-off' so that those of you who would rather concentrate solely on listening and speaking can miss it out without it affecting your understanding of other units.

At the back of the book

At the back of the book is a reference section which contains:

Key to the exercises
A **Chinese–English vocabulary** list containing all the words in the course.
An **English–Chinese vocabulary** list with the most useful words you'll need when expressing yourself in Chinese.

How to be successful at learning Chinese

1 **Little and often** is far more effective than a long session every now and then. Try to do 20–30 minutes a day if you can. If you can't manage that, then set yourself a minimum of 2–3 times a week. Try to make it at roughly the same time each day – when you get up, or at lunchtime, or before you go to bed for instance. This will make it easier for you to get into the habit of studying regularly.

2 **Revise and test yourself regularly.** Find a balance between moving through the book and revising what you have already learnt. If you move forward too quickly, you will find later units difficult and you will get discouraged. Try to avoid this.

3 **Hear yourself speak!** If at all possible, find yourself a quiet place to study where you can speak out loud. You need to build up your speaking and listening skills and your confidence, so make it as easy and as comfortable for yourself as you can.

4 **Find opportunities to speak Chinese.** You don't have to go to China to do this. Join a Chinese class to practise your Chinese with other people, find a Chinese native speaker to help you (but make sure he or she speaks **Pǔtōnghuà**) and find out about Chinese clubs, societies, and so on.

5 **Don't be too harsh on yourself!** Learning a language is a gradual process – you have to keep at it. Don't expect to remember every item of vocabulary and every new structure all at once. The important thing is to get your meaning across. Making mistakes in Chinese will not stop a Chinese person understanding you.

But most of all remember that learning and using a foreign language is fun, particularly when you find you can use what you have learnt in real situations.

Symbols and abbreviations

This indicates that the recording is needed for the following section. (But often there is an alternative way of completing the section if you don't have the recording.)

This indicates information about Chinese culture and society.

| (sing) | singular | (*lit.*) | literally |
| (pl) | plural | (MW) | measure word |

Punctuation

Chinese punctuation is very similar to that of English but a pause-mark (、) is used in lists instead of a comma, even if the list only has two items in it. A comma is used for longer pauses.

Use of apostrophe

An apostrophe (') is used to show where the break comes between
two syllables if there is any possible ambiguity in pronunciation,
for example, **shí'èr** (not **shíèr**), **nǚ'ér** (not **nǚèr**).

Use of hyphens

We have used hyphens to show how words are built up in
Chinese:

Zhōngguó *China* + **rén** *person* → **Zhōngguó-rén** *a Chinese
person*
Déguó *Germany* + **rén**   → **Déguó-rén** *a German person*

A hyphen is also used to link a verbal suffix or verbal complement
to the verb. This will encourage you to say it together with the
verb as it should be said:

Wǒ chī-**guo** Yìndù fàn.	*I've eaten Indian food.*
Tā méi qù-**guo** Zhōngguó.	*He's never been to China.*
Nǐ shuō-**de** hěn màn.	*You speak very slowly.*
Tāmen xiě-**de** bú kuài.	*They don't write quickly.*

In general we have written 'words' separately except where they
are seen as being one idea:

hǎo	*good*	but	**hǎo deduō**	*much better*
		or	**hǎo duōle**	
tā	*he, she, it*	but	**tāde**	*his, hers, its*
xīngqī	*week*	but	**xīngqīyī**	*Monday*
yuè	*month*	but	**yīyuè**	*January*
běn	*measure word for books*	but	**běnzi**	*notebook*

However, verb-objects and so on are separate for clarity:

shuō (verb)	**huà** (object)	*to speak* (speech)
shuō	**Fǎyǔ**	*to speak French*

pronunciation guide

▶ Chinese sounds

Vowels

Here is the list of the Chinese vowels with a rough English equivalent sound and then one or two examples in Chinese. There are single vowels, compound vowels or vowels plus a nasal sound, which will be listed separately.

	Rough English sound	Chinese examples
a	f<u>a</u>ther	b<u>a</u>ba, m<u>a</u>ma
ai	b<u>i</u>te	t<u>ai</u>, z<u>ai</u>
ao	c<u>ow</u>	h<u>ao</u>, zh<u>ao</u>
e	f<u>ur</u>	ch<u>e</u>, h<u>e</u>, g<u>e</u>
ei	pl<u>ay</u>	b<u>ei</u>, g<u>ei</u>, sh<u>ei</u>, f<u>ei</u>
i	t<u>ea</u>	d<u>i</u>d<u>i</u>, feij<u>i</u>, n<u>i</u>
i (after z, c, s, zh, ch, sh and r only)		z<u>i</u>, c<u>i</u>, sh<u>i</u>

The i is there more or less for cosmetic reasons – no syllable can exist without a vowel. Say the consonant and 'sit on it' and you have the sound.

ia	<u>ya</u>rrow	j<u>ia</u>, x<u>ia</u>
iao	m<u>eow</u>	b<u>iao</u>, p<u>iao</u>, <u>yao</u>
ie	<u>ye</u>s	b<u>ie</u>, x<u>ie</u>, <u>ye</u>
iu	<u>yo</u>-yo	l<u>iu</u>, j<u>iu</u>, <u>you</u>

y replaces i at the beginning of a word if there is no initial consonant.

o	m<u>ore</u>	m<u>o</u>yim<u>o</u>, map<u>o</u>
ou	g<u>o</u>	d<u>ou</u>, z<u>ou</u>

u	m<u>oo</u>	b<u>u</u>, zh<u>u</u>
ua	s<u>ua</u>ve	g<u>ua</u>, h<u>ua</u>
uo	<u>war</u>	sh<u>uo</u>, c<u>uo</u>, <u>wo</u>
uai	s<u>wipe</u>	k<u>uai</u>, <u>wai</u>
ui	<u>weigh</u>	d<u>ui</u>, g<u>ui</u>, z<u>ui</u>

w replaces **u** at the beginning of a word if there is no initial consonant.

ü	pn<u>eu</u>monia	j<u>u</u>, q<u>u</u>, l<u>ü</u>, n<u>ü</u>
üe	pn<u>eu</u>matic + <u>air</u> (said quickly)	<u>yue</u>, <u>xue</u>, <u>jue</u>

Note that **ü** and **üe** can occur only with the consonants **n, l, j, q** and **x**. As **j, q** and **x** cannot occur as j+u, q+u or x+u, the umlaut (¨) over the 'u' in **ju, qu** and **xu** has been omitted. **N** and **l**, however, can occur as both **nu** and **nü, lu** and **lü** so the umlaut (¨) has been kept.

yu replaces **ü**, and **yue** replaces **üe** if there is no initial consonant.

Here are the **vowels with a nasal sound** formed with vowels followed by **n** or **ng**. Speak through your nose when you pronounce them and listen carefully to the recording.

	Rough English sound	**Chinese examples**
an	m<u>an</u>	f<u>an</u>, m<u>an</u>
ang	b<u>ang</u>	zh<u>ang</u>, sh<u>ang</u>
en	<u>un</u>der	r<u>en</u>, h<u>en</u>
eng	h<u>ung</u>	d<u>eng</u>, n<u>eng</u>
in	b<u>in</u>	n<u>in</u>, j<u>in</u>, x<u>in</u>
ian	<u>yen</u>	t<u>ian</u>, n<u>ian</u>, q<u>ian</u>
iang	<u>Yang</u>tse (River)	l<u>iang</u>, x<u>iang</u>
ing	f<u>ing</u>er	m<u>ing</u>, q<u>ing</u>, x<u>ing</u>
iong	<u>Jung</u> (the psychoanalyst)	y<u>ong</u>, q<u>iong</u>, x<u>iong</u>
ong	<u>Jung</u>	t<u>ong</u>, c<u>ong</u>, h<u>ong</u>
uan	<u>wan</u>gle	w<u>an</u>, s<u>uan</u>, h<u>uan</u>
un	<u>won</u>	w<u>en</u>, l<u>un</u>, ch<u>un</u>
uang	<u>wrong</u>	w<u>ang</u>, h<u>uang</u>, zh<u>uang</u>
üan	pn<u>eu</u>matic + <u>en</u>d (said quickly)	<u>yuan</u>, q<u>uan</u>, x<u>uan</u>
ün	'<u>une</u>' in French	<u>yun</u>, j<u>un</u>, q<u>un</u>

Note that **ian** is pronounced '**yen**'.

The same rules about **y** replacing **i** and **w** replacing **u** at the beginning of a word if there is no initial consonant also apply to vowels with a nasal sound.

Yuan replaces **üan** and **yun** replaces **ün** if there is no initial consonant.

Consonants

Here is a list of the Chinese consonants, some of which are quite similar to English sounds, others less so. Those that are very different from the nearest English sound are explained.

	Rough English sound	**Chinese examples**
b	<u>b</u>ore	<u>b</u>ai, <u>b</u>ei
p	<u>p</u>oor	<u>p</u>ao, <u>p</u>ang
m	<u>m</u>e	<u>m</u>a, <u>m</u>ei, <u>m</u>ing
f	<u>f</u>an	<u>f</u>an, <u>f</u>eng
d	<u>d</u>oor	<u>d</u>a, <u>d</u>ou, <u>d</u>uo
t	<u>t</u>ore	<u>t</u>a, <u>t</u>ai, <u>t</u>ian
n	<u>n</u>eed	<u>n</u>a, <u>n</u>ü, <u>n</u>ian
l	<u>l</u>ie	<u>l</u>ai, <u>l</u>ei, <u>l</u>iang
z	ad<u>ds</u>	<u>z</u>i, <u>z</u>ai, <u>z</u>uo
c	i<u>ts</u>	<u>c</u>i, <u>c</u>ai, <u>c</u>uo
s	<u>s</u>ay	<u>s</u>i, <u>s</u>ui, <u>s</u>uan

The next four consonants are all made with the tongue loosely rolled in the middle of the mouth.

zh	<u>j</u>elly	<u>zh</u>ao, <u>zh</u>ong, <u>zh</u>u
ch	<u>ch</u>illy	<u>ch</u>e, <u>ch</u>i, <u>ch</u>ang
sh	<u>sh</u>y	<u>sh</u>i, <u>sh</u>ei, <u>sh</u>eng
r	<u>r</u>azor	<u>r</u>e, <u>r</u>i, <u>r</u>ong

The next three consonants are all made with the tongue flat and the corners of the mouth drawn back as far as possible.

j	<u>g</u>enius	<u>j</u>ia, <u>j</u>iao, <u>j</u>ian
q	<u>ch</u>eese	<u>q</u>i, <u>q</u>ian, <u>q</u>u
	(as said in front of the camera!)	
x	<u>sh</u>eet	<u>x</u>iao, <u>x</u>in, <u>x</u>ue
	(rather like a whistling kettle)	

Arch the back of the tongue towards the roof of the mouth for the last three consonants.

g	<u>g</u>uard	<u>g</u>e, <u>g</u>ei, <u>g</u>ui
k	<u>c</u>ard	<u>k</u>ai, <u>k</u>an, <u>k</u>uai
h	lo<u>ch</u>	<u>h</u>e, <u>h</u>uan, <u>h</u>ao

Tones

Chinese is a tonal language. Every syllable in Chinese has its own tone. **Pǔtōnghuà** has four distinct tones plus a neutral tone. This means that syllables which are pronounced the same but have different tones will mean different things. For example,

tang pronounced in the first tone means *soup* but pronounced in the second tone means *sugar*! But don't worry – all the four tones fall within your natural voice range. You don't have to have a particular type of voice to speak Chinese.

The four tones are represented by the following marks which are put over the vowel such as **nǐ** *you* or over the main vowel of a syllable where there are two or three vowels, for example, **hǎo** *good*, but **guó** *country*:

—   1st tone, high and level

╱   2nd tone, rising

∨   3rd tone, falling – rising

╲   4th tone, falling

The diagrams below will help to make this clearer.

Think of **1** as being at the bottom of your voice range and **5** at the top.

1st tone: Pitch it where **you** feel comfortable. Say 'oo' as in 'zoo' and keep going for as long as you can. You should be able to keep it up for maybe half a minute. When you have got used to that, change to another vowel sound and practise that in the same way and so on.

2nd tone: Raise your eyebrows every time you attempt a second tone until you get used to it. This is infallible!

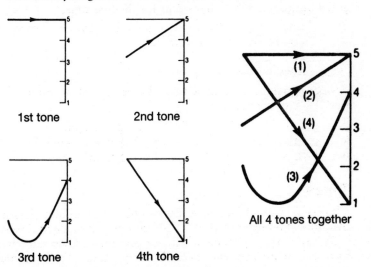

1st tone   2nd tone

3rd tone   4th tone   All 4 tones together

3rd tone: Drop your chin onto your neck and raise it again. Then practise the sound doing the movement at the same time.

4th tone: Stamp your foot gently and then accompany this action with the relevant sound.

Neutral tones: Some syllables in Chinese are toneless or occur in the neutral tone. This means they have no tone mark over the vowel. They are rather like unstressed syllables in English, such as *of a* in 'two of a kind'.

Tone changes
Occasionally syllables may change their tones.

- Two 3rd tones, one after another, are very difficult to say. Where this happens, the first one is said as a 2nd tone. We have still marked it as a 3rd tone in the book otherwise you may think that it is always a 2nd tone which it isn't:

  Nǐ hǎo! (*How do you do?*) is said as **Ní hǎo**.

- If three 3rd tones occur together, the first two are normally said as 2nd tones:

  Wǒ yě hǎo (*I'm OK too*) is said as **Wó yé hǎo**.

- Note that in the phrase **yí ge rén** (*one* measure word *person*), the **ge** is said without a tone although it is actually 4th, but it still carries enough weight to change the **yì** into a 2nd tone.

You will find a few other tone changes in the book. These will be pointed out to you when they occur for the first time.

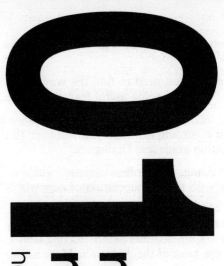

01

nǐ hǎo!
nǐ hǎo ma?

hello! how are you?

In this unit you will learn
- how to say *hello* and *goodbye*
- how to exchange greetings
- how to say *please* and *thank you*
- how to make a simple apology
- how to observe basic courtesies

Before you start

Read about the course on pp. vii–xiii. This gives useful advice on how to make the best of this course.

Everybody learns differently. You need to find the way which works best for you. You will find some useful learning tips in each unit.

Make sure you have your recording handy as you will need this to listen to the **Pronunciation guide** and **Dialogues**.

If you don't have the recording, use the **Pronunciation guide** on pp. xiv–xviii to help you with the pronunciation of new words and phrases.

It's a good idea to listen to the **Pronunciation guide** all the way through and to practise the Chinese tones before starting Unit 1. This way you can make the most of the dialogues. More advice on p. 6.

Remember that studying for 20 minutes regularly is much more effective than occasionally spending two hours in one go.

Try following this study guide and adapt it to your needs as you go along:

1 Listen to the **Dialogues** once or twice without the book (read them if you haven't got the recording).
2 Go over each one, bit by bit, in conjunction with the **Key words and phrases** and **Learning tips** underneath the dialogues.
3 Study the **Language notes** very carefully and make sure that you understand them.
4 Make sure you understand the **Learning tips** on how to pronounce and how to learn.
5 Read the ⓘ sections.
6 Go back to the **Dialogues** and **Key words and phrases** and listen and study for as long as it takes you to grasp them. This time use the pause button. Try reading a new word or phrase out loud after the speaker, then play it again to check your progress.
7 Do the **Practice** section and check your answers in **Key to the exercises** at the back of the book. Test yourself with the **Quick review**.

Now you are ready to start!

Rùkǒu
Entrance

▶ Key words and phrases

bù	*not*
bú yòng xiè	*not at all* (lit. *no need thank*)
bú zài	*not at; to be not at / in*
duìbuqǐ	*excuse me / I'm sorry*
hǎo	*good, well*
. . . hǎo ma?	*How is / are . . . ?*
hěn	*very*
jīntiān	*today*
lái	*to come*
lǎoshī	*teacher*
ma	*(question particle)*
míngtiān	*tomorrow*
míngtiān jiàn	*see you tomorrow*
nǐ	*you* (sing)
Nǐ hǎo! (sing)	*Hello!*
nǐmen	*you* (pl)
Nǐmen hǎo! (pl)	*Hello!*
Qǐng jìn!	*Please come in.*
Qǐng wèn, . . . ?	*May I ask . . . ?*
Qǐng zuò!	*Please sit down.*
tā/tā	*she / he*
tàitai	*Mrs; wife*
xiānsheng	*Mr; husband; gentleman*
xiǎo	*little, young, small*
xièxie	*thank you; to thank*
zài	*at; to be at / in*
zàijiàn	*goodbye*

Learning tips

Read the words and expressions out loud. Concentrate on the pronunciation. Turn back to the **Pronunciation guide** on pp. xiv–xviii and check anything you need to. Especially check out the four tones and the neutral tone. They're quite easy to get the hang of after a little practice.

If you have the recording, listen to the words and repeat them after the speaker using the pause button.

Dialogues

Listen to people saying *hello*, *thank you* and *goodbye* in Chinese. Press the pause button after each person has spoken and repeat out loud.

▶ Dialogue 1 Saying 'hello'

Mr Wang is a tourist guide. He prefers to be called **Xiǎo Wáng** (*lit.* little Wang) as he is only 28 years old, though his full name is Wáng Jìjūn. When Mr and Mrs Green see Xiǎo Wáng, they greet him in Chinese.

Mrs Green	Nǐ hǎo, Xiǎo Wáng!
Mr Green	Xiǎo Wáng, nǐ hǎo!
Xiǎo Wáng	Gélín xiānsheng, Gélín tàitai, nǐmen hǎo!
Mrs Green	Nǐ tàitai hǎo ma?
Xiǎo Wáng	Tā hěn hǎo, xièxie.

Try saying two 3rd tones together. Difficult isn't it? Both **nǐ** (*you*) and **hǎo** (*good*) are 3rd tones but when said together **ni** is a 2nd tone. This was explained more fully in the **Pronunciation guide** on p. xviii.

Neutral tones

Some syllables or words in Chinese are toneless or have what is called a neutral tone. The **-sheng** of **xiānsheng**, the **-men** in **nǐmen**, and the question particle **ma** in the dialogue above are good examples of this.

▶ Dialogue 2 Saying 'goodbye'

When Mr and Mrs Green have finished their visit, they thank
Xiǎo Wáng and say goodbye to him.

Mr Green	Xiǎo Wáng, xièxie nǐ.
Mrs Green	Xièxie nǐ, Xiǎo Wáng.
Xiǎo Wáng	Bú yòng xiè.
Mr Green	Zàijiàn.
Xiǎo Wáng	Zàijiàn.
Mrs Green	Zàijiàn.

How to pronounce q

This is not at all like a **q** in English as in *queen*. Q in Chinese is
pronounced like the **j** in *jeans* but with air behind it. It is rather
like the **ch** in *cheetah* but with the corners of the mouth drawn
back as far as they can go. Refer back to the **Pronunciation
guide** for more help.

▶ Dialogue 3

Mr Green comes to see his Chinese visitor. He knocks at the
door.

Lǐ	Qǐng jìn.
Green	(*enters the room*)
Lǐ	Gélín xiānsheng, nǐ hǎo!
Green	Nǐ hǎo, Lǐ xiānsheng.
Lǐ	Qǐng zuò.
Green	Xièxie.
Lǐ	Gélín tàitai hǎo ma?
Green	Tā hěn hǎo. Xièxie.

▶ Dialogue 4

Frank goes to the teachers' office to look for his teacher.

Frank	Qǐng wèn, Zhāng lǎoshī zài ma?
Lǐ lǎoshī	Duìbuqǐ, tā bú zài.
Frank	Tā jīntiān lái ma?
Lǐ lǎoshī	Bù lái. Tā míngtiān lái.
Frank	Xièxie nǐ.
Lǐ lǎoshī	Bú yòng xiè. Míngtiān jiàn.
Frank	Míngtiān jiàn.

Tone of bù

Bù (*not*) is normally a 4th tone, but it becomes a 2nd tone before another 4th tone. When this happens it is marked as such in the book, such as **bú zài** not **bù zài**.

How to practise tones

1 When you are practising words individually, pay attention to the tone and try to reproduce it. Go back and look at **Tones** on pp. xvi–xviii where you will find some useful hints on how to say each of the four tones.
2 When you are repeating phrases or sentences as in the dialogue, pay more attention to the shape of the whole sentence and copy that rather than each individual tone.
3 Don't worry if you find the idea of tones rather daunting at first – you will soon get used to them!

Language notes

1 Mr and Mrs

In Chinese the surname or family name always comes first. Traditionally this is the most important thing about your identity. The Chinese have always placed much emphasis on the family. Your title appears after your surname:

Gélín xiānsheng	*Mr Green*
Gélín tàitai	*Mrs Green*
Wáng lǎoshī	*Teacher Wang*

2 Greetings

Nǐ hǎo can be used at any time to say *Hello* or *How do you do?*. You will come across other greetings which refer specifically to the morning or the evening, such as when wishing somebody goodnight.

3 Asking somebody to do something

Qǐng is used when you want to ask somebody to do something. You use the verb **qǐng** (*to invite/request*) plus the word for whatever you want them to do. Of course **qǐng** could be translated as **please** in such cases.

Qǐng jìn.	*Please come in.*
Qǐng zuò.	*Please sit down.*

You use the verb **wèn** (*to ask*) when you want to ask a question.

Wèn wèntí	*Ask (a) question(s)*
Qǐng wèn	*May I ask . . . ?*

4 *Hǎo* Adjective or verb?

The answer is both! **Hǎo** is both an adjective (a word that describes a noun) and a verb (a word that tells you what a person, animal or thing does, or is). However, Chinese adjectives can also act as verbs so: **hǎo** means *to be good*, *to be well*, as well as *fine*, *good*, *OK*:

Nǐ **hǎo**.	*How do you do. / How are you?*
Tā hěn **hǎo**.	*He/she is (very) well. / He/she is (very) good.*

But:

hǎo tàitai	*a good wife*
hǎo lǎoshī	*a good teacher*

The use of **hěn** in **hěn hǎo** is *not* optional. If you do not use it, a comparison is implied. **Hěn** carries a lot less weight than the English 'very' unless you stress it.

5 You like me? I like you!

Pronouns (words used in place of nouns to refer to a person) are very easy in Chinese: **Wǒ** means *me* as well as *I*. **Tā** means *him*, *her*, *it* as well as *he*, *she* or *it*. To make them plural you simply add **-men**. The table overleaf will make this clearer:

wǒ	I, me	wǒmen	we, us
nǐ	you (sing)	nǐmen	you (pl)
tā	he, she, it, him, her	tāmen	they, them

Although *he*, *she* and *it* are all pronounced **tā**, each of them is written with a different character. This only affects the written language (see Unit 11), so there is absolutely nothing to worry about.

6 Simple questions with *ma*?

To make a question from any statement you just put **ma** at the end of it.

Tā míngtiān lái.	*She will come tomorrow.*
Tā míngtiān lái ma?	*Is she coming tomorrow?*
Wáng lǎoshī zài.	*Teacher Wang is around.*
Wáng lǎoshī zài ma?	*Is Teacher Wang around?*

7 How to say 'no'!

To make a verb negative in Chinese all you have to do is put **bù** in front of it. There is only **one** exception to this rule which you will meet in Unit 2. (The tone change on **bù** is explained on p. 6.)

Tāmen hǎo.	*They are well/good.*
Tāmen bu hǎo.	*They are not well/good.*
Tā zài.	*He/she's here.*
Tā bú zài.	*He/she's not here.*

8 Word order that's different but not difficult!

Basic Chinese word order is the same as in English,

| I | like | you |
| Subject | Verb | Object |

but in English, you say: *He is coming tomorrow*. Whereas in Chinese, you say:

| Tā míngtiān lái. | *He **tomorrow** comes.* |

To sum up, time words like *today*, *tomorrow*, *Wednesday*, *6 o'clock* come **before** the verb in Chinese. Other words that come before the verb are the negative **bù**, and words such as **yě** (*also*) and **hěn** (*very*).

ℹ️ Greetings

Traditionally (i.e. before 1949) the Chinese neither shook hands nor kissed when they met or said goodbye. The custom was to clasp your hands together at chest height and as you move them very slightly backwards and forwards you bow your head over them. The lower you bow your head, the higher the status of the other person. With the growing influence of the West, however, shaking hands is becoming more common.

'Please' and 'thank you'

Qǐng (*please*) and **xièxie** (*thank you*) are used much less frequently in Chinese than in English, but it is always better to use them too much rather than too little!

Practice

1 What do you say? Choose the most appropriate response for **a** from the first four boxes. Do the same for **b** and **c**.

   a When you greet a friend, you say:

   | Nǐ hǎo | Zàijiàn | Bú yòng xiè | Xièxie |

   b When you thank someone, you say:

   | Zàijiàn | Nǐ hǎo | Xièxie | Bú yòng xiè |

   c When someone thanks you for your help, you respond by saying:

   | Nǐ hǎo | Bú yòng xiè | Zàijiàn | Xièxie |

2 Responding to a Chinese person. To help you out, the first letter of the correct response is already put in.

   Example: Qǐng jìn. – Xièxie.

   a Nǐ hǎo!   N__ ___ !
   b Xièxie nǐ.   B__ ___ ___ .
   c Qǐng zuò.   X__ .
   d Zàijiàn!   Z__ !

3 This time you begin and the Chinese person responds. Now you're on your own.

   a ___ ___ .   Nǐ hǎo!
   b Lǐ tàitai ___ ___ ? Tā hěn hǎo. Xièxie nǐ.

c Lǐ xiānsheng ____ ____ ?   Duìbuqǐ, tā bú zài.
d ____ ____ .   Bú yòng xiè.

4 What would you put in each of the gaps to make them into
   words or phrases?

   Example: Duì____qǐ. – Duìbuqǐ.

   a Xiè ____ .   e Qǐng ____ .
   b ____ ____ xiè.   f ____ zuò.
   c ____ jiàn!   g ____ ____ hǎo.
   d ____ ____ jiàn!   h ____ hǎo ____ ?

5 Match the sentences on the left to those on the right.

   a Tāmen hěn hǎo.   i   They won't be in tomorrow.
   b Tāmen jīntiān bú zài.   ii They will come today.
   c Tāmen jīntiān lái.   iii They are not in today.
   d Tāmen míngtiān bú zài. iv They are very well.

▶ Quick review

Now you've arrived at the end of Unit 1. What would you say in
the following situations:

a You meet your Chinese friend, Mr Li, and you want to say
   hello.
b Then you ask how his wife is.
c You are a little bit late and you say you are sorry.
d Thank your friend (for his/her help).
e When he/she thanks you, say *You are welcome*.
f When you take your leave, what do you say?

You'll find the answers to the **Quick review** in the **Key to the
exercises** at the end of the book. If you got them correct, you are
ready to move on to Unit 2. If you found the review difficult,
spend more time revising this unit.

欢迎 **Huānyíng**
Welcome

再见 **Zàijiàn**
Goodbye

02

nǐ jiào
shénme?

what's your name?

In this unit you will learn
- how to say who you are
- how to make simple
  introductions
- how to ask who
  other people are
- how to address people
  correctly
- how to deny something

Before you start

There is a lot of practice with asking questions in this unit. Try to learn some of the questions by heart as they will be very useful. Remember what was said about tones in Unit 1 in the section **How to practise tones** on p. 6.

▶ Let's try

A Chinese visitor has knocked on the door of your office.

a What would you call out?
b How would you greet him when he comes through the door?
c How would you ask him to sit down?
d At the end of your talk you show him to the door. What do you say to him? (You have arranged to see him again tomorrow.)

Learning tips

Here are some hints for learning vocabulary. See which one works best for you:

1 Practise saying the words out loud as you read them.
2 Cover up the English and see if you can remember what any of the Chinese words mean.
3 Cover up the Chinese and see if the English words jolt your memory.
4 Listen to the recording over and over again.
5 Write the words out several times.
6 Study the new words from beginning to end then start from the bottom and work back up again.
7 Group the words in a way that will help you to remember them, such as all the verbs together, all the countries, and the language which is spoken in each one.
8 Copy the words with their tone marks on to one side of a small card with their English equivalent on the other. Go through them looking at the Chinese first and giving the English word and then vice versa. If you get one wrong, put it back in the pile and have another go at it. You can also mix up the English and Chinese.

▶ Key words and phrases

dāngrán	of course
guì	expensive, honourable
Nín guì xìng?	What's your (honourable) surname?
háizi	child / children
huì	can, to be able to
jiào	to call / be called
méi	no, not, (have not)
méi guānxi	it's OK / it doesn't matter
míngzi	name
nà/nèi (used interchangeably)	that
nán	male
Nǐ ne?	And you?
nín	you (polite form)
péngyou	friend
piàoliang	beautiful
rènshi	recognize, know (people)
shéi/shuí?	who?
shénme?	what?
shì	to be
shuō	to speak, to say
wǒ	I, me
wǒde/nǐde/nínde/tāde	my, your, his / her
xiǎojie	Miss
xìng	surname
yě	also
yìdiǎn(r)	a little
Yīngwén	English (language)
yǒu	to have
zhè/zhèi (used interchangeably)	this
zhēn	real / really
Zhōngwén	Chinese (language)
Nǐ/tā jiào shénme (míngzi)?	What is your / his / her name?
Wǒ/tā jiào . . .	I am / he is / she is called . . .
Wǒ/nǐ/tā (bú) shì . . .	I am / you are / he is / she is (not) . . .
Zhè/nà (bú) shì . . .	This / that is (not) . . .
Tā shì shéi?	Who is he / she?
Tā shì bu shì . . . ?	Is he / she . . . (or not)?

▶ **Common Chinese surnames**

Zhāng	Wáng	Lǐ	Zhào	Liú
张	王	李	赵	刘

Chén	Lín	Wú	Guō	Zhèng
陈	林	吴	郭	郑

Learning tips

1 Refer back to the **Pronunciation guide** to help you pronounce the surnames above. Repeat them out loud several times.
2 If you have the recording, listen to the names and repeat them after the speaker.

Dialogues

▶ Dialogue 1

Listen to or read the dialogue and see how you ask what another person's name is in Chinese.

Jane	Nín guì xìng?
Chén	Wǒ xìng Chén. Nín ne?
Jane	Wǒ xìng Lord. Zhè shì nínde háizi ma?
Chén	Bú shì. Wǒ méi yǒu háizi. Zhè shì Lǐ tàitai de háizi.
Jane	(to the boy) Nǐ jiào shénme míngzi?
Child	Wǒ jiào Pànpan.

▶ Dialogue 2 At a conference

White   Zhèng xiānsheng, nǐ hǎo!

Cháng   Wǒ xìng Cháng, bú xìng Zhèng. Wǒ jiào Cháng Zhèng.

White   Duìbuqǐ, Cháng xiānsheng.

Cháng   Méi guānxi. White xiānsheng, nǐ yǒu mei yǒu Zhōngwén míngzi?

White   Yǒu. Wǒ jiào Bái Bǐdé.

Cháng   Bái xiānsheng, nǐ huì bu huì shuō Yīngwén?

White   Dāngrán huì. Cháng xiānsheng, nǐ yě huì shuō Yīngwén ma?

Cháng   Huì yìdiǎnr.

▶ Dialogue 3

How do you introduce yourself and somebody else? Find out in this dialogue.

Bái   Nà shì shéi? Nǐ rènshi bu rènshi tā?

Wú   Rènshi. Tā shì Guō xiǎojie.

Bái   Tā zhēn piàoliang. *(walks over to the girl)*

Bái   Nǐ hǎo! Wǒ jiào Bái Bǐdé. Nǐ ne?

Guō   Nǐ hǎo! Wǒ jiào Guō Yùjié. *(A man walks over to her and hands her a drink.)*

Guō   Zhè shì wǒde nán péngyou. Tā jiào Liú Wénguāng. Zhè shì Bái xiānsheng.

Liú   Bái xiānsheng, nǐ hǎo!

Bái   O, nǐ hǎo!

Language notes

1 How to be courteous

In Chinese, when you don't know somebody very well (or at all) or you wish to show respect (usually for older people, teachers, etc.), you use **nín** instead of **nǐ**. It is, however, used less frequently than it used to be and it is not usually used in the plural. This means that the plural form of both **nǐ** and **nín** is **nǐmen**, **nǐmen** being both heard and read frequently in daily life.

2 'You' and 'yours'!

Nǐ means *you* (sing). If you add the little word de to it, it means *your* or *yours*:

nǐde háizi	*your child*
wǒde xiānsheng	*my husband*
zhè shì nǐde	*this is yours*
Lǐ tàitai de háizi	*Mrs Li's child*
tāde háizi	*her/his child*

In close personal relationships: nǐ tàitai (*your wife*), wǒ māma (*my mum*), the de may be omitted (**Dialogue 1**, p. 4 where Mrs Green asks Xiǎo Wáng, Nǐ tàitai hǎo ma?).

3 How to say 'No' with *Yǒu*!

To say *do not have* in Chinese you put méi in front of the verb yǒu *to have*.

For present or future actions all other verbs are negated by putting bù in front of them (p. 8).

Wǒ **méi yǒu** háizi.	*I have no children.*
Tā **méi yǒu** Zhōngwén míngzi.	*She doesn't have a Chinese name.*

4 Another way of asking questions

If you put the positive and negative forms of the verb together (in that order) you can make a question:

Nǐ **yǒu mei yǒu** háizi?	*Do you have children?*
Nǐ **shì bu shì** lǎoshī?	*Are you a teacher?*

This is a popular alternative to the question form with ma on p. 8. The negative form of the verb is normally unstressed when it is used to make a question in this way. It **is** stressed, however, if the question is said slowly or with emphasis.

5 'Yes' and 'No' in replies

Yes and *no* don't exist as such in Chinese. If you are asked a question the answer is either the positive form of the verb (to mean *yes*) or the negative form of the verb (to mean *no*):

Nǐ yǒu méi yǒu háizi?	*Do you have children?*
Yǒu.	*Yes, I do.*
Méi yǒu.	*No, I don't.*

Nǐ rènshi tā ma?   *Do you know her?*
Rènshi.   *Yes, I do.*
Bú rènshi.   *No, I don't.*

6 To be or not to be?

Shì, the verb *to be* in English, is used much less in Chinese than in English. This is because adjectives in Chinese can also act as verbs as you saw in Unit 1, p. 7. For example, **hǎo** means *to be good* as well as *good* so there is no need for the verb *to be*.

Zhè **shì** nǐde háizi ma?   *Is this your child?*
Bú **shì**. Zhè **shì** Lǐ tàitai de háizi. *No, it's Mrs Li's.*
Tā **shì** nǐde nǚ péngyou ma?   *Is she your girlfriend?*
Bú **shì**. Tā **shì** wǒ tàitai.   *No, she is my wife.*

7 Who and what?

In Chinese, question words such as **shéi** (*who*) and **shénme** (*what*) appear in the sentence in the same position as the word or words which replace them in the answer:

Nǐ jiào **shénme** míngzi?   *What are you called?*
                             (*lit.* You are called what?)
Wǒ jiào **Pànpan**.   *I'm called Pànpan.*
Nà shì **shéi**?   *Who is that (young lady)?*
                             (*lit.* That [young lady] is who?)
Tā shì **wǒ (de) péngyou**. *She is my friend.*

This is different from the word order in English where the question word is at the beginning of the sentence.

8 Follow-up questions

To avoid having to ask a question in full or to repeat the same question you can use the little word **ne** at the end of a phrase to take a short cut!

Nǐ jiào shénme míngzi?   *What's your name?*
Wǒ jiào Wú Zébì. Nǐ **ne**? *I'm called/My name is Wu Zebi.*
                             What about you?
                             (i.e. what's your name?)
Wǒ jiào Bái Bǐdé. Tā **ne**? *My name's Peter White.*
                             What's hers?

i As you saw in Unit 1, the surname or family name comes before your title in Chinese. This means that your given name (first name) comes **after** your surname:

Cháng (family name) **Zhèng** (given name)
Bái (family name) **Bǐdé** (given name)

The use of first names is generally reserved for family members and close friends. Colleagues or people in your peer group are addressed on an informal basis by their surnames prefaced by **lǎo** (*old*) or **xiǎo** (*young*), largely depending on whether the person in question is older or younger than you.

Practice

1 Complete the following exchanges by filling in the blanks in the sentences below:

a Tā jiào ____ míngzi? Tā ____ Fāng Yuán.
b Nǐ ____ shuō Zhōngwén ma? Huì. Wǒ huì ____ yìdiǎnr.
c Tāde nán péngyou ____ shéi? Wǒ bú ____ tā.

2 Look at the pictures and answer the following questions in Chinese:

a Tāmen shì shéi?
← b Tā jiào shénme?
   c Tā xìng Yīng ma? →
← d Tā yě xìng Yīng ma?
e Nǐ rènshi tāmen ma?

Lǐ Jīnshēng

Yīng Zǐpéng

▶3 Listen to the recording and answer the following questions about the Chinese woman in the passage either in Chinese or English. If you don't have the recording, read the passage below and then answer the questions.

a What's her surname?
b What's her first name?
c How much English does she speak?
d What is her occupation?
e Does she know you?
f What does she look like?
g Does she have a boyfriend?

Wǒde Zhōngwén lǎoshī jiào Wáng Lányīng. Tā hěn piàoliang. Tā yǒu nán péngyou. Tāmen bú rènshi nǐ. Tāmen huì shuō yìdiǎnr Yīngwén.

4 Who is who? State the names and the occupation of each person pictured below. You can get more practice if you use both of the patterns given in the example:

Tā jiào Yán Lóng. Tā shì xuésheng (*student*).
Zhè/nà shì Yán Lóng. Tā shì xuésheng.

a **Zhào Huá**	b **Liú Guāng**	c **Guō Jié**
jǐngchá	sījī	yīshēng
d **Lǐ Mínglì**	e **Zhōu Jiābǎo**	f **Wū Zébì**
lǎoshī	xuésheng	chúshī

5 According to the pictures in exercise 4, are the following statements true or false? If it's true, say **duì** meaning *correct*. If it's not true, say **bú duì**, meaning *not correct*. Tick the right box in each case.

Example: Zhào Huá xìng Huá.   (bú duì)

		duì	bú duì?
a	Zhào Huá shì lǎoshī.	☐	☐
b	Liú Guāng bú shì sījī.	☐	☐
c	Nà ge yīshēng jiào Wú Zébì.	☐	☐
d	Zhōu Jiābǎo xìng Jiābǎo.	☐	☐
e	Lǐ lǎoshī jiào Lǐ Míng.	☐	☐
f	Wú Zébì shì chúshī.	☐	☐

6 You have learnt two ways to ask questions. With each set of words use these different question forms to make up two questions. The example will make this clear.

Example: Tā/huì shuō/Fǎwén (*French*)
– Tā huì shuō Fǎwén ma?
– Tā huì bu huì shuō Fǎwén?

a Nǐ/huì shuō/Yīngwén
b Nǐmen/shì/lǎoshī
c Xiǎo Zhèng/zài
d Lǐ xiānsheng/jīntiān/lái

e Wáng Fāng/yǒu/Yīngwén míngzi
f Lín lǎoshī/jiào/Lín Péng

▶ Quick review

How would you say the following?

a Ask what a person's surname is.
b Say *My name is xxx*.
c Say that you haven't got a Chinese name.
d Say that you don't know her.
e Say *That's OK* when someone apologizes to you.
f Say that your friend is not a teacher.

Lā *Pull*	**Tuī** *Push*
拉 ·	· 推

03
nǐ shì nǎ guó rén?
where are you from?

In this unit you will learn
- how to say where you come from and what nationality you are
- how to ask for and give an address
- the numbers 0–10
- how to ask for, and give, a telephone number
- how to fill out a form

Before you start

Talking about where you come from, what nationality you are, where you live and what your telephone number is in Chinese is straightforward with the necessary vocabulary and a few of the basic rules about word order. Chinese numbers are very easy as you will discover in this unit.

It is important to have short-term goals to encourage yourself. In this unit keep practising how to ask other people where they come from, where they live and what their telephone number is. Make sure you can answer these questions yourself! Aim at answering them without thinking.

Let's try

You are at a party where you hardly know anyone.

a How do you introduce yourself and how do you ask somebody his/her name?
b If you find out that one of the guests is married, how do you ask if they have any children?

► Key words and phrases

diànhuà	telephone (lit. electric speech)
duì	yes, correct
Dōngchéng (Qū)	Eastern City (District)
duōshao?	what's the number of?
fàndiàn	hotel
fángjiān	room
fēijī	plane
Guǎngdōng	Canton (province)
guó	country
hào	number
hàomǎ	number (often used for telephone, telex, fax numbers and car registration plates)
hépíng	peace
jǐ hào?	which number?
lù	road, street

Lúndūn	London
míngpiàn	namecard
năr?	where?
piào	ticket
qū	district
rén	person
Xīchéng (Qū)	Western City (District)
xǐhuan	to like
yìsi	meaning
zhù	to live
zhù zài	to live in / at a place

Learning tips

1 Try pronouncing the names of the countries on pp. 25–26. Repeat them out loud over and over again.
2 Every time you stumble over the pronunciation of a word or syllable go back to the **Pronunciation guide** and check it out on pp. xiv–xviii.
3 Foreign names, such as the names of countries and cities, can be expressed in Chinese in three main ways:

- Based on the original sound, such as **Yìdàlì** (*Italy*)
- Based on the meaning, such as **Niújīn** (*Oxford*) (*lit.* ox/ cow ford)
- A mixture of the orginal sound and its meaning, such as **Xīn** (*new*) **Xīlán** (*New Zealand*)

Dialogues

▶ Dialogue 1

Mr Peter White (Bái Bǐdé) meets a Chinese person, Lín Jiànmù, at a conference.

Lín	Nín shì nă guó rén?
Bái	Wǒ shì Yīngguó-rén. Zhè shì wǒde míngpiàn.
Lín	Xièxie. O, Bái xiānsheng, nín zhù zài Lúndūn?
Bái	Duì. Nín shì Zhōngguó-rén ba?
Lín	Shì, wǒ shì Guǎngdōng-rén.

▶ Dialogue 2

Bái xiānsheng goes to collect his plane ticket at a Chinese travel agency.

Assistant	Zhè shì nínde fēijī piào.
Bái	Xièxie. Wǒ zhù zài shénme fàndiàn?
Assistant	Nín zhù zài Hépíng Fàndiàn.
Bái	Hépíng shì shénme yìsi?
Assistant	Hépíng shì '*peace*' de yìsi.
Bái	Hěn hǎo. Wǒ xǐhuan hépíng.

▶ Numbers 0–10

líng	0	sān	3	liù	6	jiǔ	9
yī	1	sì	4	qī	7	shí	10
èr	2	wǔ	5	bā	8		

一　二　三　四　五　六　七　八　九　十

yī　èr　sān　sì　wǔ　liù　qī　bā　jiǔ　shí

- Practise saying 1 to 5: yī èr sān sì wǔ. Then say 6 to 10: liù qī bā jiǔ shí. Then put them altogether: yī èr sān . . . jiǔ shí.
- Now say: yī sān wǔ qī jiǔ. Then say: èr sì liù bā shí.
- Now try this: yī èr sān, sān èr yī, yī èr sān sì wǔ liù qī.

▶ Dialogue 3

Mr White and Mr Lin decide to further their business association.

Lín	Nǐ zhù zài nǎr?
Bái	Wǒ zhù zài Hépíng Fàndiàn.
Lín	Jǐ hào fángjiān?
Bái	Wǔ-líng-bā hào fángjiān. Nǐ zhù zài nǎr?
Lín	Wǒ zhù zài Píng'ān Lù qī hào.
Bái	Píng'ān Lù zài nǎr?
Lín	Píng'ān Lù zài Xīchéng Qū.
Bái	Hépíng Fàndiàn yě zài Xīchéng Qū shì bu shì?
Lín	Bú zài. Zài Dōngchéng Qū.
Bái	Nǐde diànhuà hàomǎ shì duōshao?
Lín	Liù-wǔ-wǔ-èr jiǔ-sān-èr-sì. Nǐde ne?
Bái	Wǒde shì liù-liù-qī-sān bā-bā-sān-líng.

Language notes

1 Where are you from?

To give your nationality you say the name of the country and then add -rén *person* after it:

Zhōngguó | *China, Chinese*
Zhōngguó-rén | *Chinese person*
Měiguó | *America (US)*
Měiguó-rén | *American*

Look at the two maps and the table between them to see exactly how this works.

Country	Nationality	Country/Nationality
Ài'ěrlán	Ài'ěrlán-rén	Ireland/Irish
Déguó	Déguó-rén	Germany/German
Fǎguó	Fǎguó-rén	France/French
Měiguó	Měiguó-rén	USA/American
Rìběn	Rìběn-rén	Japan/Japanese
Sūgélán	Sūgélán-rén	Scotland/Scottish
Yīngguó	Yīngguó-rén	Britain/British
Yuènán	Yuènán-rén	Vietnam/Vietnamese
Wēi'ěrshì	Wēi'ěrshì-rén	Wales/Welsh
(Xiānggǎng)	(Xiānggǎng-rén)	(Hong Kong/from HK)
Zhōngguó	Zhōngguó-rén	China/Chinese

You do exactly the same thing when you wish to say which province or town you come from:

Wǒ shì Lúndūn-rén.   *I'm a Londoner.*
Nǐ shì Luómǎ-rén ma?   *Are you from Rome?*
Tā shì bu shì Běijīng-rén?   *Is he from Beijing?*
Wǒmen shì Fújiàn-rén.   *We're from Fujian province.*
Tāmen shì Guǎngdōng-rén.   *They're from Canton province.*

2 Question tag: *ba*

Ba is placed after a verb or phrase to make a suggestion or to ask for confirmation of a supposition:

Nǐ shì Zhōngguó-rén **ba**?   *You're Chinese, I take it?*
Hǎo **ba**?   *Is that all right then?*

3 Linking word *de*

You have to reverse the word order in Chinese to translate a phrase such as: *the meaning of peace.* The two words **hépíng** (*peace*) and **yìsi** (*meaning*) are linked by the little word **de**.

hépíng **de** yìsi   *the meaning of* hépíng

Some people call this the possessive **de** to distinguish it from another **de** you will meet in Unit 8.

Look carefully at the following examples:

Fàndiàn **de** yìsi shì *hotel*.   *The meaning of **fandian** is hotel.*

Bái xiānsheng **de** diànhuà   *Mr White's telephone number*
hàomǎ

Mǎ tàitai **de** háizi   *Mrs Ma's child*

4 Room 508

Room 508 is said as *508 Room* in Chinese (the reverse of English word order) with the addition of the word **hào** (*number*) after 508. More examples of this are given below:

10 (shí) **hào**   *No. 10*
5 (wǔ) **hào** fángjiān   *Room 5*

Room numbers up to 100 are generally said as one number. You will meet numbers from ten to 100 in the next unit.

Numbers over 100 are broken down into single digits:

374 (sān-qī-sì) hào fángjiān   *Room 374*
896 (bā-jiǔ-liù) hào fángjiān   *Room 896*

5 Question tag: *shì bu shi?*

Making a question by putting **shì bu shi** at the end of a sentence in Chinese conveys the idea of *Am I right?* or *Is it true?*:

Hépíng Fàndiàn yě zài   *The Peace Hotel is also in the*
Xīchéng Qū **shì bu shì**?   *Western City District, isn't it?*
Nǐ shì Yīngguó-rén   *You're English/British,*
shì bu shì?   *aren't you?*

6 Telephone numbers

Telephone numbers are often made up of seven or eight digits each of which is usually said separately:

551 8274   wǔ-wǔ-**yāo** bā-èr-qī-sì
8228 9436   bā-èr-èr-bā jiǔ-sì-sān-liù

Yāo is used instead of **yī** when telephone numbers or large numbers for rooms, buses, trains, and so on, are broken down into single digits. This avoids any confusion with **qī** (seven).

Learning tips

1 Have imaginary conversations with yourself in Chinese using the material in the dialogues and the structures you have covered.

2 Think of somebody and say everything you can about them in Chinese: what their name is, what nationality they are, where they live, what their telephone number is, whether they have children, if you like them, and so on. Then do the same thing with somebody else, and so on, until you can go through the whole routine without hesitation.

3 **Don't worry about making mistakes!**

Anybody who has successfully learnt a foreign language knows that the way to make progress is to listen and speak as much as possible. Don't worry if you don't understand a lot of what is said to you in the beginning – just respond to what you do understand.

You will find the following two sentences very useful. Practise them over and over again:

Qǐng nǐ shuō màn yìdiǎn.	*Please speak more slowly.* (*lit.* invite you say slow a little)
Qǐng nǐ **zài** shuō yí biàn.	*Please say it again.* (*lit.* invite you again say one time)

This **zài** is not the **zài** which means *to be in/at*; it is the **zài** which means *again* as in **zàijiàn** (*goodbye*) (*lit.* again see). Words like **zài** (*again*) are called adverbs. They come before the verb in Chinese.

i Chinese people are very direct with their questions. It is not considered rude to ask how old you are, how much you earn, how much your house cost to buy or what the rent is, how much the clothes you are wearing cost, and so on.

Even questions as to why you are so fat or so thin or why you haven't married or why you got divorced (have you got a bad temperament?!) are all considered perfectly legitimate. Things are changing, however, as those people who have increasing contact with Westerners realize that the latter are uncomfortable with such questions.

Practice

1 Answer the following questions. If you don't know, say **Wǒ bù zhīdao** (*lit.* I not know.):

   a Nǐ shì Měiguó-rén ma?
   b Nǐ māma (*mum*) shì Fǎguó-rén ma?
   c Nǐde lǎoshī shì Zhōngguó-rén ba?
   d Nǐ bàba (*dad*) bú shì Déguó-rén ba?
   e Dèng Xiǎopíng shì Zhōngguó-rén ma?
   f Shāshìbǐyà (*Shakespeare*) shì bu shì Yīngguó-rén?

▶2 You are going to hear three people introducing themselves. Listen to the recording twice and take notes while you are doing so. Then fill in as many details about each of the three speakers as you can. Listen again paying particular attention to the bits you have not been able to catch. Listen for a fourth time to check what you have written.

	Speaker 1	Speaker 2	Speaker 3
Surname:			
Given name:			
Nationality:			
Telephone no:			
Address:			
– city:			
– street:			
– number:			

If you're still not sure of what you've heard, have a look at what the three people say in the **Key to the exercises** on p. 234.

NB: Chinese addresses are written in the reverse order to the way addresses are written in English. In English you give the number of your flat/house first, then the street or road and then the town or city. In Chinese it is city, street, number, as you can see from the chart above.

3 **a** Follow the same pattern as the passage you heard in exercise 2 and say something about yourself. Fill in your details on the chart overleaf as you did in exercise 2. You can do this exercise even if you don't have the recording.
   b Think of one of your friends and fill in his/her details.
   c If you are doing this with another person, ask him/her questions and fill in his/her details.

	Yourself	Friend A	Friend B
Surname:			
Given name:			
Nationality:			
Telephone no:			
Address:			
– city:			
– street:			
– number:			

4   You often see Chinese addresses written in English as in the following examples. How would these addresses be said (or written) in Chinese?

a   Mingli Li
    (Lecturer)
    2, Chaoyang Lu
    BEIJING

b   Mr. Hua Zhao,
    Room 384, Dongfang
    Hotel, 9 Longhai Lu,
    Suzhou

c   Miss Jiabao Zhao,
    5, Heping Lu,
    Xicheng Qu
    Nanjing

5   Match the words in the left-hand column with the ones on the right to make words you've already seen. (We've done one for you.)

a	fēijī	i	Fàndiàn
b	Lúndūn	ii	jiàn
c	Hépíng	iii	piào
d	èr-líng-wǔ	iv	Qū
e	míngtiān	v	fángjiān
f	Dōngchéng	vi	hàomǎ
g	diànhuà	vii	rén

▶ Quick review

a You meet someone you don't know. How do you ask your friend who he is?

b How do you ask someone where he/she lives?

c Tell someone that you don't live in London.

d Ask someone to give you his/her telephone number.

e Ask what the meaning of **diànhuà** is.

f Say to the Chinese air hostess that this is your (plane) ticket.

You'll find the answers in the **Key to the exercises**. How have you done? If most of them are correct, you will be ready to go on to Unit 4. Congratulations! Before you do so, spend some time revising Units 1, 2 and 3. Regular revision will help to consolidate what you have learnt and give you more confidence.

04

nǐ yǒu xiōngdì jiěmèi ma?

do you have brothers and sisters?

In this unit you will learn
- how to talk about yourself and your family
- how to ask other people about their family
- how to ask someone if they are married and/or have children
- how to say how old you are
- how to ask how old somebody is
- how to count up to 100

Before you start

You'll find that speaking about yourself and your family in Chinese is very easy. Remember how to say *I have* or *I don't have* (**wǒ yǒu, wǒ méi yǒu**)? Using this and the basic vocabulary you will learn in this unit, you have all you need!

You will also be able to count up to 100 by the end of this unit. Having mastered one to ten in Unit 3 you will be surprised how easy it is. 11 is 10 + 1, 12 is 10 + 2, 20 is 2 × 10, 30 is 3 × 10, all the way up to 99 which is 9 × 10 + 9. There is a special word **bǎi** for *hundred* so 100 is **yìbǎi** (*one hundred* – you have to use **yī** *one*).

Let's try

You have just been introduced to a Chinese business associate who is on a week's visit to London.

a Ask her which hotel she is staying in and what the number of her room is.
b What do you say when you give her your card?

Key words and phrases

bú kèqi	you are welcome (lit. *not guest air*)
dà	big
. . . duō dà?	How old . . . ?
. . . duō dà niánjì?	How old . . . ? (respectful) (lit. *how old year record*)
gè	(measure word)
hé	and
jié hūn	marry
. . . jié hūn le ma?	. . . married?
. . . jǐ suì?	How old . . . ? (for children)
jīnnián	this year
le	grammatical marker
liǎng	two (of anything)
. . . suì	. . . years old; age
xiàng	(to look) like
bú xiàng	not to look (like) it
xiǎo	small
yí ge . . . yí ge	one . . . , the other
zhēnde	really

▶ Family members

bàba	*dad, father*
māma	*mum, mother*
érzi	*son*
nǚ'ér	*daughter*
gēge	*elder brother*
jiějie	*elder sister*
dìdi	*younger brother*
mèimei	*younger sister*
xiōngdì	*brothers*
jiěmèi	*sisters*
dà dìdi	*the older one of the younger brothers*
xiǎo dìdi	*younger one of the younger brothers*

▶ Numbers 11–100

shíyī	11	shíliù	16	sānshí	30	bāshí	80
shí'èr	12	shíqī	17	sìshí	40	jiǔshí	90
shísān	13	shíbā	18	wǔshí	50	yìbǎi	100
shísì	14	shíjiǔ	19	liùshí	60		
shíwǔ	15	èrshí	20	qīshí	70		

Dialogues

▶ Dialogue 1

Dīng Fèng is carrying out a family planning survey and Liú Fúguì (from the Miáo national minority) has agreed to answer a few questions:

Dīng Nín jiào shénme míngzi?
Liú Wǒ jiào Liú Fúguì.
Dīng Liú xiānsheng jié hūn le ma?
Liú Jié hūn le.
Dīng Yǒu mei yǒu háizi?

Liú	Yǒu liǎng ge, yí ge érzi, yí ge nǚ'ér.
Dīng	Tāmen jǐ suì?
Liú	Érzi liǎng suì, nǚ'ér wǔ suì.

Learning tips

Practise saying 11 to 15: **shíyī, shí'èr, shísān, shísì, shíwǔ.** Then say 16 to 20 **shíliù, shíqī, shíbā, shíjiǔ, èrshí.** Then put them together: **shíyī, shí'èr, shísān, . . . èrshí.** Do the same for 21 to 25, 26 to 30, and so on.

Tones on *yī*

Yī (*one*) is a 1st tone when it is part of a number, such as **yī** (*one*), **shíyī** (*eleven*), **èrshíyī** (*twenty-one*). When it occurs before a measure word it is normally a 4th tone, for example **yì tiān** (*one day*), **yì běn shū** (*one book*), but it turns into a 2nd tone before another 4th tone, for example **yí suì** (*one year old*). In **yí ge háizi**, **gè** is said without a tone, although it is actually 4th, but it still carries enough weight to change **yī** into a 2nd tone.

Suì (*year of age*), **tiān** (*day*) and **nián** (*year*), all act as measure words and nouns combined (refer to p. 37 for an explanation of what a measure word is). Note that **yìbǎi** is *one hundred*.

▶ Dialogue 2

Dīng Fèng asks Liú Fúguì some more questions. By reading/listening to the dialogue can you find out whether Liú Fúguì has any brothers or sisters? How old are they?

Dīng	Nín yǒu xiōngdì jiěmèi ma?
Liú	Yǒu liǎng ge dìdi, yí ge mèimei. Méi yǒu gēge hé jiějie.
Dīng	Nín dìdi, mèimei duō dà?
Liú	Dà dìdi èrshíliù, xiǎo dìdi èrshísì.
Dīng	Mèimei ne?
Liú	Mèimei èrshíbā.
Dīng	Hěn hǎo, xièxie nín.
Liú	Bú kèqi.
Dīng	Zàijiàn.
Liú	Zàijiàn.

▶ Dialogue 3

Wú and Lù are looking at a photo of Lù's family.

Wú   Nǐ bàba、 māma duō dà niánjì?
Lù   Bàba wǔshísān, māma sìshíjiǔ.
Wú   Bú xiàng, bú xiàng. Zhè shì nǐ mèimei ba. Tā zhēn piàoliang.
Lù   Tā jīnnián èrshí'èr.
Wú   Zhēnde? Tā jié hūn le ma?
Lù   Méi yǒu. Kěshì yǒu nán péngyou le.
Wú   O.

Language notes

1 Sentences ending in . . . *le*

If you put the little word **le** at the end of a sentence, it shows that something has happened or has already taken place:

Wǒ jié hūn **le**.	*I'm married.*
Wǒ qǐng tā **le**.	*I invited him.*
Wǒ wèn tā **le**.	*I asked her.*

If you want to make a question, simply add **ma** or **méi you** to the end of a sentence. **Yǒu** is unstressed.

Nǐ jié hūn le **ma**?	*Are you married?*
Nǐ jié hūn le **méi you**?	*Are you married?*

If you want to say something has not happened, you use **méi yǒu** (*not have*) plus the verb:

Wǒ **méi yǒu** jié hūn.	*I'm not married.*
Wǒ **méi** qǐng tā.	*I didn't invite him.*
Wǒ **méi** wèn tā.	*I haven't asked her.*

The **yǒu** can be omitted.

2 One or two

In Chinese something called a measure word (MW) or classifier has to be used between a number and the noun following it.

In English you can say:

two children
three daughters
four books

But in Chinese you have to put the measure word/classifier in between the number and the item:

two measure word/classifier children
three measure word/classifier daughters
four measure word/classifier books

liǎng **ge** háizi	*two children*
sān **ge** nǚ'ér	*three daughters*
sì **běn** shū	*four books*

Different measure words are used with different categories of nouns. For example, **běn** is used for books and magazines whereas **zhāng** is used for rectangular or square, flat objects such as tables, beds, maps and so on, but it is not a true measure as to length or anything else:

wǔ **běn** zázhì	*five magazines*
liù **zhāng** zhuōzi	*six tables*
qī **zhāng** chuáng	*seven beds*

Gè is by far the most common measure word. It is used with a whole range of nouns which do not have their own specific measure word. When in doubt use **gè**! The noun accompanying the number and measure word is often omitted when it is clear from the context what this is:

Nǐ yǒu mei yǒu háizi?	*Have you any children?*
Yǒu liǎng **ge** (háizi), yí **ge** érzi, yí **ge** nǚ'ér.	*Two, a son and a daughter.*

3 Two for tea!

Liǎng meaning *two of a kind* is used with measure words instead of **èr** (*two*), so *two children* is **liǎng ge háizi** and not **èr ge háizi**.

4 How old are you?

When asking small children how old they are, you use **jǐ** (*how many*) when you are expecting a small number (generally less than 10) as an answer plus the word for years (of age) **suì**:

| Háizi **jǐ suì**? | *How old is/are the children?* |
| Tā **wǔ suì**. | *He/she's five years old.* |

Note that no verb is necessary in such sentences. When asking teenagers or young adults how old they are you use **duō** (*how*) together with **dà** (*old/big*):

| Nǐ **duō dà**? | *How old are you (of teenager/young adult)?* |
| Wǒ èrshí suì. | *I'm twenty.* |

Again, note that no verb is necessary.

When asking older(!) adults how old they are, the phrase **duō dà niánjì** (*lit.* how big year record) is used:

| Nǐ bàba、māma **duōdà niánjì**? | *How old are your Mum and Dad?* |
| Bàba wǔshísān, māma sìshíjiǔ. | *Dad is 53, Mum is 49.* |

Bàba (*dad*) comes before **māma** (*mum*) in Chinese word order, as does **fùqin** (*father*) before **mǔqin** (*mother*)!

5 Punctuation – when is a comma not a comma?

When it's a pause-mark! In Chinese, if two or more items are listed together, a pause-mark、is used between the items and not a comma. A comma is reserved for longer pauses:

| Wǒ yǒu liǎng ge dìdi、yí ge mèimei. | *I have two younger brothers and a younger sister.* |
| Nǐ bàba、māma duō dà niánjì? | *How old are your Mum and Dad?* |

6 Apostrophe for clarity

To prevent you saying **nǚer** instead of making a pause between the two syllables **nǚ** and **èr**, the Chinese insert an apostrophe (') between the two, so it is:

nǚ'èr
shí'èr (*not* shíèr)
èrshí'èr (*not* èrshíèr)

7 Brothers and sisters

The collective term for *sisters* (without saying whether they are older or younger) is **jiěmèi**, combining half of **jiějie** with half of **mèimei**. Similarly there is a collective term **xiōngdì** for *brothers*, although in this case a more literary term for elder brother is used:

Wǒ méi yǒu xiōngdì jiěmèi.   *I don't have any brothers or sisters.*

8 Polite talk

In Unit 1, when Mrs Green thanked Xiǎo Wáng he responded by saying:

Bú yòng xiè (*lit.* not need/use thank)   *Don't mention it / Not at all.*

He could also have said **Bú xiè.**

An equally appropriate response to thanks would be:

Bú kèqi. (*lit.* not guest air/polite)   *It's nothing, not at all.*

Chinese people tend to say 'thank you' rather less than in the West so they feel obliged to respond when somebody says 'thank you' to them.

Learning tips

Create opportunities to speak Chinese as much as you can.

1 Try to find other learners of Chinese to practise with. Find out about classes in your local area or where you work. (Your public library will usually be able to help you.)
2 If you have the recording, listen to it as much as you can – in the car, on public transport.
3 Advertise a language exchange in your local newspaper – offer to give English conversation lessons in return for Chinese ones. Make sure that you say you are learning Modern Standard Chinese (or Mandarin as it is called by many overseas Chinese) as many Chinese people in the UK are Cantonese speakers who have come from Hong Kong.

ℹ The Chinese zodiac

The Chinese zodiac works in a 12-year cycle rather than in months as the Western one does. You probably know whether you are a Capricorn or a Leo or whatever but do you know which **Animal Year** you belong to? The order is as follows:

Rat (*shŭ*)	1996	1984	1972	1960	1948	1936
Ox (*niú*)	1997	1985	1973	1961	1949	1937
Tiger (*hŭ*)	1998	1986	1974	1962	1950	1938
Rabbit (*tù*)	1999	1987	1975	1963	1951	1939
Dragon (*lóng*)	2000	1988	1976	1964	1952	1940
Snake (*shé*)	2001	1989	1977	1965	1953	1941
Horse (*mǎ*)	2002	1990	1978	1966	1954	1942
Sheep (*yáng*)	2003	1991	1979	1967	1955	1943
Monkey (*hóu*)	2004	1992	1980	1968	1956	1944
Cockerel (*jī*)	2005	1993	1981	1969	1957	1945
Dog (*gǒu*)	2006	1994	1982	1970	1958	1946
Pig (*zhū*)	2007	1995	1983	1971	1959	1947

Can you work out which animal you are?! For instance if you were born in 1976 you are a dragon, if you were born in 1971 you are a pig (but make sure you take the Lunar New Year into account on p. 217). Each Animal Year is said to possess certain characteristics. It might be fun to get hold of a book on Chinese astrology and read up on your particular animal. Such books are now relatively easy to obtain at any reputable bookshop.

Practice

1 Choose the right number:

   a Which is the smallest number?
      wǔshíbā
      èrshíjiǔ
      sìshíliù

   b Which is the odd one out?
      qīshíyī
      bāshíbā
      jiǔshíjiǔ

   c Which number is the largest?
      sānshí'èr
      èrshísān
      sānshíyī

2 Now try the following calculations. Find the number to replace the question marks and say it out loud in Chinese.

   a $7 \times 3 = ?$ c $10 + ? = 76$
   b $? - 40 = 30$ d $98 \div 2 = ?$

   You can also say equations in Chinese:

   + **jiā** *plus*   × **chéng** *times*
   − **jiǎn** *minus*   ÷ **chú** *divide*

   What would you say to fill these blanks?

   e Shíwǔ chéng èr shì ___.
   f ___ jiǎn wǔshí shì shí.
   g Èrshí jiā ___ shì sānshíwǔ.
   h Jiǔshíjiǔ chú sān shì ___.

3 Listen to the recording (or read the passage below if you haven't got the recording) and say or write down the names and ages of Dīng's children. If you're still not sure of what you've heard, check it out in the **Key to the exercises** on p. 235.

   Dīng Fèng jié hūn le. Tā yǒu liǎng ge háizi, yí ge érzi, yí ge nǚ'ér. Érzi jiào Dīng Níng, jīnnián shí'èr suì. Nǚ'ér jiào Dīng Yīng, jīnnián shísì suì.

4 You are an only child and you are neither married nor have any children. Your father is a doctor (**yīshēng**), and your mother a teacher. How would you answer the following questions in Chinese?

a Nǐ yǒu gēge ma?
b Nǐ jié hūn le ma?
c Nǐ bàba shì lǎoshī ma?
d Nǐ yǒu jǐ ge háizi?
e Nǐ dìdi jiào shénme?

5 Match the questions in the left-hand column with the answers on the right.

a Nǐ jié hūn le ma?   i   Wáng Yìfū.
b Tā jǐ suì?   ii   Tā méi yǒu nǚ'ér.
c Wáng lǎoshī jiào shénme míngzi?   iii Tā wǔ suì.
d Nǐmen yǒu háizi ma?   iv   Wǒ jié hūn le.
e Lǐ tàitai yǒu nǚ'ér ma?   v   Wǒmen méi
                                                              háizi.

▶6   The following is what Hēnglì (Henry) said about himself, his brother and his sister. Imagine you are Hēnglì's sister and talk about yourself and your brothers.

Wǒ jiào Hēnglì, jīnnián èrshí suì. Wǒ méi yǒu gēge, méi yǒu jiějie. Wǒ yǒu yí ge dìdi, yí ge mèimei. Wǒ dìdi jiào Bǐdé (*Peter*). Tā shíwǔ suì. Wǒ mèimei jiào Mǎlì (*Mary*). Tā jīnnián shíqī suì. Wǒmen dōu (*all*) shì xuésheng (*student*).

▶ Quick review

You see a little Chinese girl and say the following to her:

a Hello!
b What's your name?
c How old are you?
d Have you got any brothers and sisters?
e Thank you.
f Goodbye!

05

jǐ diǎn le?

what time is it now?

In this unit you will learn
- the days of the week
- the months of the year
- how to tell the time
- how to ask what time it is
- some useful expressions of time
- how to give the date
- how to make arrangements

Before you start

In China, or any Chinese-speaking environment, you'd need to be able to find out when shops and banks are open. You also need to be able to recognize the Chinese characters for opening times **Yíngyè shíjiān** 营业时间 and the numbers 1 to 12 (plus the characters for *o'clock*) and the days of the week. You will be able to do all this by the end of the unit.

Let's try

1 You are at a reception where you meet a Chinese acquaintance of a friend of yours. He does not speak any English so you take the opportunity to try out your Chinese. You know he is called Chén. Think of at least ten questions you can ask him in Chinese. Go back to Units 1 to 4 if you need to review vocabulary.

2 Revise the following numbers and say them out loud. 64 – 29 – 57 – 38 – 12 – 95 – 40 – 2 – 73 – 10. Check your answers with the numbers on p. 34.

Key words and phrases

bàn	*half*
bāng	*help*
chà	*lacking, short of*
Chūnjié	*the Spring Festival*
dào	*to*
dì	*(for ordinal numbers)*
dōu	*all, both*
guān (mén)	*close (door)*
hái	*still*
hái yǒu	*still have, there are still*
huì	*meeting*
huǒchē	*train*
jǐ?	*how many? (usually less than ten)*
jiù shì	*to be precisely; to be nothing else but*
kāi huì	*to have a meeting*
kāi (mén)	*open (door)*
kāishǐ	*start*

kàn(yi)kàn	to have a look
kěxī	it's a pity
míngnián	next year
qù	go
shàng	on
shēngrì	birthday
yǐjīng	already
yǐwéi	thought, assume
zhàntái	platform
zhīdào	know
zhù (ni)	wish (you)
Zhù nǐ yílù shùnfēng!	Have a safe journey!

Time expressions

diǎn	o'clock
fēn(zhōng)	minute
jǐ diǎn?	what time . . . ?
(Xiànzài) jǐ diǎn le?	What time is it now?
Jǐ yuè jǐ hào?	What's the date?
	(lit. how many month, how many numbers?)
shàngwǔ	morning
shíjiān	time
wǎnshang	evening
xiànzài	now
xiàwǔ	afternoon
xīngqī	week
Xīngqī jǐ?	What day is it?
yíkè	a quarter (time)
yuè	month
zǎoshang	morning
zhōngwǔ	noon
zhōumò	weekend

一月 yīyuè January	二月 èryuè February	三月 sānyuè March	四月 sìyuè April
五月 wǔyuè May	六月 liùyuè June	七月 qīyuè July	八月 bāyuè August
九月 jiǔyuè September	十月 shíyuè October	十一月 shíyīyuè November	十二月 shí'èryuè December

Liǎng diǎn bàn   **Sān diǎn yí kè**   **Chà wǔ fēn sì diǎn**   **Chà yí kè liù diǎn**
Wǔ diǎn sān kè

Learning tips

1   Months of the year are very easy to say in Chinese. You already know the numbers 1 to 12. All you then need is the word for **yuè** 月 (*moon*). January is **yī-yuè**, February is **èr-yuè** and so on. Be careful not to confuse **yí ge yuè** *one month* with **yīyuè** *January*, **liǎng ge yuè** *two months* with **èryuè** *February*.

yīyuè	January	**qīyuè**	July
èryuè	February	**bāyuè**	August
sānyuè	March	**jiǔyuè**	September
sìyuè	April	**shíyuè**	October
wǔyuè	May	**shíyīyuè**	November
liùyuè	June	**shí'èryuè**	December

2   Days of the week are also easy to say in Chinese. They all start with **xīngqī** 星期 (*week*) (*lit.* star period) and then you use the numbers 1 to 6 for Monday to Saturday. Sunday is special! You add the word **rì** 日 (*sun*) or **tiān** 天 (*day*) to **xīngqī** to make it into Sunday.

xīngqīyī	Monday	**xīngqīwǔ**	Friday
xīngqī'èr	Tuesday	**xīngqīliù**	Saturday
xīngqīsān	Wednesday	**xīngqītiān**	Sunday
xīngqīsì	Thursday	**xīngqīrì**	

3 Repeat the days of the week and the months of the year several times out loud until you have mastered them or listen to them on the recording and say them after the speaker.

Dialogues

▶ Dialogue 1

A customer is ringing a shop to find out the opening hours.

营业时间

星期一至星期五 8:30 – 19:30
星期六、星期日 9:00 – 18:30

Yíngyè shíjiān
Opening hours

Customer	Qǐng wèn, nǐmen jǐ diǎn kāi mén?
Assistant	Shàngwǔ bā diǎn dào xiàwǔ wǔ diǎn bàn.
Customer	Zhōngwǔ guān mén ma?
Assistant	Bù guān.
Customer	Zhōumò kāi bu kāi?
Assistant	Xīngqīliù kāi, xīngqītiān bù kāi.

早上 上午 中午 下午 晚上

< ---------------- 8am ---------------- 12pm ---------------- 6pm ----------- >

zǎoshang   **shàngwǔ**   **zhōngwǔ**   **xiàwǔ**   **wǎnshang**

▶ Dialogue 2

Two colleagues, Xiǎo Xú and Lǎo Wàn, are in the office when Xiǎo Xú suddenly remembers something.

Xiǎo Xú	Xiànzài jǐ diǎn le?
Lǎo Wàn	Liǎng diǎn yí kè le.
Xiǎo Xú	O, huì yǐjīng kāishǐ le.
Lǎo Wàn	Shénme huì? Nǐ bú shì míngtiān kāi huì ma?
Xiǎo Xú	Jīntiān xīngqī jǐ?
Lǎo Wàn	Xīngqīsān.
Xiǎo Xú	O, wǒ hái yǐwéi shì xīngqīsì ne.

ℹ️ In overseas Chinese communities, and also in China, especially in the South, you may well hear the word **lǐbài** 礼拜 used instead of **xīngqī**. So Monday would be **lǐbàiyī** instead of **xīngqīyī**, Tuesday would be **lǐbài'èr** and so on. The word **lǐbài** has certain Christian connotations as 'to go to church' is **zuò (do) lǐbài**.

▶ Dialogue 3

Departure
LIVERPOOL
Platform 6
15.15
16.20

At a train station, Jane sees a Chinese person looking at the departure and arrivals board, obviously very perplexed. She decides to help him if she can.

Jane	Nǐ qù nǎr?
Chinese	Wǒ qù Lìwùpǔ.
Jane	Jǐ diǎn de huǒchē?
Chinese	Wǒ bù zhīdao. Piào shang méi yǒu shíjiān.
Jane	Wǒ bāng nǐ kànkan. (*looks at the notice board*) Ah, sān diǎn yí kè, zài dì-liù zhàntái.
Chinese	Xiànzài sān diǎn chà wǔ fēn, hái yǒu èrshí fēnzhōng.
Jane	Zhù nǐ yílù shùnfēng.
Chinese	Xièxie nǐ. Zàijiàn.

▶ Dialogue 4

Ann wants to find out whether her birthday happens to fall on Chinese New Year. Read the dialogue and see if you can find the answer.

Ann	Míngnián Chūnjié shì jǐ yuè jǐ hào?
Friend	Èryuè shí'èr hào.

Ann	Zhēn kěxī. Wǒde shēngrì shì èryuè shíyī hào.
Friend	Méi guānxi. Yīngguó shíyī hào de wǎnshang jiù shì Zhōngguó shí'èr hào de zǎoshang.

Language notes

1 Telling the time

Xiànzài jǐ diǎn (zhōng) le?   *What time is it/now?* (*lit.* now how many points clock)

To reply to this question you use the 12-hour clock in Chinese. **Zhōng** is normally left out except when asking the time or (as in English) on the hour where it is optional. The use of **xiànzài** is also optional.

11.00 (Xiànzài) shíyī diǎn (zhōng).
11.05 (Xiànzài) shíyī diǎn (líng) wǔ fēn. **Líng** (*zero*) is optional.
11.10 Shíyī diǎn shí fēn.
11.15 Shíyī diǎn shíwǔ fēn *or* shíyī diǎn yí kè (*one quarter*).
11.20 Shíyī diǎn èrshí fēn.
11.25 Shíyī diǎn èrshíwǔ fēn.
11.30 Shíyī diǎn sānshí *or* shíyī diǎn bàn (*half*).

1.35 Yì diǎn sānshíwǔ.
1.40 Yì diǎn sìshí *or* chà èrshí (fēn) liǎng diǎn.
1.45 Yì diǎn sìshíwǔ fēn *or* yì diǎn sān kè (*three quarters*) *or* chà yí kè liǎng diǎn *or* liǎng diǎn chà yí kè.
1.50 Yì diǎn wǔshí fēn *or* chà shí fēn liǎng diǎn.
1.55 Yì diǎn wǔshíwǔ fēn *or* chà wǔ fēn liǎng diǎn.

Formal announcements of time are given using the 24-hour clock.

2 Dates

Months of the year, days of the week and parts of the day are easy (pp. 46–47) but you still need to learn dates. In Chinese the order for a date is the reverse of that used in English:

It is year, month, day, time of day (morning, afternoon, etc.), hour.

In Chinese you move from the general to the particular.

The year is read as single numbers followed by the word **nián** 年 (*year*):

yī-jiǔ-yī-sì nián	*1914*
yī-jiǔ-sì-wǔ nián	*1945*

You ask what the date is by saying: **Jǐ yuè jǐ hào?** (*lit.* how many months how many numbers).

Jīntiān jǐ yuè jǐ hào?	*What's the date today?*
Jīntiān bāyuè shí hào.	*Today's August 10th.*
Xīngqīsān jǐ hào?	*What's the date on Wednesday?*
(Xīngqīsān) èrshíbā hào.	*It's 28th (on Wednesday).*

You can now work out how to say 12 noon on Tuesday, July 23rd 1989:

Yī-jiǔ-bā-jiǔ nián qīyuè èrshísān hào xīngqī'èr zhōngwǔ shí'èr diǎn.

Note that when you're telling the time and giving dates no verb is necessary. You have already met this in Unit 3 when dealing with ages.

3 Another type of *le*

You will have noticed the little word **le** appearing after **Xiànzài jǐ diǎn?** and **Liǎng diǎn yí kè** in **Dialogue 2**. It is used to indicate that a new state of affairs or situation has appeared. It is used at the end of such sentences as:

Nǐmen yǐjīng hěn dà **le**.	*You're already pretty grown up* (whereas previously you weren't).
Tā xiànzài (hěn) piàoliang **le**.	*He's very good looking now* (whereas previously he wasn't!).

The Chinese stretch this idea of a change of state to its limits by often using it with questions and answers about age and time:

Háizi jǐ suì **le**?   *How old is the child?* (*lit.* child
                          how many years become)
Xiànzài jǐ diǎn **le**?   *What time is it?* (*lit.* now how
                          many o'clock become)

4 Linking word *de*

This is the same **de** you looked at in Unit 3, p. 26. The main idea
– what you are talking about – comes after the **de**, and what
describes this main idea or tells you more about it, comes before
the **de**:

Jǐ diǎn **de** huǒchē?   *The train at what time?*
Xīngqītiān kāi **de** shāngdiàn *Shops which open on Sundays*
Zài Lúndūn kāi **de** huì   *The meeting held in London*

5 Ticket on – on the ticket

Piào shang (*lit.* ticket on) *on the ticket*. Again the reverse of the
English word order. Do the Chinese do everything back to front,
you may be tempted to ask? No wonder they used to write from
top to bottom and from right to left (and still do in Taiwan and
Hong Kong)! Thus in Chinese you say:

shāngdiàn **lǐ**   *inside the shop*
lù **shàng**   *on the road / on the way*
huǒchē **xià**   *underneath the train*

Words such as **lǐ**, **shàng** and **xià** are normally unstressed when
used in this way.

6 Repeating the verb: *kànkan!*

Repeating the verb has the effect of softening the suggestion,
question or statement. Thus the repeated verb is often unstressed.
It conveys the idea of *having a little go* at doing the action of the
verb in both the sense of a trial and in not making a big fuss
about doing something. Verbs of one syllable often have **yi**
inserted in the middle when they are repeated.

Kànyikàn.   *Have a little look.*
Shuōyishuō. *Try saying.*

Verbs of two syllables cannot have **yi** inserted in this way; so
you cannot say **rènshiyirènshi** or **kāishǐyikāishǐ**.

7 First or second

To make the numbers one, two, and so on into *the first, the second*, and so on, you only have to put the word **dì** in front of the number. **Èr** does not change into **liǎng** in such cases as there are not two seconds! An expression which used to be very common in China when any form of competition was involved is:

Yǒuyì **dì-yī**, bǐsài **dì-èr**.　　*Friendship first, competition second.*

Learning tips

Have fun while you're learning!

1 What have you learnt about the Chinese language so far? How is it different from any other language you've learnt? Take some time to reflect on this and jot down your thoughts. See if your ideas change as you learn more.

▶2 Tongue-twisters are fun in any language. Try the following. Repeat them until you can say them off by heart:

Sì shì sì.	*4 is 4.*
Shí shì shí.	*10 is 10.*
Sì bú shì shí.	*4 is not 10.*
Shí yě bú shì sì.	*10 is not 4 either.*
Shísì bú shì sìshí.	*14 is not 40.*
Sìshí yě bú shì shísì.	*40 is not 14 either.*

The last one is the hardest of all:

Sìshísì ge shí shīzi　　*44 stone lions*

Practice

▶1 Can you say the dates of the following festivals (**jié**) in Chinese?

a New Year's Day (**Xīnnián**)
b Christmas Day (**Shèngdàn jié**)
c International Women's Day (**Guójì Fùnǚ jié**)
d National Day of China (**Zhōngguó de Guóqìng jié**)
e National Day of your country (**X X Guóqìng jié**)

2 Give the birthdays of five people using the following structures:

Sòng lǎoshī de shēngrì shì sìyuè shísì hào.
Sìyuè shísì hào shì Sòng lǎoshī de shēngrì.

You can use these structures to talk about dates when you have learned more words such as those in Exercise 1.

▶3   You will hear some dates and times. Repeat them and write them down. If you haven't got the recording, read the dates and times below and write them down in English.

a jiǔyuè jiǔ hào
b xīngqītiān shàngwǔ
c shíyīyuè èrshíbā hào xīngqīsì
d xīngqīliù shàngwǔ shí diǎn sìshíwǔ
e qīyuè liù hào xīngqīwǔ xiàwǔ sān diǎn bàn
f shí'èryuè sānshíyī hào xīngqīyī shàngwǔ shíyī diǎn

4 Based on the assumption that the time is now 5.05 in the afternoon (**wǔ diǎn líng wǔ fēn**), answer the following questions in Chinese:

a What will the time be in ten minutes?
b What time was it ten minutes ago?
c How long is it before it is 5.45?
d What time is it in 12 hours' time?
e The train is leaving in two minutes. What time is the train scheduled to leave?

5 Answer the following questions in Chinese based on the day of the week it is when you are doing this exercise.

a What day is it tomorrow?
b And yesterday?
c Five days from today?
d How many days is it before next Tuesday?

6 We don't know the answers to the following questions, but you do:

a Which months are Spring in the part of the world you are living in?
b When is Summer (i.e. what months)? Autumn? Winter?
c How many months is it before your next birthday?
d How many months is it before the New Year? (**Hái yǒu X ge yuè.**)

Quick review

Answer the following questions in Chinese according to the information on the boards.

a What's the date today?
b What day is it today?
c What's the time now?
d When does the train from Oxford (**Niújīn**) arrive? At which platform?
e When does the train to Cambridge (**Jiànqiáo**) leave? From which platform?

Thursday March 30th
16.27
Departure
CAMBRIDGE
Platform 1
16.50

Thursday March 30th
16.27
Arrival
OXFORD
Platform 3
16.45

06

nǐ jīntiān xiǎng zuò shénme?

what do you want to do today?

In this unit you will learn
- how to say what you want to do
- how to understand and ask for advice
- how to express similarities
- how to compare and contrast

Before you start

Word order is very important in Chinese so there's plenty of help with some of the basic rules in this unit. You'll also learn different ways of making comparisons.

Let's try

1 It is often very difficult to get train tickets in China. You are in Běijīng and want to go to Tiānjīn in a couple of days' time. A Chinese friend offers to get your ticket for you as he knows you are very busy. Tell him you want a train ticket for the 9.30am train on Thursday.

2 Say the following dates in Chinese:
   a 6 January 1997
   b 21 March 2000 (líng = *zero*)
   c 15 August 1943

3 When is your birthday?

4 When were your parents born?

Key words and phrases

Běihǎi Gōngyuán	*Beihai Park*
bǐ	*compared to*
chē	*vehicle (bus, bike, car)*
dìng (piào)	*to book (a ticket)*
dōngxi	*thing, object*
fúwùyuán	*assistant, housestaff (lit. service person)*
gěi	*for; to give*
gēn	*and*
háishi	*or (used in question forms)*
huàn qián	*to change money*
kàn	*to watch, to look at*
mǎi	*to buy*
nàme	*in that case, then*
nán	*difficult*
qián	*money*
ránhòu	*afterwards*
róngyì	*easy*
shāngdiàn	*shop*
tīng	*to listen to*

wèntí	question, problem
méi wèntí	no problem
xiān	first
xiǎng	would like to; to think
Xīfāng	the West, Western
xiūxi	to rest, rest
yào	to want, to need, will
yínháng	bank
yíyàng	same
yǒu yìsi	interesting (lit. have meaning)
zài	(indicating continuing action)

Leisure activities

dǎ tàijíquán	to do Tai Chi
diànyǐng	film, movie
jīngjù	Peking opera
yīnyuè	music
yīnyuèhuì	concert
tīng yīnyuèhuì	to attend a concert
zájì	acrobatics
zuò	to do
zuò qìgōng	to do qigong

Questions and phrases

shénme shíhou?	What time?, When?
Zǎoshang hǎo!	Good morning!
Zhōngguó Yínháng	Bank of China
zuò chē	to take the bus (lit. sit vehicle)
A bǐ B nán/róngyì	A is more difficult / easier than B
A gēn B (bù) yíyàng	A is the same as (different from) B
Nǐ xiǎng zuò shénme?	What do you want to do?
Tā zài zuò shénme?	What's he / she doing?
Tài hǎo le!	Excellent!

Learning tips

1 Go back to the **Pronunciation guide** and read the notes there. The best way of learning this selection of sounds is in pairs, as follows:

b and **p**	**zh** and **ch**
d and **t**	**j** and **q**
z and **c**	**g** and **k**

2 Take a sheet of A4 paper and hold it vertically in front of you. Say **b** . . . If you are saying it correctly the sheet will not move. Then say **p** and the top of the sheet should be blown away from you. The same should happen with **d** and **t**, i.e. the sheet should not move when you say **d** but it should move with **t**! Repeat this with each remaining pair. The sheet should not move with **z**, **zh**, **j** and **g** but it should move with **c**, **ch**, **q** and **k**.

Dialogues

▶ Dialogue 1

Frank is attending a conference in China. Today he is free. His Chinese host, Xiǎo Wú, is asking him about his plans. Listen to or read the dialogue and note down his plans:

Frank's plans	
Shàngwǔ:	
Xiàwǔ:	
Wǎnshang:	

Xiǎo Wú	Jīntiān xiūxi. Nǐ xiǎng zuò shénme?
Frank	Wǒ xiǎng qù mǎi dōngxi. Kěshì wǒ yào xiān huàn qián.
Xiǎo Wú	Hǎo. Wǒmen xiān zuò chē qù Zhōngguó Yínháng huàn qián, ránhòu qù shāngdiàn mǎi dōngxi.
Frank	Hǎo. Xiàwǔ wǒ xiǎng qù Běihǎi Gōngyuán.
Xiǎo Wú	Méi wèntí. Wǎnshang ne?
Frank	Wǎnshang wǒmen qù kàn zájì hǎo bu hǎo?
Xiǎo Wú	Tài hǎo le. Wǒ qǐng fúwùyuán gěi wǒmen dìng piào.

▶ Dialogue 2

Frank has changed his money, done the shopping and been to Beihai Park. Unfortunately there are no tickets for the acrobatics this evening. So Frank and Xiǎo Wú are planning what to do instead.

Xiǎo Wú	Jīntiān wǎnshang nǐ xiǎng kàn diànyǐng háishi kàn jīngjù?
Frank	Wǒ bù xǐhuan jīngjù.
Xiǎo Wú	Nàme wǒmen kàn diànyǐng ba. Diànyǐng bǐ jīngjù yǒu yìsi.
Frank	Yǒu mei yǒu yīnyuèhuì?

Xiǎo Wú	Nǐ xiǎng tīng Zhōngguó yīnyuè háishi tīng Xīfāng yīnyuè?	
Frank	Zài Zhōngguó dāngrán tīng Zhōngguó yīnyuè.	

▶ Dialogue 3

A whole range of activities goes on in Chinese parks in the early morning. Tai Chi is especially popular. Frank decides to go and see for himself.

Frank	Zǎoshang hǎo!
Passer-by	Zǎoshang hǎo!
Frank	(*pointing to someone doing Tai Chi*) Tā zài zuò shénme?
Passer-by	Tā zài dǎ tàijíquán.
Frank	Nèi ge rén yě zài dǎ tàijíquán ma?
Passer-by	Bù. Tā zài zuò qìgōng.
Frank	Qìgōng gēn tàijíquán yíyàng ma?
Passer-by	Bù yíyàng.
Frank	Qìgōng bǐ tàijíquán nán ma?
Passer-by	Bù yídìng. Wǒ shuō qìgōng bǐ tàijíquán róngyì.

北海公园   Běihǎi Gōngyuán

Language notes

1 Word order again!

In some ways the Chinese language is much more logical than English in its word order. In English you can say:

First I want to change some money. *or*
I want to change some money *first*.

In Chinese the position of **xiān** (*first*) is not changeable. It comes after **Wǒ yào** (*I want*) but before **huàn diǎnr qián** (*change some money*):

Wǒ yào **xiān** huàn diǎnr qián.

This is because **xiān** is connected with what you want to do, not with what you want; and adverbs like **xiān** precede the verb to which they refer.

2 Time before manner before place (TMP)

In Chinese you say:

I *tomorrow at 9am* (time) *by plane* (manner) go *to China* (place).

You can't say:

I'm going to China by plane at 9am tomorrow.
or I'm going by plane to China at 9am tomorrow.

In Chinese the word order is logical: first you establish *when* you're going to do it, then *how* you're going to do it, and then *where* you're going to do it. So the rule to remember is **Time** (**T**) comes before **Manner** (**M**) and **Manner** (**M**) comes before **Place** (**P**); TMP for short:

Wǒmen xiān (**T**) zuò chē (**M**)   *We'll go to the Bank of China*
   qù Zhōngguó Yínháng (**P**)   *in the car to change money*
   huàn qián.   *first (lit. we first sit car go*
   China Bank change money).

Wǒmen shí'èr diǎn zhōng (**T**)   *We'll have lunch at the Peace*
   zài Hépíng Fàndiàn (**P**)   *Hotel at 12.*
   chī wǔfàn.

As you can see from the second example sometimes only two out of the three elements (TMP) are present but the rule still applies.

3 Either . . . or?

Do you want to go to a film *or* to the opera?

To express the *or* in the sentence above you use **háishi** in Chinese. Of course, you don't have to reverse the subject/verb order to make a question as in English.

All you do is put **háishi** between two statements thereby making them alternatives from which the listener must choose *one*:

Nǐ xiǎng kàn diànyǐng **háishi** kàn jīngjù?	*Would you like to go to a film or to the Peking opera?* (*lit.* you fancy see film or see Peking opera)
Nǐ xiǎng tīng Zhōngguó yīnyuè **háishi** (tīng) Xīfāng yīnyuè?	*Would you like to listen to Chinese music or Western music?*

If the subject or object in both halves is the same you don't need to repeat it (this holds true for any two clauses, not just ones using **háishi**, and is a feature of Chinese), but there should be a verb in both halves even if it is the same one. However, in colloquial Chinese the second verb is sometimes left out if it is the same as the first one. This is shown in the two examples above.

An exception to this rule is if the verb is **shì** (*to be*). In this case, the second **shì** may be left out. Here is an example of this:

Tā shì nǐde péngyou **háishi** nǐde lǎoshī?	*Is he your friend or your teacher?*

Try saying **háishi shì** and you'll understand why!

4 To be in the middle of doing something

To show that an action is in progress the word **zài** is put in front of the verb:

Tā **zài** dǎ tàijíquán.	*He's doing Tai Chi.*
Wǒ **zài** zuò qìgōng.	*I'm doing qigong.*
Nǐ **zài** kàn diànshì.	*You're watching TV.*

You will sometimes find the words **zhèng** or **zhèng zài** used in exactly the same way instead of **zài**. They are simply alternatives. **Ne**, at the end of a sentence, can also convey the idea that the action is in progress; or you might find **ne** occurring with any of the above. Here are a few examples to illustrate this:

Xiǎo Liú **zhèngzài tīng**
   yīnyuè (**ne**).

Xiao Liu is listening to music.

Tāmen **zhèng** chī wǔfàn **ne**.

They're in the middle of lunch.

Wǒmen kāi huì **ne**. Qǐng nǐ
   míngtiān zài lái.

*We're in the middle of a
meeting. Please come again
tomorrow.*

Note that this action in progress can take place in the past, present or future and it is the use of time-words (plus context) which tells us when the action actually takes place:

Míngtiān shàngwǔ tā yídìng
   zài yóuyǒng (**ne**).

*She'll certainly be swimming
tomorrow morning.*

Zuótiān wǎnshang wǒ **zài**
   kàn xì (**ne**).

*I was at the theatre yesterday
evening.*

5 The same or not the same?

In Chinese, to express that one thing is the same as another, or *A is the same as B* you say **A gēn** (*with*) **B yíyàng** (*the same*).

A gēn B yíyàng gāo.
A is as tall as B.

Wáng tàitai **gēn** Lǐ xiǎojie
   yíyàng gāo.
Mrs Wang is as tall as Miss Li.

Zhāng xiānsheng **gēn** tā jiějie
   yíyàng pàng.
*Mr Zhang is as fat as
his elder sister.*

To say that A is *not* the same as B you simply put **bù** in front of **yíyàng**:

A gēn B bù yíyàng gāo.
A is not as tall as B.

6 Making comparisons

To say that something is *more . . . than* use **bǐ**:

A **bǐ** B nán.	*A is more difficult than B.*
Qìgōng **bǐ** tàijíquán nán.	*Qigong is more difficult than Tai Chi.*
Kàn diànyǐng **bǐ** kàn jīngjù yǒu yìsi.	*Going to the cinema (lit. see/watch film) is more interesting than watching Peking opera.*

It is important to note that **bù bǐ** does not mean *less . . . than*. Look carefully at the following examples:

Tā **bù bǐ** wǒ dà.	*He is no older than I.*
Wǒ jiějie **bù bǐ** nǐ gāo.	*My elder sister is no taller than you.*

7 Helping verbs

Helping verbs or modal verbs such as *want, ought to, must, can* occur before action verbs or verbal expressions:

Nǐ **xiǎng** zuò shénme?	*What would you like to do?*
Wǒ **xiǎng** qù mǎi dōngxi.	*I'd like to go shopping.*
Wǒ **gāi** qù.	*I should go.*
Tā **yào** zǒu.	*She wants to leave.*
Nǐ **huì** shuō Hànyǔ ma?	*Can you speak Chinese?*
Tāmen **xǐhuan** mǎi dōngxi.	*They like shopping.*

Note the difference between **xiǎng** (*would like to do, fancy doing, something*) and **xǐhuan** (*like*).

Unlike other types of verbs which can take endings to indicate, for example, that something has taken place or to show direction, these 'helping' or auxiliary verbs cannot have anything added to them.

8 To give or not to give

Gěi basically means *to give*, but it can be used with a noun or pronoun (referring to a person or living thing) *before* the verb to mean *to do something for someone or something*.

Wǒ **gěi** nǐ kànkan.	*I'll take a look for you.*
Tā **gěi** wǒ kāi mén.	*He opened the door for me.*
Wǒ qǐng fúwùyuán **gěi** wǒmen dìng piào.	*I'll ask the attendant to book tickets for us.*

i Chinese traditional music sounds very different from Western music. If you ever have the chance to see Peking opera, do take it. You may decide never to go again but it is certainly worth trying once, just for the experience! The make-up and costumes are very elaborate and give you all sorts of information about the characters being portrayed, so try to go with somebody who knows something about Peking opera. Most people enjoy the battles and the acrobatics if not the singing!

Examples of Peking opera masks

You might have heard of **tàijí** (often written **Tai Chi** in the West) or of **qìgōng** which are forms of exercise practised for hundreds of years in China. Some forms of **qìgōng** are thought to be beneficial to cancer sufferers and people are encouraged to go to regular classes (usually in the local park early in the morning around 6am) as part of their treatment and recovery programme.

Why not try out a **tàijí** or **qìgōng** class yourself? Ask at your local library for information. You are likely to meet other people in the class who are interested in learning Chinese and with whom you can practise, chat and exchange ideas.

Practice

1 Tā/tāmen zài zuò shénme? *What is he/she doing? What are they doing?*
Look at the pictures below and say what the people are doing using the pattern above.

a mǎi dōngxi   **b kàn zájì**   **c huàn qián**

d dǎ tàijíquán   **e kàn diànyǐng**   **f tīng yīnyuè**

2 Look at the pictures in Exercise 1. Suppose these are the things you plan to do at the weekend. Draw up a plan and say when you are going to do what. Expressions of time can either occur before the verb, or at the beginning of the sentence if you want to give them more emphasis. Look at these examples:

Xīngqīliù shàngwǔ wǒ yào qù zuò qìgōng.
Xīngqītiān wǎnshang wǒ xiǎng qù kàn diànyǐng.

3 **Tāmen yíyàng ma?** *Are they the same?*

gāo	*tall*
dà	*old (of age) (. . . duō dà?*
	How old . . .?)
xiǎo	*young (of age)*
zhòng	*heavy*

Answer the following questions using **yíyàng** or **bù yíyàng**.

Qū   Hú   Xǔ

AGE 70   AGE 25   AGE 25
60 kg   76 kg   60 kg
1·66m   1·75m   1·76m

a Qū gēn Xǔ yíyàng gāo ma?
b Xǔ gēn Hú yíyàng dà ma?
c Qū gēn Hú yíyàng zhòng ma?
d Xǔ gēn Hú yíyàng gāo ma?
e Qū gēn Xǔ yíyàng zhòng ma?
f Hú gēn Qū yíyàng dà ma?

4 According to the information in Exercise 3 are the following statements true or false? If true, say **duì**. If false, say **bú duì** and say what is true.

	duì	bú duì
a Hú bǐ Xǔ gāo.	☐	☐
b Hú bù bǐ Qū zhòng.	☐	☐
c Xǔ bǐ Hú dà.	☐	☐
d Qū bǐ Xǔ dà.	☐	☐
e Hú gēn Xǔ bǐ Qū xiǎo.	☐	☐

5 The following is what Mr Jones (Qióngsī xiānsheng) has put in his diary. Answer the questions below according to what is written in the diary.

Monday evening - learn Chinese
Tuesday morning - meeting
Wednesday morning - go to a concert
Thursday afternoon - meet a friend
Friday evening - see a film
Saturday - shopping
*   - change money*
Sunday - learn Tai Chi

a Qióngsī xiānsheng xīngqīliù háishi xīngqītiān xué tàijíquán?

b Tā shénme shíhou qù kàn (*to visit*) péngyou?

c Tā xīngqīsān wǎnshang qù tīng yīnyuèhuì háishi xīngqīsì wǎnshang qù?

d Tā xīngqī'èr shàngwǔ kāi huì háishi xiàwǔ kāi huì?

e Tā shénme shíhou qù mǎi dōngxi?

▶ Quick review

a Ask your Chinese friend what she would like to do tomorrow.

b Say Xiǎo Mǎ and her elder sister are as tall as each other.

c Say you find acrobatics more interesting than Peking opera.

d Ask Xiǎo Zhào where he would like to go this evening.

e Ask Ms Lǐ whether she would like to see a film or go to a concert.

The following signs should come in useful.

Gentlemen

Nán cèsuǒ

Ladies

Nǚ cèsuǒ

07

duōshao qián?

how much is it?

In this unit you will learn
- how to ask for things (in shops)
- how to ask the price
- how to state quantities
- numbers 100–1,000
- how to express the distance between two points

Before you start

You will get to grips with Chinese money in this unit and be able to comment on the prices of things. You will also master basic colours and learn how to make more complex comparisons.

Let's try

Tomorrow evening it is your turn to entertain your business colleagues from China.

a You don't know whether to take them to a concert or to a play (**kàn xì**) so what do you ask them?
b They want to go to a concert. How do you ask them whether they like Western music?
c They assure you that in the West they want to listen to Western music so what do **they** say to you?'

Key words and phrases

bǎi	*hundred*
búcuò	*pretty good, not bad*
cái	*not . . . until, only then*
dào	*to arrive, to go to*
. . . deduō/. . . duōle	*much (more)*
jǐ	*crowded*
jiàn	*(measure word for clothes)*
jīn	*half a kilogram*
jìn	*near, close*
jiù	*just; only*
kěshì	*but*
kuài	*(unit of money)*
lí	*distance from*
lóu	*floor*
mài	*to sell*
máoyī	*woollen pullover*
něi/nǎ?	*which?*
nèi/nà	*that*
shìchǎng	*market*
shìhé	*to suit*
shìshi	*to try*
tài . . . le!	*too . . . !*
tián	*sweet*
xīnxiān	*fresh*

yuǎn	*far*
zánmen	*we / us (including listener)*
zhàn	*(bus) stop, station*
zhèi/zhè	*this*
zhèr	*here, this place*
zhème (guì)	*so (expensive)*
zìyóu	*free, freedom*
zǒu lù	*to walk, on foot*
zuì	*the most*

Fruits

cǎoméi	*strawberry*
píngguǒ	*apple*
pútao	*grape*
xiāngjiāo	*banana*

Questions and phrases

A lí B duō yuǎn?	*How far is A from B?*
A lí B hěn jìn/yuǎn.	*A is close to / far from B*
duō cháng?	*how long?*
duō yuǎn?	*how far?*
duōshao?	*how much? how many?*
Duōshao qián yì jīn? **Yì jīn duōshao qián?**	*How much is it for half a kilo?*
. . . kěyǐ ma?	*Can I . . . ? Is it allowed . . . ?*
Nín mǎi shénme?	*What would you like (to buy)?*
Wǒ yào . . .	*I want . . .*
shénme yánsè (de)?	*what colour?*
. . . xíng ma?	*Is it OK? Can I . . . ?*
X zěnme mài?	*How much is X?*

Colours

hóng(sè) (de)	*red*		**lán(sè) (de)**	*blue*
huáng(sè) (de)	*yellow*		**bái(sè) (de)**	*white*
lǜ(sè) (de)	*green*		**hēi(sè) (de)**	*black*

Learning tips

Here are two more pairs: **lu** and **lü**, **nu** and **nü**.

Go back to the **Pronunciation guide** and read the notes there. You will need a mirror for the next exercise.

First of all push out your lips and say *oo*. Then tighten them and say *you*. Repeat this but put l in front of the *oo*. Now you have the sound **lu**. To say **lü** say the word *lewd* without the d. For **nu** and **nü** say the *noo* of *noodles* and the *nu* of *nude*! Now look in the mirror and say the sounds again. What do you notice about your lips when you say the two different sounds?

You have to tighten them to say the **ü** sound don't you? For those of you who know a little French or German the **ü** in Chinese is like the *u* in *tu* (French) or the *ü* in *über* (German).

Ju, qu and **xu** are also pronounced as though they were written with **ü**. Don't confuse them with **zhu, chu,** and **shu** where the **u** is the *oo* sound.

▶ Numbers 100–1,000

100	yìbǎi	300	sānbǎi
200	èrbǎi/liǎngbǎi	308	sānbǎi líng bā
202	èrbǎi líng èr	410	sìbǎi yīshí
210	èrbǎi yīshí	794	qībǎi jiǔshísì
225	èrbǎi èrshíwǔ	1,000	yìqiān

Think of a number as being made up of units, tens and hundreds. If there is a zero in the tens column, you have to say **líng** (*zero*) in Chinese.

Ten is **shí** in Chinese but when it occurs with *one hundred*, *two hundred*, and so on you have to say *one ten*: **yīshí**, so 110 is **yìbǎi yīshí**.

Dialogues

▶ Dialogue 1

It may not be easy to get what you want in a shop despite the polite service you get. This customer knows what she wants and what she doesn't want, as this dialogue shows:

	(*at the information point*)
Customer	Qǐng wèn, zài nǎr mǎi máoyī?
Assistant	Zài èr lóu.
	(*at knitwear counter*)
Assistant	Nín mǎi shénme?
Customer	Wǒ xiǎng mǎi yí jiàn máoyī.
Assistant	Yào něi jiàn? Nín xǐhuan shénme yánsè de?

Customer	Nèi jiàn hóngsè de gěi wǒ kànkan xíng ma?
Assistant	Zhèi jiàn hěn hǎo.
Customer	O, tài dà le. Nèi jiàn huángsè de wǒ shìshi kěyǐ ma?
Assistant	Zhèi jiàn yě búcuò.
Customer	O, tài xiǎo le.
Assistant	Zhèi jiàn lánsè de hěn shìhé nǐ.
Customer	Tài hǎo le. Duōshao qián?
Assistant	Wǔbǎi kuài.
Customer	Nn, tài guì le. Duìbuqǐ, xièxie nǐ.
Assistant	... ...

Wǔxīng chāojí shìchǎng
Five star supermarket

i In Chinese the ground floor is **yī lóu**, (*lit.* one floor), the first floor is **èr lóu** (*lit.* two floor), the second floor **sān lóu** (*lit.* three floor), the third floor **sì lóu** (*lit.* four floor) and so on.

▶ Dialogue 2

If you can't get what you want in one shop, you can try somewhere else. This is what Xiǎo Fāng is suggesting to Ann.

Fāng	Wǒmen qù zìyóu shìchǎng kànkan ba.
Ann	Hǎo. Zìyóu shìchǎng lí zhèr duō yuǎn?
Fāng	Hěn jìn. Zuò chē liǎng、sān zhàn jiù dào le.
Ann	Chē tài jǐ le. Zánmen zǒu lù qù ba.
Fāng	Kěshì zǒu lù tài yuǎn le.
Ann	Zǒu lù yào duō cháng shíjiān?
Fāng	Zǒu lù èr、sānshí fēnzhōng cái néng dào.
Ann	Hǎo ba. Nàme zánmen zuò chē qù ba.

▶ Dialogue 3

There are markets throughout China where you can probably bargain. This is what you might hear at a fruit stall.

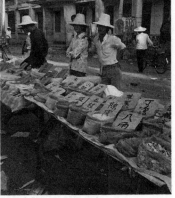

Buyer	Píngguǒ zěnme mài?
Seller	Sì kuài yì jīn.
Buyer	Zhēn guì! Tāmende píngguǒ sān kuài bā yì jīn.
Seller	Kěshì wǒde píngguǒ bǐ tāmende dà yìdiǎnr.
Buyer	Pútao duōshao qián yì jīn?
Seller	Sì kuài liǎng máo wǔ yì jīn.
Buyer	Zhème guì! Tāmen de sì kuài yì jīn.
Seller	Kěshì wǒde pútao bǐ tāmende tián duōle.
Buyer	Cǎoméi yì jīn duōshao qián?
Seller	Bā kuài èr.
Buyer	Tài guì le!
Seller	Kěshì wǒde cǎoméi bǐ tāmen de xīnxiān deduō.
Buyer	Nǐde dōngxi zuì guì.
Seller	Kěshì wǒde dōngxi zuì hǎo!

斤斤计较 **Jīn jīn jìjiào** (Chinese proverb)

Haggle over every ounce, quibble over small differences

Language notes

1 More on measure words

You have already met in Unit 4 the measure words **běn** (for books and magazines) and **zhāng** (for rectangular or square flat objects), together with the most common measure word of all, **gè**.

Some measure words like **jīn** (*half a kilogram*) and **bēi** (*cup*) are actually indicators of quantity. The table below lists some of the more common of these:

Pinyin	Category	Examples
bǎ	objects with a handle, chairs	*knife, umbrella, toothbrush, chair*
bāo	parcel, packet	*cigarettes, noodles*
bēi	cup, glass	*tea, coffee, wine*
běn	volume	*book, dictionary*
fēng		*letter*
gè	people, things which do not fall into other categories; substitute MW	*person, student*
jiàn	piece, article	*clothes, luggage*
jīn	indicator of quantity (0.5 kilogram)	*fruit, vegetables*
kuài	piece	*soap, land*
lǐ	indicator of length ($\frac{1}{3}$ mile, 0.5 km)	*road*
liàng	things with wheels	*car, bicycle*
píng	bottles, jars	*beer, wine, jam*
tiáo	long and winding; carton (e.g. 200)	*towel, trousers, fish; cigarettes*
wèi	people (*polite*)	*teacher, lady, gentleman*
zhāng	flat, rectangular objects	*ticket, blanket, table, paper, map*

Note that **gōngjīn** (*lit.* public pound) is a *kilogram*, **gōnglǐ** (*lit.* public li) is a *kilometre* and **yīnglǐ** (*lit.* English li) is a *mile*.

2 Money, money, money . . . !

Chinese money operates the decimal system and the currency in China is known as **rénmínbì** (*the people's currency*). Foreign currency is known as **wàibì** (*lit.* external/outside currency).

The largest single unit is the **yuán** 元 (written as ¥ in many transactions). There are ten **jiǎo** 角 in one **yuán** and ten **fēn** 分 in one **jiǎo**. These are the words (and Chinese characters) used in the written language and printed on banknotes, tickets, etc. so it is important to recognize them.

You saw how the characters for 1 to 10 were written in Unit 3. Don't be put off by the more complex characters you will see on Chinese banknotes. This also goes for the character 元 which is written 圓 on banknotes. These prevent confusion (and forgery!) when numbers are being written out in financial transactions.

In spoken Chinese, **kuài** 块 piece/lump is used for **yuán** and **máo** 毛 for **jiǎo** but **fēn** remains unchanged.

RMB	Spoken	Written
0.01 yuán	yì fēn (qián)	yì fēn
0.1 yuán	yì máo (qián)	yì máo
1.00 yuán	yí kuài (qián)	yì yuán
5.5 yuán	wǔ kuài wǔ	wǔ yuán wǔ jiǎo
14.32 yuán	shísì kuài sān máo èr	shísì yuán sān jiǎo èr fēn
30.09 yuán	sānshí kuài líng* jiǔ fēn	sānshí yuán líng* jiǔ fēn

* If a sum of money involves **kuài** and **fēn** but no **máo** the absence of **máo** is marked by a **líng** (*zero*).

When two or more different units of currency are used together, the last one is often omitted:

sì kuài liù	rather than	sì kuài liù máo	¥4.60
bā máo qī	rather than	bā máo qī fēn	¥0.87

3 Too much?

Tài (*too*) is almost always with **le**:

tài xiǎo le	*too small*
tài guì le	*too expensive*
tài hǎo le	*excellent, great*

It is probably better just to accept this as a rule rather than try to analyze it!

4 How far is A from B?

To say A is a long way from B, where A and B are fixed points, use:

A **lí** (*separate*) B **hěn yuǎn** (*far*)

If you don't use **hěn** (*very*), some sort of comparison is implied, i.e. A is a long way from B (but near to C). Thus in Chinese, as we have said before, **hěn** is very weak.

Lúndūn **lí** Àidīngbǎo **hěn yuǎn**.	*London is a long way from Edinburgh.*

To say A is near B use: A **lí** B **hěn jìn** (*near*).

Niújīn **lí** Lúndūn hěn **jìn**.	*Oxford is close to London.*

To say exactly how far A is from B use: A **lí** B (**yǒu**) the distance.

Yǒu (*to have*) can also have the meaning *there is/there are*.

Jiànqiáo (*Cambridge*) **lí** Niújīn **yǒu yìbǎi liùshí gōnglǐ**.	*Cambridge is 160 kilometres from Oxford.*

A and B can also be fixed points in time. To say how far A is from B *in time* use: A **lí** B **yǒu** + time difference.

Nǐde shēngrì lí jīntiān hái **yǒu sì tiān**.	*There are still four days to go to your birthday* (*lit.* your birthday separate today still have four days).

5 Approximate numbers

If you want to say *two or three* (people) in Chinese, you put the words for *two* (of a pair) and *three* one after another with a pause-mark in between them:

liǎng、sān ge rén   *two or three people*
wǔ、liù běn shū   *five or six books*

20 or 30 is **èr、sānshí**: the **shí** is only said *once*.

45 or 46 is **sìshíwǔ、liù**: the **sìshí** is only said *once*.

6 More on comparisons

You have already met **bǐ** in Unit 6, p. 63:

Chī fàn **bǐ** hē jiǔ yǒu yìsi.   *Eating is more interesting than consuming alcohol.*

To say that A is *much* more . . . than B use:

A **bǐ** B adjective/verb **duōle**.
    or
A **bǐ** B adjective/verb **deduō**.

Zhè jiàn máoyī **bǐ** nèi jiàn   *This sweater is much bigger than that one.*
    dà **duōle**.
Cǎoméi **bǐ** píngguǒ guì   *Strawberries are much more expensive than apples.*
    deduō.

To say that A is a little more . . . than B use: A **bǐ** B adjective/verb **yìdiǎnr**.

Wǒde shuǐguǒ (*fruit*) **bǐ** tāde   *My fruit is a little fresher than his.*
    shuǐguǒ xīnxiān **yìdiǎnr**.

7 Be the best!

You only have to put the little word **zuì** (*most*) in front of **hǎo** to make it into *the best*! Look carefully at the following examples using **zuì**:

zuì hǎo   *the best* (lit. most good)
zuì guì   *the most expensive*
zuì tián   *the sweetest*

You can put **de** + noun after the examples to make such phrases as:

zuì hǎo **de** pútao   *the best grapes*
zuì guì **de** cǎoméi   *the most expensive strawberries*
zuì tián **de** píngguǒ   *the sweetest apples*

8 *Cái* and *jiù*

Both **cái** and **jiù** are adverbs indicating something about time.
Cái indicates that something takes place later or with more
difficulty than had been expected. **Jiù**, on the other hand,
indicates that something takes place earlier or more promptly
than expected:

Tā sì diǎn zhōng **cái** lái.	*He didn't come until four* (though I had asked him to come at 3.15).
Tāmen liù diǎn bàn **jiù** lái le.	*They were there by 6.30* (though we had invited them for seven).

Cái often translates as *not . . . until*. **Jiù** usually has a **le** at the
end of the sentence to convey a sense of completion whereas
cái does not. **Jiù** will sometimes have **zǎo** (*early*) in front of it as
well as **le** at the end.

Both **cái** and **jiù** must come immediately before the verb whatever
else there is in the sentence. Look carefully at the following
examples:

Zuò chē liǎng、sān zhàn **jiù** dào le.	*It's only two or three stops on the bus.*
Zǒu lù èr、sānshí fēnzhōng **cái** néng dào.	*It will take as much as 20 or 30 minutes on foot (if we walk).*
Zuótiān hěn lěng dànshi jīntiān **cái** xià xuě.	*Yesterday was very cold but it didn't snow until today.*
Wǒ xiànzài **cái** zhīdao Fǎguó dōngxi guì.	*It's only now that I know things in France are expensive.*
Wǒ **zǎo jiù** zhīdao le.	*I knew ages ago (that things in France are expensive).*

Learning tips

What do you do if you don't understand?

1 Don't panic and don't give up listening.
2 Try to concentrate on what you do understand and guess the
  rest. If there comes a point where you really feel you can't
  understand anything, isolate the phrase or word(s) that is
  causing you problems and say to the speaker:

. . . shì shénme yìsi?	*What does . . . mean?*

Hopefully he or she will say it in another way that you will be able to understand. Remember the two useful sentences you learnt in Unit 3:

Qǐng nǐ zài shuō yí biàn.   *Please say it again.*
Qǐng nǐ shuō màn yìdiǎn.   *Please speak more slowly.*

i Most Chinese people are expert bargainers. A lot of selling is done from street stalls or with articles laid out on a piece of cloth on the ground. In these circumstances it is possible to bargain. If you are interested in buying something, point to it and say:

Zhè ge duōshao qián?   *How much is this?*

Having got a price, one way is to start by halving it and to say:

Wǒ zhǐ néng gěi nǐ X kuài.   *I can only give you X kuai.*

And then the fun starts with the two of you negotiating a price that you both find acceptable. It is a good policy to decide from the outset how much you are prepared to pay for something so that you have that in mind when bargaining. If neither of you can agree on a price, you can finish the bargaining by saying:

Xièxie, wǒ bù mǎi le.   *Thank you, I won't buy it then.*

and walking away. Sometimes if you are lucky, the vendor will rush after you and offer it to you for the last price you offered or one very similar.

Fruit and vegetables sold from stalls are normally offered at a certain price and if you think it's too expensive, you just don't buy them. Don't buy from anyone whose prices are not shown until you have ascertained how much they are. The Chinese are very good at charging fellow-Chinese one price and foreigners another (naturally more expensive). Unfortunately it is very hard to check whether they are giving you the correct weight as they often use a pole with weights on one end and a pan (to hold the purchased fruit on) on the other. There is no bargaining in ordinary shops and department stores.

Practice

1 Say the following prices in Chinese.
   Example: ¥4.03 sì kuài líng sān fēn

   a ¥0.52   c ¥12.76   e ¥205.54
   b ¥2.25   d ¥99.99   f ¥8.07

2 **Duōshao qián?** *How much is it?*

Tell your Chinese friend how much these fruits cost in your local town. You need to know the words **yīng bàng** (*a pound in money*) and **biànshì** (*pence*).

Example: Píngguǒ yì jīn wǔshíbā biànshì.
            Pútao yí bàng sì-jiǔ yì jīn.

Note that in prices over £1 which include pence, **shí** (*ten*) is left out where the number of pence is ten or more. The number of pence are treated as separate digits, for example, £1.45 is **yí bàng sì-wǔ**. One **jīn** (used all over China) is equivalent to half a kilogram or a little over a pound in weight.

3 You want to buy the following vegetables in a Chinese market, but they are not priced. Ask the greengrocer the prices by filling in the blanks in the following questions:

xīhóngshì (*tomato*)	¥0.65 a jin
báicài (*Chinese leaves*)	¥0.42 a jin
tǔdòu (*potato*)	¥0.28 a jin

a **You** ____ ____ mài?
Greengrocer Liù máo wǔ yì jīn.
b **You** ____ yì jīn ____ qián?
Greengrocer Yì jīn sì máo èr.
c **You** ____ ____ qián yì jīn?
Greengrocer Liǎng máo bā yì jīn.

▶4 Listen to the recording and write down the items mentioned and their prices. We've done the first for you. If you get really stuck look at what is said in the **Key to the exercises**.

a yú (*fish*) ¥7.09
b ¥
c ¥
d ¥
e ¥

5 What would you say in the following situations?

Example: Situation – It's freezing today.
You could say – **Jīntiān tài lěng** (*cold*) **le.**

a You've tried on a pullover and found it too big.
b It is 30°C today. (**rè** = *hot*)
c She's got too much money!
d The ticket to a match costs £150.
e You have studied French for years and still cannot speak it. (i.e. *French is too difficult*).

6 Make comparisons with the information given using the pattern

A bǐ B adjective

or

A bǐ B adjective (yìdiǎnr, deduō or **duōle):**

Example: cǎoméi ¥8.50/jīn, pútao ¥6.30/jīn
Cǎoméi bǐ pútao guì duōle.

a Nǎ ge guì? (**bǐ**) Píngguǒ ¥4.00/jīn;
Pútao ¥4.10/jīn

b Tāmen shéi gāo? (**yìdiǎnr**) Xiǎo Wáng 1.73m;
Lǎo Lǐ 1.70m

c Nǎ ge dìfang rè? (duōle)   Běijīng 29°C; Lúndūn 17°C
d Tāmen shéi dà? (deduō)   Bái xiānsheng 58;
Bái tàitai 48

7 Use either **cái** or **jiù** to fill in the blanks.

a Wǔ diǎn kāi huì, tā sì diǎn bàn ____ lái le.
b Nǐ hái bù zhīdao ma? Wǒ zuótiān (*yesterday*) ____ zhīdao le.
c Duìbuqǐ, Lǐ lǎoshī jīntiān bù néng lái. Tā míngtiān ____ lái.
d Tā bù xiǎng míngtiān qù, tā xiǎng xiànzài ____ qù.
e Yīnyuèhuì qī diǎn kāishǐ (*start*), tā qī diǎn yíkè ____ lái.

▶ Quick review

How do you say:

a It will take only five minutes to get there.
b It will take (as long as) 50 minutes to get there.
c In my family my father is the oldest.
d The cinema is not far from my home.
e Bananas cost 49p per pound.

08

zěnmeyàng?

what's it like?

In this unit you will learn
- how to ask about sizes
- how to talk about clothes
  and shoes
- how to describe things
- how to express likes and
  dislikes
- how to make comparisons

Before you start

This unit will give you the necessary vocabulary and structures to ask people their opinions about things: **Nǐ kàn zěnmeyàng?** (*What's it like?*) and to make comparisons **Zhè ge méi yǒu nà ge hǎo** (*This one is not as good as that one*).

Let's try

Refer back to **Dialogue 1** and **Dialogue 3** in Unit 7 and answer the following questions:

1 Did the customer buy a pullover? Why?
2 How did the fruitseller justify his prices being higher than other people's? Give four reasons.

Key words and phrases

bù zěnmeyàng	*not so good*
dàxiǎo	*size*
fēicháng	*extremely*
gèng	*even more*
guò	*to pass or spend* (of time)
hái kěyǐ	*just so so*
héshì	*suitable*
jiàqī	*holiday, vacation*
juéde	*to feel, think*
kuài	*fast*
màn	*slow*
měi	*every*
měi tiān	*every day*
mō(mo)	*to feel, touch*
nǎli nǎli	*not really* (response to a compliment)
nánkàn	*ugly*
piányi	*cheap*
xià yǔ	*to rain*
xīn	*new*
xīn mǎi de	*newly bought*
xué(xí)	*to learn, study*
yánsè	*colour*
Yìdàlì	*Italy*

yǐhòu	*later, in future*
yǐqián	*before, in the past*
Yīngwén	*English language*
yǒu yìdiǎn(r)	*a little*
yòu . . . yòu . . .	*both . . . and . . .*
zǎo jiù	*ages ago, for ages*
zěnme le?	*what is / was the matter?*
zěnmeyàng?	*how is it? how about it?*
zhāng	*(measure word for flat objects)*
zhìliàng	*quality*
zhǐ yào	*only need / cost*
zhǔyì	*idea*
zúqiú	*football*

Learning tips

Here's another set of pairs:

j and **q**
zh and **ch**
sh and **r**

Go back to the **Pronunciation guide** again and read the notes there.

The **j** in Chinese is the same as our own. Say *jeans*, in the same way as you would say 'cheese' to the camera, a few times and observe your mouth in a mirror. You will notice that the corners of your mouth are drawn back as far as they can go.

Q bears no resemblance to our **q**. It is pronounced *in exactly the same way as* **j** but you put air behind it to make the **q**. You have already done some practice on **q** in Unit 1, p. 5, but as it is so different from **q** in English it is worth looking at again.

For **zh, ch, sh** and **r** you must curl your tongue back in a loose sausage-roll. They are all pronounced with the tongue in this position. **Zh** and **ch** are identical sounds except the **ch** is said with air behind it.

R is the one to watch. Listen to the recording carefully and try to reproduce the sounds you hear as closely as possible. Recording your own voice and then comparing it with the original would be extremely helpful at this stage.

Dialogues

▶ Dialogue 1

Sùlán is showing her newly bought pullover to her boyfriend Colin. She is very pleased with it as the price was reduced. But what does Colin think of it?

Sùlán	Zhè shì wǒ xīn mǎi de máoyī. Nǐ kàn zěnmeyàng?
Colin	Búcuò, búcuò.
Sùlán	Dàxiǎo héshì ma?
Colin	En, yǒu diǎnr dà.
Sùlán	Yánsè hǎokàn ma?
Colin	En, bù nánkàn.
Sùlán	Nǐ mōmo. . . . Nǐ juéde zhìliàng zěnmeyàng?
Colin	En, hái kěyǐ. Duōshao qián?
Sùlán	Bú guì, zhǐ yào yìbǎi wǔshí kuài.
Colin	Shénme?! Yìbǎi wǔshí kuài wǒ kěyǐ mǎi sān zhāng zúqiú piào!

大减价

Dà jiǎn jià
Big reductions

▶ Dialogue 2

Mr Li and Mrs Law are just back from holiday. How were their respective holidays?

Mrs Law	Jiàqī guò-de hǎo ma?
Mr Lǐ	Fēicháng hǎo, jiù shi dōngxi bù piányì.
Mrs Law	Wǒ zǎo jiù zhīdao le.
Mr Lǐ	Wǒ yǐqián juéde Yīngguó de dōngxi guì, xiànzài cái zhīdao Fǎguó de dōngxi gèng guì.
Mrs Law	Yìdàlì de dōngxi yě hěn guì shì bu shì?
Mr Lǐ	Yìdàlì de dōngxi yě bù bǐ Fǎguó de piányi. Nǐ de jiàqī guò-de zěnmeyàng?
Mrs Law	Bù zěnmeyàng.
Mr Lǐ	Zěnme le?
Mrs Law	Měi tiān dōu xià yǔ.

▶ Dialogue 3

Martin is learning Chinese. He has met a Chinese girl who is studying English. What is their plan?

Bǎojié	Nǐde Zhōngwén shuō-de zhēn hǎo.
Martin	Nǎli, nǎli. Wǒde Zhōngwén méi yǒu nǐde Yīngwén hǎo.
Bǎojié	Bù. Nǐde Zhōngwén bǐ wǒde Yīngwén hǎo deduō.
Martin	Yǐhòu wǒ bāng nǐ xué Yīngwén, nǐ bāng wǒ xué Zhōngwén, zěnmeyàng?
Bǎojié	Hǎo zhǔyì. Kěshì wǒ xué-de bú kuài.
Martin	Méi guānxi, wǒ xué-de yě hěn màn.

Language notes

1 A bit . . . ?

To say something is *a little/bit* . . . use:

adjective + (yì)**diǎnr**

hǎo (yì)**diǎnr**	*a bit better*
dà (yì)**diǎnr**	*a little older/bigger*

(See also p. 77 where adjective + **yìdiǎnr** is used in comparisons.)

When you wish to convey a negative feeling even if it is only subjective on your part, then **yǒu (yì)diǎnr** is put in front of the adjective:

Yǒu (yì)diǎnr guì.	*It's a bit on the expensive side.*
Yǒu (yì)diǎnr dà.	*It's a little on the big side.*

In all these examples you can miss out the **yì** to sound more colloquial.

2 How well do you speak Chinese?

When you are describing how the action of a verb is carried out, such as *quickly, slowly, well*, you use **de** after the verb and *then* the word for *quick, slow, good*, and so on.

You do *not* have to change them into adverbs as in English – quick-quickly, good-well.

Nǐde Zhōngwén shuō-**de** zěnmeyàng?	*What's your Chinese like?*
Wǒde Zhōngwén shuō-**de** bù hǎo.	*I don't speak Chinese well.*
Wǒ xué-**de** bú kuài.	*I don't learn fast.*

This **de** is different from the **de** you met in Units 3 and 5 but they are written the same in pinyin and both are toneless. They are represented by two entirely different Chinese characters however.

When sentences of this kind have an object you can either repeat the verb after the object adding **de** to the second verb:

Wǒ   xué   Zhōngwén **xué-de** hěn màn.
subject   verb   object
(*I'm learning Chinese very slowly.*)
Tā kàn shū **kàn-de** hěn duō.   *He reads a lot.*

Or you can miss out the first verb and have the object coming straight after the subject followed by the verb with **de**:

Nǐ Rìyǔ shuō-de zěnmeyàng?   *What's your Japanese like?*
   object
Wǒ Rìyǔ shuō-de bù hǎo.   *My Japanese is not very good.*

3 What's it like?

Zěnmeyàng (*What's it like? How?*) is a useful question word in Chinese. As you saw in Unit 2, p. 17 with **shéi** (*who*) and **shénme** (*what*), question words appear in the same position as the word or words which replace them in the answer:

Nǐ kàn **zěnmeyàng?**	*What do you think?*
Nǐ mōmo. Nǐ juéde zhìliàng **zěnmeyàng?**	*Feel it. What do you think of the quality?*
Jiàqī guò-de **zěnmeyàng?**	*How was your holiday?*
(Guò-de) bù **zěnmeyàng.**	*Not very good / not up to much.*

Note the neat expression **bù zěnmeyàng** (*not up to much*) in response to a question containing the question word **zěnmeyàng**.

4 Even more!

To say *even more expensive* in Chinese you only have to put the little word **gèng** in front of **guì**:

gèng guì	*even more expensive*
gèng piányi	*even cheaper, still cheaper*
gèng kuài	*even quicker, even more quickly*
Tā bǐ wǒ xué-de **gèng** màn.	*He learns even more slowly than I do.*

You will sometimes find **hái** (*still*) used instead of **gèng**, but the meaning remains exactly the same:

Nǐ bǐ tā xiě-de **hái** hǎo.   *You write even better than she does.*

5 Even more on comparisons!

You have already met **bǐ** in Unit 6, p. 63 and in Unit 7, p. 77. If you wish to say that something (A) is not up to a certain standard as represented by another person, living thing or object (B) use:

A **méi yǒu** B *adjective/verb*

Wǒde Zhōngwén (A) **méi yǒu**   *My Chinese is not as good* nǐde Yīngwén (B) **hǎo**.   *as your English.*
Nǐde qìchē **méi yǒu** wǒde   *Your car is not as fast as* (qìchē) **kuài**.   *mine.*

You will sometimes find **nàme** or **zhème** (*so*) in front of the adjective:

Zhè jiàn máoyī de dàxiǎo   *This sweater doesn't fit as* **méi yǒu** nà jiàn (máoyī   *well as that one* (lit. This MW de dàxiǎo) **nàme héshì**.   *sweater's size not up to that MW (sweater's size) so suitable).*

This construction can also be used in the positive form by omitting **méi**, but it is not nearly so common as the negative form:

Wǒ jiějie **yǒu** nǐ gēge   *My elder sister is as tall as your* **nàme gāo**.   *elder brother.*

6 Each and every!

Měi (*each/every*) is often reinforced by putting **dōu** (*both/all*) before the verb:

Měi tiān **dōu** xià yǔ.   *It rains/rained every day.*
Tā **měi** nián **dōu** qù   *He goes to China every year.* Zhōngguó.

In the example above, it is clear that **dōu** has to refer back to **měi nián** rather than to **tā** which is singular.

Tiān and **nián** don't need a measure word between **měi** and themselves because they act as measure words as well as nouns, but other nouns do:

měi ge jiàqī *every holiday*; **měi jiàn** máoyī *every sweater*

Note that the measure word between **měi** and **rén** is optional.

Learning tips

Don't worry about making mistakes!

The important thing is to keep talking. People quickly lose interest in talking to you if you look at them blankly and don't respond. Say something. Use gestures to help you out and don't worry about the mistakes. Don't be too ambitious in the initial stages – use vocabulary you know even if it means you have to keep the conversation simple. If all else fails, use a word in English (the foreign language most likely to be known by Chinese speakers), clearly pronounced, to keep things moving.

The Chinese are normally so delighted that someone has made the effort to learn their language that they are very patient and make enormous allowances for your accent and poor tones (or lack of them!), and are always very complimentary about your efforts.

Chéngjī **Quēdiǎn** **Cuòwu**
Achievements *Shortcomings* *Mistakes*

ℹ️ Following on from the above, even if your Chinese is very poor you will usually be told how good it is! The correct response to such compliments is either **Guòjiǎng, guòjiǎng** (*you praise me too much*), or **Nǎli, nǎli** lit. *where, where?* (meaning that you don't see it the way they do!). Self-deprecation is definitely a Chinese art – you are invited to somebody's house and the table is groaning with delicious food and you are told that it is only **biànfàn** (*simple/convenience food*). The cook asks you to forgive his/her poor cooking when you can see that the opposite is the case. Examples such as these are endless and come under the general heading of **kèqi huà** (*polite talk*). You will find more examples of **kèqi huà** later on in the book. Why not start making a list of them for your own interest? Note people's self-deprecatory remarks and other people's responses to them.

Never give Chinese friends white flowers. White is the colour for mourning in China. Be circumspect with red too – it's the colour associated with weddings (the bride's dress is traditionally red though with Western influence this is also changing). At Chinese New Year presents of money are given in little red envelopes (**hóng bāo**), and couplets expressing good luck and good fortune for the coming year are written on red paper and pasted on people's doors.

Practice

1 Match up the opposites:

a	yǐqián	i	nánkàn
b	dà	ii	màn
c	guì	iii	róngyì
d	hǎokàn	iv	piányi
e	kuài	v	yǐhòu
f	zǎo	vi	xiǎo
g	nán	vii	wǎn

▶ **Items of clothing**

Item	Measure word	
chènyī	(jiàn)	shirt
dàyī	(jiàn)	overcoat
jiākè	(jiàn)	jacket
kùzi	(tiáo)	trousers
nèikù	(tiáo)	underpants
qúnzi	(tiáo)	skirt
shuìyī	(jiàn)	nightdress, pyjamas
xié	(shuāng)	shoes (a pair of)
xīfú	(tào)	suit (Western)
yǔyī	(jiàn)	raincoat

2 Refer to the list of colours (Unit 7, p. 70) and items of clothing above. How would you ask for the following things in Chinese? (Note the measure words.)

Example: *a green jacket* yí jiàn lǜ jiākè

a a white shirt
b a yellow overcoat
c a blue suit
d a green skirt
e a pair of black shoes
f a pair of red trousers

3 Listen to the recording and answer the following questions. If you don't have the recording, read the passage below and then answer the questions.

a Xiǎo Cài jīntiān chuān (*wear*) shénme?
b Xiǎo Zhào jīntiān chuān shénme?
c Lǎo Fāng jīntiān chuān shénme?

Materials

bù	cotton / cloth
bùxié	cloth shoes
pí	leather
píxié	leather shoes
sīchóu	silk
rénzào gé	imitation leather

Xiǎo Cài jīntiān chuān yí jiàn bái chènyī, yì tiáo lán qúnzi. Xiǎo Cài hěn xǐhuan chuān píxié. Jīntiān tā chuān yì shuāng hóng píxié.

Xiǎo Zhào jīntiān chuān yí jiàn lán de sīchóu chènyī, yì tiáo hēi kùzi. Xiǎo Zhào zuì bù xǐhuan chuān píxié. Tā jīntiān chuān yì shuāng lǜ bùxié.

Lǎo Fāng jīntiān chuān yí tào hēi xīfú, yí jiàn bái chènyī, yì shuāng hēi píxié. Xīngqīyī dào xīngqīwǔ tā dōu chuān xīfú hé píxié.

4 Describe what the following people are wearing with the information provided:

Example: Xiǎo Wáng / white shirt / black trousers / yellow shoes.

Answer: Xiǎo Wáng chuān yí jiàn bái chènshān, yì tiáo hēi kùzi, yì shuāng huáng píxié.

a Lǎo Mǎ / black leather shoes / blue shirt.

b Xiǎo Qián / red shirt / black trousers / cloth shoes.

c Liú xiānsheng / grey (**huī**) suit / yellow shirt / brown (**zōng**) leather shoes.

5 How well do they do the following things? Answer each of the following questions using the information given in brackets.

Example: Xiǎo Zhū Fǎyǔ shuō-de zěnmeyàng? (*not at all well*)

Answer: Tā Fǎyǔ shuō-de bù zěnmeyàng.

a Lǐ xiānsheng Déwén (*German*) shuō-de zěnmeyàng? (*very well*)

b Zhāng tàitai jiàqī guò-de hǎo bu hǎo? (*not very well*)

c Cháo xiǎojie Yīngwén xué-de kuài bu kuài? (*extremely quickly*)

d Mǎlì yòng kuàizi (*chopsticks*) yòng-de zěnmeyàng? (*not at all well*)

e Hēnglì shuō Rìyǔ (*Japanese*) shuō-de hěn qīngchu (*clearly*) ma? (*very clearly*)

6 Look carefully at the pictures of Zhāng Tóng and Mǎ Fēng overleaf and the sentences comparing their height, age and weight. Then make up similar sentences comparing their cars, TVs (**diànshì**) and handwriting (**zì**) using **méi yǒu . . .** and the adjectives given in brackets.

Zhāng Tóng's car (dà, guì)   Mǎ Fēng's car

Example: Mǎ Fēng de chē **méi yǒu** Zhāng Tóng de chē **dà**.
Zhāng Tóng de chē **méi yǒu** Mǎ Fēng de chē **guì**.

Zhāng Tóng's TV   Mǎ Fēng's TV

a **diànshì** (*TV*) (dà, guì)

Zhāng Tóng

Mǎ Fēng

b (gāo, dà, zhòng)

5 July 2002 Dear Jack, Weather here sunny and warm. Having a great holiday. See you soon! Zhang Tong	8/C. Hello Susan Raining again today. Why did I have to come to Scotland for my holidays? Miss you— MaFeng

c zì (*handwriting*) (qīngchu *clear*)

▶ Quick review

What do you say?

a Say to someone that she speaks English very well.
b Say that something, e.g. a shirt, is a bit small.
c Ask someone how her holiday was.
d Say that England (**Yīnggélán**) is bigger than Ireland (**Ài'ěrlán**).
e Say that Germany is not as big as France.

Bù gōngpíng *Unfair*

09

qù . . . zĕnme zŏu?

how do I get to . . . ?

In this unit you will learn
- how to ask for and understand directions
- how to use public transport
- how to ask people if they have ever done something
- how to express how long something happens for

Before you start

You will be able to say all sorts of things about where you are going, where you are coming from and by what means of transport, by the time you have worked your way through this unit. You will also be able to say which order you are going to do things in and whether you have ever done them before.

Let's try

1 Refer back to **Dialogue 1** in Unit 8 and answer the following questions in Chinese:

a How much was the pullover?
b What could Colin have bought for the money instead?

2 a Somebody asks you whether French goods are more expensive than British ones. What do you reply?
b The same person compliments you on your spoken Chinese. What is your response?

Key words and phrases

Àomén	*Macao*
biān	*side*
xībiān(r)	*west side*
chēzhàn	*bus / train stop or station*
chuán	*ship, boat*
cóng	*from*
dǎsuàn	*to plan*
dìfang	*place*
dù jià	*to take a holiday*
duìmiàn	*opposite*
-guo	*have ever* (verb suffix)
hái	*still*
háishi	*would be better*
huàn (chē)	*to change* (bus)
jià	*holiday*
jiù	*emphatic*
X lù (chē)	*the number X bus*
mǎlù	*road*
méi shénme	*it's nothing, don't mention it*

nàr/nàli	there (used interchangeably)
qián	front, ahead
tiān	day
Tiāntán	Temple of Heaven
tīngshuō	I heard, I am told
tuìxiū	to retire
wǎng	in the direction of
wǎng nán kāi de chē	southbound bus
xià chē	to get off the bus
Xiānggǎng	Hong Kong
xiànmu	to envy
xíng	OK
yǐhòu	after
yòng	to need, to use
zěnme	how
zhōumò	weekend
cóng A dào B	from A to B
... jiù dào le.	It takes only ... to get there.
Qù X zěnme zǒu?	How do (I) get to X?
xiān ... zài ...	first ... then ...

Learning tips

1 z is pronounced like the -ds in *adds* or the z in *zoo*.
2 c is not at all like the c in English so be very careful with it. It is pronounced like the -ts in it*s*. It is useful to practise it together with z and to say them one after the other so that you can hear the difference clearly. Remember the top of your sheet of A4 (see Unit 6, p. 58) should be blown away from you when you say c but not when you say z.

Dialogues

▶ Dialogue 1

Xiǎo Féng and Lǎo Qiáo are talking about taking their holidays. Where is Xiǎo Féng going and how will she get to those places? What about Lǎo Qiáo? How long is his holiday?

Qiáo   Tīngshuō nǐ kuài yào qù dù jià le.
Féng   Duì. Wǒ yǒu sān ge xīngqī de jià, cóng liùyuè èrshíqī hào dào qīyuè shíbā hào.

Qiáo	Nǐ dǎsuàn qù nǎr?
Féng	Xiānggǎng hé Àomén. Zhèi liǎng ge dìfang wǒ dōu méi qù-guo.
Qiáo	Nǐ zěnme qù?
Féng	Wǒ xiān zuò fēijī dào Xiānggǎng, zài nàr zhù wǔ tiān. Zài cóng Xiānggǎng zuò chuán dào Àomén.
Qiáo	Wǒ zhēn xiànmu nǐ.
Féng	Nǐ shénme shíhou dù jià?
Qiáo	Wǒ? O, shí'èryuè.
Féng	Duō cháng shíjiān?
Qiáo	Bù zhīdao.
Féng	Zěnme huì bù zhīdao?
Qiáo	Jīnnián shí'èryuè wǒ jiù yào tuìxiū le.
Féng	Wǒ zhēn xiànmu nǐ.

i As China is situated in the East, the most important cardinal point is east rather than north. In the West we say *north, south, east, west* but the Chinese start with **dōng** (*east*) and say **dōng、 nán** (*south*), **xī** (*west*), **běi** (*north*).

South-west in Chinese is **xīnán** (*west, south*), *north-east* is **dōngběi** (*lit.* east, north) and so on.

▶ Dialogue 2

Ann is touring in Beijing. Today she is going to visit Tiantan. Can you follow the directions given to her by a passer-by?

Ann	Qǐng wèn, qù Tiāntán zěnme zǒu?
Passer-by	Tiāntán zài xīnán biānr. Zuò chē sì zhàn jiù dào le.

Ann	Zuò jǐ lù chē?
Passer-by	Nǐ xiān cóng zhèr wǎng dōng zǒu, zài zuò wǎng nán kāi de chē, shíwǔ lù、èrshísān lù dōu xíng. Chēzhàn zài yínháng duìmiànr.
Ann	Yòng huàn chē ma?
Passer-by	Bú yòng. Xià chē yǐhòu wǎng qián zǒu yìdiǎnr. Tiāntán jiù zài mǎlù xībianr.
Ann	Xièxie nín.
Passer-by	Méi shénme.

公共汽车站

Gōnggòng qìchēzhàn *Bus stop*

i When giving you directions, the Chinese (especially in the north) usually use the points of the compass rather than left and right. So it's good to know where north and south are when you ask somebody the way!

Dialogue 3

James is suggesting something adventurous to his friend, Huáng Zìlì. What is his suggestion and does Huáng accept it?

James	Nǐ qù-guo Tiānjīn ma?
Huáng	Méi qù-guo.
James	Xià ge zhōumò zánmen yìqǐ qù ba.
Huáng	Hǎo'a. Nǐ dǎsuàn zěnme qù? Zuò qìchē háishi zuò huǒchē?
James	Zánmen qí chē qù zěnmeyàng?
Huáng	Shénme? Nǐ fā fēng le! Qí chē qù Tiānjīn yào liǎng、sān tiān, yòu lèi yòu wēixiǎn.
James	Wǒ bú pà lèi, yě xǐhuan màoxiǎn!
Huáng	Fǎnzheng wǒ bù gēn nǐ yìqǐ qù. Wǒ zài jiā kàn diànshì, yòu shūfu yòu ānquán.

ānquán	safe
diànshì	TV
fā fēng	mad
fǎnzheng	no way, in any case
gēn	with
jiā	home
lèi	tired, tiring
màoxiǎn	adventurous, to take the risk
pà	afraid
qí	to ride (bicycle, motorbike, horse)
qìchē	vehicle, bus, car
shūfu	comfortable
wēixiǎn	dangerous
xià ge	next
yào . . .	it takes . . .
yìqǐ	together
yòu . . . yòu . . .	both . . . and . . .
zìxíngchē	bicycle

Language notes

1 About to

To say something is about to happen or is going to happen soon use:

yào (*want, will*) + verb . . . **le**

| Nǐ **yào** qù dù jià **le**. | *You're going on holiday soon.* |
| Wǒ **yào** qù Xiānggǎng **le**. | *I'm about to leave for Hong Kong.* |

Kuài (*quick*) or **jiù** (*then*) can also be put in front of **yào** to make the imminence of the action even clearer:

| Jīnnián shí'èr yuè wǒ **jiù yào** tuìxiū **le**. | *I'll be retiring in December.* |
| Tā **kuài yào** kàn diànshì **le**. | *He's about to watch TV.* |

2 From . . . to . . .

Simply use **cóng** (*from*) and **dào** (*to*).

| **cóng** Xiānggǎng **dào** Àomén | *from Hong Kong to Macao* |
| **cóng** Běijīng **dào** Tiānjīn | *from Beijing to Tianjin* |

And from one time to another:

cóng sānyuè shíbā hào **dào**   *from 18 March to 9 April*
  sìyuè jiǔ hào

There are only two small points to remember.

- The word order cannot be reversed in Chinese. You cannot say *I am going to* (**dào**) *China from* (**cóng**) *Japan*. So **cóng** must always precede **dào**.
- In the sentence, *I am going to* (**dào**) *Macao from* (**cóng**) *Hong Kong by* (**zuò**) *boat*, 'from Hong Kong' must come first followed by the means of transport 'by boat' and then 'to Macao' last:

  Wǒ **cóng** Xiānggǎng **zuò** chuán **dào** Àomén.

The Chinese are very logical – you cannot get to Macao unless you 'sit on the boat' **zuò chuán** first so that should come before 'to Macao' **dào Àomén**.

3 Have you ever . . . ?

If you put the little word **guo** after the verb it will emphasize a past experience:

Wǒ qù-**guo** Yìdàlì.   *I've been to Italy*
                                  (at some time or other).

Tā chī-**guo** Yìndù fàn.   *He has eaten Indian food*
                                  (at some time in the past).

You make the negative by putting **méi yǒu** in front of the verb:

Wǒ **méi** (yǒu) qù-**guo**   *I have never been to China.*
  Zhōngguó.

You make the question by putting **ma** or **méi you** at the end of the statement:

Nǐ qù-**guo** Tiānjīn **ma**?   *Have you (ever) been to*
                                  Tianjin?

Nǐ zuò-**guo** fēijī **méi you**? *Have you (ever) travelled*
                                  by plane?

Hái **méi yǒu** (qù-guo).   *Not yet.*
Méi zuò-guo.   *No, never.*

Note the two possible ways of answering a question with -**guo**.

4 First . . . then . . .

By using **xiān** (*first*) + verb followed by **zài** (*then*) + verb you show that the two actions are linked:

Wǒ **xiān** zuò fēijī dào Xiānggǎng, **zài** zuò huǒchē qù Běijīng.	*First I'll go Hong Kong by plane then I'll go by train to Beijing.*
Nǐ **xiān** cóng zhèr wǎng dōng zǒu, **zài** zuò wǎng nán kāi de chē.	*You walk eastwards from here first. Then you get on a bus going south* (lit. then sit towards south drive on bus).

The **xiān** + verb and the **zài** + verb may occur in two separate sentences but the idea of sequence of actions is still there:

(Wǒ) **xiān** zuò fēijī dào Xiānggǎng . . . **Zài** cóng Xiānggǎng zuò chuán dào Àomén.	*First I'll go to Hong Kong by plane . . . Then from Hong Kong I'll go to Macao by boat.*

By the way, this **zài** is written like the **zài** in **zàijiàn** not as in **zài** (*at, in*).

5 How long?

As you saw in Unit 1, time-words like *today, Wednesday, 6 o'clock* come before the verb in Chinese. However, when you want to say how long you do the action of the verb, the time-word comes after the verb:

Wǒ zài nàr zhù **wǔ tiān.**	*I'll stay there five days.*
Tā zài zhèr gōngzuò le **liǎng nián.**	*She worked here for two years.*

The **le** after the verb shows that the action of the verb has been completed.

6 Huì *Can*

You met **huì** (*can*) in Unit 6, p. 63 with the meaning *to know how to do something* (having learnt to do it). Its other meaning is *to be likely to* or *to be possible*:

Tā xiàwǔ **huì** lái.	*He'll (is likely to) come in the afternoon.*
Zěnme **huì** bù zhīdao?	*How could (you) not know?* (lit. how possible not know?)

7 Both . . . and . . .

To express *both . . . and . . .* you put **yòu** in front of the two adjectives or verbs:

yòu lèi yòu wēixiǎn	*both tiring and dangerous*
yòu shūfu yòu ānquán	*both comfortable and safe*
yòu hǎo yòu bú guì	*both good and inexpensive*

8 Added 'r'

You will find **r** added to some words in this unit in order for you to get used to seeing and reading it. It is used a great deal by people in the north of China especially around Beijing. You certainly don't have to use it but it is important to know that it exists. It is to be found on the ends of words such as:

(yì) diǎn	(yì)diǎnr	*a little bit*
yì wǎn	yì wǎnr	*one bowl*
tiān	tiānr	*day*
duìmiàn	duìmiànr	*opposite*
biān	biānr	*side*
xībian	xībianr	*west side*
wán (verb)	wánr	*to enjoy oneself*

Learning tips

Learn from your mistakes and keep trying

1 Everyone makes mistakes when learning a language. If you didn't make mistakes, you wouldn't have to learn it! Small children also make mistakes when learning their own language so accept that this is perfectly normal and natural.

2 Some mistakes affect the meaning of what you say more than others. For instance, it is important not to confuse **mǎi** (3rd tone) (*to buy*) with **mài** (4th tone) (*to sell*) for obvious reasons. But surprisingly enough, poor tones don't seem to affect the ability of most Chinese people to understand what you are saying. There is also a wide variety of pronunciation across the whole of China because it is so vast.

So concentrate on getting your message across rather than on not making any mistakes. Learning to speak a foreign language is one case where quantity (as long as it is comprehensible) is better than quality! That is the way you will learn.

Nevertheless when a standard speaker of Chinese corrects your Chinese, make a mental note of it and at the first opportunity write it down, learn it and try to use it.

3 It is good to deliberately try out new constructions and vocabulary. Practise them beforehand so that you won't be too hesitant the first time you try something. If it doesn't work as well as you'd hoped, look at them again and have another go. It's like learning to ride a bicycle. When you fall off you have to get on again straight away so that you don't lose confidence.

> **i** It is still sometimes very difficult to buy return tickets in China especially for trains and long-distance buses. Normally you have to think when you are going to leave a place as soon as you have arrived in it and organize your return (or ongoing) ticket accordingly. China's large population makes queuing inevitable unless you book your ticket through an agency (hotel, China Travel Service and so on) which may require plenty of notice and a commission charge.

Practice

1 Answer the following *Have you ever . . . ?* questions:

Example: Nǐ qù-guo Zhōngguó ma?
Qù-guo or **Méi qù-guo.**

a Nǐ qù-guo Rìběn ma?   [ever been to Japan?]
b Nǐ zuò-guo fēijī ma?   [ever travelled by plane?]
c Nǐ kàn-guo Déguó   [ever seen German films?]
  diànyǐng ma?
d Nǐ chī-guo Zhōngguó   [ever had Chinese food?]
  fàn ma?
e Nǐ hē-guo Měiguó   [ever drunk American wine?]
  pútáojiǔ ma?

▶2 Listen to the recording (or read the following passage) and draw the way to the cinema (**diànyǐngyuàn**) on the plan overleaf. Which letter represents the cinema?

Xiān wǎng nán zǒu. Dào Dōnghǎi Lù zuò wǎng dōng kāi de chē. Zuò liǎng zhàn. Diànyǐngyuàn jiù zài Dōnghǎi Lù de nánbianr, shāngdiàn de duìmiànr.

3 You are now in the cinema. You have just seen a film. Can you say in Chinese how you get back on foot or by bus to the hotel you are staying in (A)? It may help to listen to the recording once again.

4 Read the directions below which tell you where various places are situated. Then go back to the sketch and identify the buildings represented by the letters (B), (C), (D) and (E).

a **Zhōngguó Yínháng** zài diànyǐngyuàn de xībianr.
b **Shāngdiàn** zài diànyǐngyuàn de duìmiàn.
c **Dōnghǎi Gōngyuán** zài Zhōngguó Yínháng de xībian.
d **Xuéxiào** (*school*) zài Zhōngguó Yínháng de běibian, fàndiàn de dōngbian.

5 Answer the following questions using (**cóng**) . . . **dào** . . . . If you don't know, say **Wǒ bù zhīdao**. (But you could find out.)

Example: When is Mr Wang's next holiday?
(**Cóng**) wǔyuè sānshí hào **dào** liùyuè bā hào.

a When is **your** next holiday?
b What are the opening hours of **your** local (or school) library during the weekdays and weekends?
c Which days of the week do **you** work? (e.g. from Monday to Friday)
d What are **your** working hours during the week?

6 How do you get there?
Choose an appropriate means of transport from the list overleaf to make complete sentences in Chinese according to the information given in a–e. Take care with the word order!

zuò gōnggòng qìchē	by bus
zuò huǒchē	by train
zuò dìtiě	by underground
zuò fēijī	by plane
zuò chuán	by ship
qí (zìxíng)chē	to cycle
kāi chē	to drive
zǒu lù	to walk

Example: to go to work (qù shàng bān)
Wǒ **qí zìxíngchē** qù shàng bān.

a to go to work   [qù shàng bān]
b to go to school   [qù xuéxiào]
c to do shopping   [qù mǎi dōngxi]
d to go to see a film   [qù kàn diànyǐng]
   (at your local cinema)
e to go to X train station   [qù X huǒchē zhàn]

7 In the box below you will find some useful words to describe things. Which pair would you use to describe the following things? Try to use **yòu . . . yòu . . . .**

Example: Zuò fēijī **yòu** guì **yòu** bù shūfu.
Zuò fēijī **yòu** kuài **yòu** shūfu.

guì	expensive	bú guì	not expensive
piányi	cheap	bù piányi	not cheap
fāngbiàn	convenient	máfan	troublesome
kuài	fast	màn	slow
wēixiǎn	dangerous	ānquán	safe

a Cóng Rìběn zuò chuán dào Zhōngguó
b Zài Lúndūn/Bālí (*Paris*) qí zìxíngchē
c Zuò gōnggòng qìchē qù shàng bān
d Cóng Yīngguó zuò fēijī dào Měiguó
e Kāi chē qù mǎi dōngxi

▶8 Listen to the recording and answer the following questions about Mr White's holiday.

See first if you can answer the questions in Chinese. If you find them too difficult, read the questions in English below and answer them either in English or in Chinese.

If you haven't got the recording, read the passage after the questions and then answer the questions. If you need to refer to it, the English script is in the **Key to the exercises**.

a Bái xiānsheng dǎsuàn qù shénme dìfang?
b Tā zài Bālí zhù jǐ tiān?
c Tā gēn shéi yìqǐ qù Yìdàlì? Tāmen zěnme qù Yìdàlì?
d Bái xiānsheng dǎsuàn zài Yìdàlì zhù jǐ tiān?
e Tā zěnme huí Yīngguó?
f Tā péngyou zěnme huí Fǎguó?

a *Where did Mr White plan to go?*
b *How long does he plan to stay in Paris?*
c *Who will he go to Italy with? How will they travel to Italy?*
d *How long does Mr White plan to stay in Italy?*
e *How will he get back to the UK?*
f *How will his friend get back to France?*

Bái xiānsheng de jiàqī *Mr White's holidays*

Bái xiānsheng yào qù dù jià le. Tā yào qù liǎng ge dìfang. Tā xiān cóng Lúndūn zuò huǒchē dào Bālí. Tā dǎsuàn zài Bālí zhù sì tiān. Ránhòu tā gēn tāde Fǎguó péngyou kāi chē qù Yìdàlì. Tāmen dǎsuàn zài Yìdàlì zhù yí ge xīngqī. Zuìhòu tā cóng Yìdàlì zuò fēijī huí Lúndūn. Tāde péngyou kāi chē huí Fǎguó.

▶ Quick review

a Ask how to get to the Bank of China (**Zhōngguó Yínháng**).
b Tell the Chinese person who has asked you the way to take the number 10 bus.
c Then tell her that it will be five stops (before she gets there).
d Say that your friend has never been to China.
e Say it's going to rain soon.

Jìnzhǐ xī yān
禁止吸烟

10

nín xiăng chī shénme?

what would you like to eat?

In this unit you will learn
- how to order a meal and drinks
- how to pay the bill
- how to say you have given up something (such as smoking)
- more about verb endings

Before you start

By the end of this unit you will be able to get yourself various things to eat and drink and even to question the bill! There's lots of very useful vocabulary so take your time.

Let's try

1 You need to tell a Chinese friend your itinerary once you have left home so she can book your hotel in Beijing and arrange your programme.

   a Tell her that you are going by air to Hong Kong first and staying there two days.
   b Then you are going from Hong Kong to Shanghai by train.
   c You plan to travel by air to Beijing on the morning of 10th August.

2 The same friend asks if you have ever been to Shanghai before. What does she say to you?

Key words and phrases

àiren	husband / wife (sometimes used in the People's Republic)
bēi	a cup of; cup
bié	don't
cài	dish
càidān	menu (lit. dish list)
Chángchéng	the Great Wall
chī	to eat
chī-wán/chī-bǎo/chī-hǎo le	to have finished eating / be full / satisfied
chī sù	to be vegetarian (lit. eat non-meat food)
chōu (yān)	to smoke (a cigarette)
duì	to, for
duō	more; many
gēn wǒ lái	follow me
hǎochī	delicious, tasty
hē	to drink
jiè (yān)	to give up (smoking)
jié zhàng	to ask for the bill
là (de)	hot, spicy (food)

lái	(I'll) have (colloquial)
pàng	fat
ràng	to let, allow
rè	hot
shǎo	less; few
shēntǐ	health
shōu	to accept, to receive
tiānqi	weather
xiànjīn	cash
xìnyòng kǎ	credit card
yùdìng	to book (a room)
zhī	(measure word for cigarettes)
zhǐ	only
zhīpiào	cheque / check
Nǐmen chī/hē diǎnr shénme?	What would you like to eat / drink?
Jiǔ lái le	Here comes the wine

Food and Drinks

dòufu	beancurd
bīngqílín	ice-cream
júzizhī	orange juice
mápó dòufu	spicy beancurd / tofu
pútáojiǔ	wine (lit. grape alcohol)
qīngcài	vegetables
ròu	meat
tāng	soup
suānlà tāng	hot and sour soup
yú	fish

Learning tips

1 Practise the difference between -uo and -ou as in duō (*much/many*) and dōu (*both/all*).

2 Practise the difference between -an and -ang as in fàn (*food*) and fàng (*to put*) and between -en, -eng as in fēn (*minute/smallest unit of Chinese currency*) and fēng (*wind*).

▶3 Now go back and revise all the vowels with a nasal sound in the Pronunciation guide, p. xv. Listen to the recording if you have it.

Hold your nose gently as you practise these sounds. You should be able to feel the vibration in it when you say -ang, -eng, -iang, -ing, -iong, -ong and -uang. This is particularly obvious when you say the sound in the 1st tone and hang on to it.

Dialogues

Sìchuān cāntīng
Sichuan restaurant

▶ Dialogue 1

Mr Brown and his friend Yúqiáo are going to have a Chinese meal. What drinks and food have they ordered?

Waiter	Nǐmen yùdìng le ma?
Brown	Yùdìng le. Wǒ jiào John Brown.
Waiter	Wǒ kànyikàn. . . . Mr Brown, qī diǎn bàn, liǎng ge rén.
Brown	Duì, duì.
Waiter	Hǎo, qǐng gēn wǒ lái.
Waiter	Zhè shì càidān. Nǐmen xiān hē diǎnr shénme?
Yúqiáo	Wǒ yào yì bēi júzizhī.
Brown	Nǐmen yǒu shénme pútáojiǔ?
Waiter	Wǒmen yǒu Chángchéng bái pútáojiǔ hé Zhōngguó hóng pútáojiǔ.
Brown	Lái yì bēi bái pútáojiǔ ba.
Waiter	Jiǔ lái le. Nǐmen yào shénme cài?
Yúqiáo	Wǒ bù chī ròu.
Brown	Nǐ chī bu chī yú?
Yúqiáo	Bù chī. Wǒ zhǐ yào qīngcài hé dòufu.
Brown	Shénme? Nǐ xiànzài chī sù le.
Yúqiáo	Shì'a. Wǒ yǐjīng hěn pàng le.
Waiter	Nǐmen xǐhuan chī là de ma?
Yùqiáo	Xǐhuan. Kěshì bié tài là le.
Waiter	Lái yí ge mápó dòufu ba.
Brown	Hǎo'a. Xiān lái liǎng ge suānlà tāng.
Yúqiáo	Jīntiān tiānqi yǐjīng hěn rè le. Wǒmen yīnggāi shǎo chī là de.
Waiter	Méi guānxi. Chī-wán fàn yǐhòu, nǐmen duō chī diǎnr bīngqílín. Wǒmen de bīngqílín fēicháng hǎochī.

ℹ The custom when eating Chinese food is that all the dishes are put in the middle of the table and shared. The host helps her/his guest to the best titbits. Too bad if you don't share his/her taste! The soup is always eaten last in China except for some areas in the south.

▶ Dialogue 2

Mr Brown and Yúqiáo are chatting over the meal. Listen to or read their conversation and find out why Yúqiáo has given up smoking and Mr Brown hasn't.

Brown	Chōu zhī yān ba.
Yúqiáo	Wǒ bù chōu yān le.
Brown	Wèishénme?
Yúqiáo	Wǒ àiren bú ràng wǒ chōu le. Tā shuō chōu yān duì wǒde shēntǐ bù hǎo, duì tāde shēntǐ yě bù hǎo.
Brown	Wǒ yě bù xiǎng chōu le. Kěshì wǒ yǒu yí ge péngyou, jiè yān yǐqián bú pàng, jiè yān yǐhòu jiù pàng le. Wǒ pà pàng.
Yúqiáo	Wǒ yě pà pàng, kěshì jīntiān de cài tài hǎochī le.
Brown	Nǐ chī-bǎo le ma?
Yúqiáo	Chī-bǎo le.
Brown	Wǒmen jié zhàng ba. Fúwùyuán, qǐng jié zhàng.
Waiter	Nǐmen chī-hǎo le ma?
Yúqiáo	Chī-hǎo le, xièxie.
Brown	Nǐmen shōu bu shōu xìnyòng kǎ hé zhīpiào?
Waiter	Duìbuqǐ, wǒmen zhǐ shōu xiànjīn.

▶ Dialogue 3

Ann and Xiǎo Fāng have arrived at the street market (see **Dialogue 3, Unit 7**). What are they going to do next? Are they going to get a bargain this time?

Ann	Wǒ **è** le. Wǒmen **suíbiàn** chī diǎnr ba.
Fāng	Nàr yǒu ge xiǎo **tānzi**. Tāmen de **chǎomiàn** hǎochī-**jíle**. *(At the food stall)*
Ann	*(whispering)* Wǒ kàn zhèr bú tài **gānjìng**.
Fāng	Méi guānxi, tāmen huì gěi wǒmen **wèishēng kuàizi**.

* * *

Fāng	Qǐng lái liǎng **wǎnr** chǎomiàn、liǎng **tīng kěkǒukělè**.
Waitress	Qǐng xiān **fù qián**. Liǎng wǎnr chǎomiàn shí'èr kuài, liǎng tīng kěkǒukělè shísì kuài, **yígòng** èrshíliù kuài.
Fāng	Shénme? Nǐ **suàn-cuò** le ba. **Shàng cì** chǎomiàn wǔ kuài yì wǎnr.
Waitress	Méi suàn-cuò. Shàng cì shì shàng cì, xiànzài yì wǎnr liù kuài le.

Words in **bold** are listed overleaf.

è	*hungry*
chǎomiàn	*fried noodles*
fù qián	*to pay (money)*
gānjìng	*clean*
-jíle	*(suffix) extremely*
kěkǒukělè	*Coca-Cola*
kuàizi	*chopsticks*
shàng cì	*last time*
suàn-cuò le	*to have calculated wrongly*
suíbiàn	*casually*
tānzi	*stall*
tīng	*(measure word for cans (of drink))*
wǎn(r)	*bowl*
wèishēng	*hygiene, hygienic*
yígòng	*altogether*

i When eating from street stalls or fast-food outlets you usually get **wèishēng kuàizi** (*hygienic*, i.e. disposable, *chopsticks*) which should, of course, come wrapped. You have to break them apart which shows you that they are still unused.

Language notes

1 Already and *le*

Remember using **le** in Unit 4 to show that something has happened or has already taken place? When **yǐjīng** (*already*) appears in front of a verb it reinforces this idea of something having happened so you will find **le** at the end of such sentences:

Wǒ **yǐjīng** hěn pàng **le**.	*I'm already very fat.*
Jīntiān **yǐjīng** hěn rè **le**.	*It's already very hot today.*

2 More before the verb!

To say *eat more*, put the little word **duō** (*much/many*) in front of the verb *to eat*:

duō chī	*eat more*

This works with all full verbs, i.e. verbs that cannot also act as adjectives such as **hǎo** (*good*), **pàng** (*fat*) and so on.

duō hē	*drink more*
duō yào	*want more*
duō gěi	*give more*

You do exactly the same thing if you want to say *eat less, drink less*, and so on but you put **shǎo** (*less/few*) in front of the verb instead of **duō**:

shǎo chī	*eat less*
shǎo hē	*drink less*
shǎo yào	*want less*
shǎo gěi	*give less*

3 Not any more!

To say that you don't do something any more use:

bù verb (+ object) **le**

Wǒ **bù** chōu yān **le**.	*I don't smoke any more/ I've given up smoking.*
Wǒ tàitai **bú** ràng wǒ chōu **le**.	*My wife doesn't let me smoke any more.*
Tā **bù** hē jiǔ **le**.	*She's given up drinking.*
Tāmen **bù** niánqīng **le**.	*They're no longer young.*

If the verb is **yǒu** (*to have*), you have to use **méi** instead of **bù**:

You	Nǐ yǒu **mei** yǒu hóng chènshān? *Do you have a red shirt?*
Shop assistant	**Méi** yǒu **le**, mài-wán **le**. *(We're) out of stock. They're sold out. (lit. not have any more, sell finish le).*

4 Smoking is not good for your health!

As you know, **duì** means *right, correct*. In certain contexts it also means *to* or *for*. Learn the following useful phrases:

A **duì** shēntǐ (bù) hǎo.	*A is (not) good for the health/body.*
Y **duì** X (bù) hǎo.	*Y is (not) good to X.*

Thus **Chōu yān duì wǒde shēntǐ bù hǎo** means *Smoking is not good for my health*.

5 After . . .

In English you say *after I've been to the restaurant* but in Chinese you say *I've been to the restaurant after* – the reverse of the English word order:

| Jiè yān **yǐhòu** | *After giving up smoking* |
| Chī fàn **yǐhòu** | *After eating* |

The same happens with **yǐqián** (*before*) and **de shíhou** (*when*). (You will meet **de shíhou** later in Units 12–21):

Jiè yān **yǐqián**	*Before giving up smoking*
Fù qián **yǐqián**	*Before paying*
Jié zhàng **de shíhou**	*When working out the bill*

6 To eat your fill

To say that you *have eaten your fill* in Chinese you put **bǎo** (*full*) after the verb **chī** (*to eat*):

| Wǒ chī-**bǎo** le. | *I'm full (lit. I eat full le).* |

The **le** after the verb shows completed action. (See Unit 4, p. 36.)

To make the verb negative, use **méi** not **bù** and drop the **le** as the verb is then no longer completed.

Other little words, or endings, which appear after the verb in this way have other meanings:

Nǐmen chī-**hǎo** le ma?	*Have you finished eating (to your satisfaction)?*
Chī-**hǎo** le.	*Yes, we have (finished eating to our satisfaction).*
Nǐ suàn-**cuò** le ba.	*You must have got it wrong (lit. you calculate wrong le, haven't you).*
Méi suàn-**cuò**.	*No, I haven't (lit. not have calculate wrong).*
Nǐmen hē-**wán** le ma?	*Have you finished your drinks (lit. you drink finish le ma)?*
Wǒmen hē-**wán** le.	*Yes, we have (lit. we drink finish le).*
Nǐ kàn-**jiàn** tā le ma?	*Did you see him/her (lit. you look perceive him/her le ma)?*
Wǒ méi kàn-**jiàn** ta.	*I didn't see him/her (lit. I not have look perceive him/her).*

If you put **bù** between the verb and **one** of these endings as in the examples below, you have the meaning of **cannot + verb + ending**:

Wǒ kàn-**bu**-jiàn. *I can't see.*
Tā tīng-**bu**-dǒng. *She can't understand.*
  (lit. she listen cannot understand).
Wǒmen hē-**bu**-wán. *We can't finish (our drinks).*

If on the other hand you put **de** (yes, **de** again!) between the verb and one of these endings, you have the meaning of **can + verb + ending**:

Wǒ kàn-**de**-jiàn. *I can see.*
Tāmen tīng-**de**-dǒng. *They can understand.*
  (lit. they listen can understand)
Wǒmen hē-**de**-wán. *We can drink up.*

This is the same **de** as the one used in Unit 8, pp. 87–8.

7 Tins, bowls and bottles

You should be familiar with measure words by now but did you spot the ones for *bottle, bowl* and *tin* in this unit?

yì **píng** Fǎguó jiǔ *a **bottle** of French wine*
liǎng **wǎn(r)** chǎomiàn *two **bowls** of fried noodles*
liǎng **tīng** kě(kǒukě)lè *two **tins** of Coke*

8 Don't . . . !

To tell somebody not to do something, all you have to do is put the word **bié** (*don't*) in front of what you don't want them to do:

Bié shuō huà. *Don't speak.*
Bié zǒu. *Don't go.*

Adding **le** at the end of such sentences helps to soften the idea of giving an order or command.

Learning tips

Do you feel comfortable with the grammar?

Having now got to the halfway mark in the book it is probably a good idea to see how well you're doing with grammar and how to revise and consolidate what you know.

1. Units 1 to 10 contain all the grammar you will need to know to study Units 12 to 21 so it is important that you feel comfortable with it before proceeding. Go back to the **Practice** sections of Units 1 to 10 and pick out one or two exercises from each unit and do them again. If you find any particular exercise difficult, revise the relevant **Language notes** carefully and try the exercise again.

2. By the time you have completed **Language tip 1** you should be feeling more confident. When you go on to study Units 12 to 21 look at the structures in the dialogues and fit them into the patterns you have already learnt. You might like to jot these down so that you have a list of examples under each structure. You will find this helps the consolidation process.

Practice

▶1 Listen to the dialogue and tick on the menu what Mr Jones has ordered for his meal. You will need to know the word for *beer*, which is **píjiǔ** in Chinese.

Fúwùyuán	Nín xiǎng chī diǎnr shénme?
Jones	Wǒ xǐhuan chī là de.
Fúwùyuán	Wǒmen yǒu yúxiāng ròusī hé mápó dòufu.
Jones	Wǒ yào yí ge yúxiāng ròusī ba.
Fúwùyuán	Nín yào tāng ma?
Jones	Nǐmen yǒu shénme tāng?
Fúwùyuán	Suānlà tāng hé zhàcài tāng.
Jones	Lái yí ge suānlà tāng ba.
Fúwùyuán	Yào jiǔ ma?
Jones	Yào yì píng píjiǔ.
Fúwùyuán	Wǔxīng píjiǔ háishi Qīngdǎo píjiǔ?
Jones	Lái yì píng Wǔxīng píjiǔ.
Fúwùyuán	Hǎo de.

Càidān

mápó dòufu
yúxiāng ròusī
········
········
suānlà tāng
zhàcài tāng
········
········
Wǔxīng píjiǔ
Qīngdǎo píjiǔ

2 How many? Put the correct number and measure word under each of the items in the pictures below. You may not be able to use all of these measure words: **píng, gè, bēi, zhāng, wǎn, jiàn, tīng, zhī**.

Example: yì **běn** shū (*a book*)

3 Have things changed?
   If something has changed, you use . . . **le**.
   If it has not changed, you say **méi yǒu**, or **gēn yǐqián yíyàng**
   (*the same as before*).

   Example: Dōngxi guì le ma?
   Guì **le** (yìdiǎnr).
   Méi yǒu or Gēn yǐqián yíyàng.

   a Dōngxi guì le ma?   (compared with five years ago)
   b Nǐ pàng le ma?   (compared with five years ago)
   c Tiānqi lěng le ma?   (compared with a month ago)
   d Nǐ zhǎng (*to grow*)   (compared with five years ago)
   gāo le ma?

4 The following dialogue is between you and a waitress.
   Complete your part.

   a **You**   (*Waiter! The bill please.*)
   Fúwùyuán Nǐmen chī-hǎo le ma?
   b **You**   (*Yes. Thank you.*)
   Fúwùyuán Yígòng sānbǎi kuài.
   c **You**   (*I think you've got it wrong.*)
   Fúwùyuán Wǒ zài kànkan (*let me look at it again*).
   Duìbuqǐ. Wǒ suàn-cuò le.
   d **You**   (*That's all right.*)

5 Which is correct, **méi** or **bù**, in the following sentences?

a Tā yǐqián chōu yān, xiànzài **méi/bù** chōu yān le.
b Wǒ liùyuè qù dù jià le, xiànzài **méi/bù** yǒu jià le.
c Yǐqián wǒ yǒu yì tiáo gǒu (*dog*), xiànzài **méi/bù** yǒu le.
d Tiānqi tài rè le, wǒ **méi/bù** chī là de le.

Halfway review

▶1 On the recording, you will hear different years being said.

Example: yī-jiǔ-jiǔ-qī nián *1997*

Repeat each one and write them down.

2 You have learned two ways of asking *yes* or *no questions*.
Can you try to turn the following statements into questions
using both ways?

Example: Statement – Jīntiān tiānqi hěn hǎo.
            Question 1 – Jīntiān tiānqi hǎo ma?
            Question 2 – Jīntiān tiānqi hǎo bu hǎo?

a Tāmen shì jiěmèi.
b Tāde chǎomiàn zhēn hǎochī.
c Míngtiān tā tàitai qù mǎi dōngxi.
d Nǐ bú rènshi tā.
e Xiǎo Lǐ yǒu yì tiáo hóng kùzi.

3 Which of the following statements talk about habitual
things one does or does not do (call these X), and which
state things one has done at some point or has never done
(call these Y)?

a Xiǎo Fāng chōu-guo yān.
b Tā měi tiān chōu yān.
c Tā méi chī-guo Yìdàlì fàn.
d Tā bù xǐhuan chī Yìdàlì fàn.

4 Pair up the question words in Chinese with their English
equivalents.

a shéi   i   *where*
b nǎr   ii   *what*
c shénme   iii *which*
d zěnme   iv   *how many*
e nǎ   v   *who*
f jǐ   vi   *how*

5 Can you answer the following questions about Jane?

JANE

Jane went to the USA in 1995. She studied German for one year
in 2000 and visited France in 2002. In 2003, she had Vietnamese
food for the first time, and she stopped smoking in 2004. She will
visit China and Japan for the first time next year.

a Tā qù-guo Zhōngguó ma?
b Tā 1995 qù nǎr le?
c Tā huì shuō Déyǔ ma?
d Tā qù-guo Fǎguó ma?
e Tā xiànzài hái chōu yān ma?
f Tā chī-guo Yuènán fàn ma?
g Tā míngnián qù nǎr?

(tíng)
No stopping

Jìnzhǐ tíng chē
No parking (*lit.* forbid stop vehicle)

Good luck with the rest of the book!

wǒmen kànkan Hànzì ba!

let's look at Chinese characters!

In this unit you will be introduced to the Chinese writing system and learn
- the structure of Chinese characters
- the rules of writing
- how to write the numbers 1–99
- how to write the days of the week and the date
- how to write the time

Before you start

You will remember from the introduction that this unit is largely independent of the rest of the book, so if you have decided not to get involved with the Chinese script, you can miss it out. Alternatively, you can choose to come back to it later when you have finished the other units. Even if you don't do any of the exercises in this unit it would be a good idea to read it through, so that at least you have some idea what the Chinese script is all about. This will help your understanding of the Chinese language as a whole and hence of the people who speak it.

The Chinese writing system

Chinese characters (**Hànzì**) are the symbols used to write the Chinese language. Written Chinese does not use a phonetic alphabet. This means that you cannot guess how a character (**zì**) is pronounced just by looking at it. The Chinese script is very, very old. Its earliest written records date back over 3,500 years. These are the markings on oracle bones (tortoise shells and animal bones) on which the priests used to scratch their questions to the gods. The earliest characters were pictures representing easily recognizable objects, such as the sun, the moon, fire, water, a mountain, a tree, and so on.

火 fire　水 water　山 mountain　雨 rain

Such characters (**zì**) were known as *pictographs*. Some of them are still in use even today.

The next step was for *pictographs* to be combined to form new characters known as *ideographs* because they express an idea:

日 *sun* + 月 *moon*　= 明 *bright*
女 *woman* + 子 *child* = 好 *good*
日 *sun* + 木 *tree*　= 東 *east* (the sun coming up behind a tree)
人 *person* + 木 *tree* = 休 *to rest* (a person leaning up against a tree)

So far so good! Unfortunately only a limited number of ideas could be expressed in this way so then characters were created which contained a *meaning* element (often known as the *radical*) and a *phonetic* element which was to help with the pronunciation of the character. Of course, pronunciation has changed over the centuries, so that now this phonetic element is only of limited help. Let's look at a few of these *radical-phonetic* or compound characters. You can see how such characters came into being and what they look like today.

fēn *divide; separate*   **fěn** *powder*

Both the characters above are pronounced the same, although they have different tones. This is quite normal. The next pair have the same pronunciation and the same tone, but this is unusual.

lǐ *village; mile; inside*   **lǐ** *polish; reason; principle*

At the opposite end of the spectrum we have the following three characters, which have a common phonetic element 母 mu, but are pronounced quite differently. This is the worst scenario!

mǔ *mother*   **měi** *every*   **hǎi** *sea*

The basic rules for writing Chinese characters

As you can imagine, there are some basic rules for writing Chinese characters which you need to master. This is important if you are to remember them, and so the brain needs to operate a kind of orderly filing system. To do this, it needs help. Chinese characters should always be written the same way, so that they become fixed in your imaginary filing system. Most characters are made up of two or more basic structural parts called 'character components', although of course some character components such as 日 **rì** (*sun*) can stand by themselves, as we have mentioned earlier. Although the total number of characters is quite large, the number of character components is limited. These components are written with a number of basic strokes, which are illustrated below:

Stroke	Name	
丶	diǎn	*dot*
一	héng	*horizontal*
丨	shù	*vertical*
丿	piě	*left-falling*
乀	nà	*right-falling*
丿	tí	*rising*
亅乚乚	gōu	*hook*
乛	zhé	*turning*

These strokes are basically straight lines and were traditionally written in ink with a hair brush. The main directions are from top to bottom and from left to right. The arrows on the basic strokes overleaf show how the characters are written by indicating the direction each stroke takes:

The rules of stroke order in writing Chinese characters and character components are as follows:

Example	Stroke order						Rule
十	一					十	First horizontal, then vertical
人	丿					人	First left-falling, then right-falling
三	一	二				三	From top to bottom
州	丶	丿	丬	州	州 州	州	From left to right
月	丿	刀	月			月	First outside, then inside
四	丨	冂	冋	四		四	Finish inside, then close
小	亅	小				小	Middle, then the two sides

Numbers 1–10

Now let's try writing the numbers 1 to 10. We have shown the direction and sequence of each stroke to help you. It is helpful to think of each character, however simple or complex, as occupying a square of the same size.

Numbers 11–99

11 is	10 + 1	=	十一
12 is	10 + 2	=	十二
20 is	2 × 10	=	二十
30 is	3 × 10	=	三十
65 is	6 × 10 + 5	=	六十五
99 is	9 × 10 + 9	=	九十九

It is worth noting that Arabic numerals are being used more and more in China. Newspapers and magazines in the People's Republic all use Arabic numerals for dates and (large) numbers. The traditional Chinese characters are still widely used in Hong Kong and Taiwan.

Practice

1 Which numbers do the following characters represent?

a 二   f 二十四
b 六   g 八十三
c 十   h 六十九
d 五   i 五十七
e 十一   j 三十六

2 Write out the following numbers in Chinese characters:

a 3   b 8   c 10   d 15   e 42   f 98   g 67

(The answers to all the exercises are in the **Key to the exercises** at the back of the book.)

Days of the week

All you need to know to write the characters for the days of the week are the two characters **xīng** (*star*) and **qī** (*period*) which, when combined together, form the word for *week*; plus the numbers 1 to 6 and the characters for *sun* (**rì**) or *day* (**tiān**). **Xīng** is made up of the radical 日 **rì** (*sun*) and 生 **shēng** (*to give birth*):

Qī is made up of the phonetic element 其 **qí** and the radical 月 **yuè** (*moon*).

You have already met 日 **rì** (*sun*).

Tiān (*day*) is also a nice easy character:

It is actually made up of one horizontal stroke plus the character 大 **dà** (*big*).

Revise the days of the week (see p. 46) and then do the following exercises.

Practice

3 Which day of the week . . .

a do people go to church? 星期 ☐

b comes after Tuesday? 星期 ☐

c are many football matches played in the UK? 星期 ☐

d comes before Friday? 星期 ☐

4 Now fill in the missing characters for the days of the week given below:

a Sunday 星期 ☐ or 星期 ☐

b Tuesday 星 ☐ 二

c Friday 星 ☐ 五

d Thursday ☐ 期四

e Saturday ☐ 期六

How to write the date

For this you need to revise your numbers (1–31) and the characters for *moon* or *month* (**yuè** 月). Having done that, check up on how to say the date in Chinese (see p. 50). In formal *written* Chinese **rì** 日 is used instead of **hào** 号. Thus, 21 February is:

二月二十一日   èryuè èrshíyī rì

Practice

5 Can you recognize the following dates?

a 十一月三日
b 六月十八日
c 七月十一日
d 十月十四日
e 八月二十九日

6 Can you write out the following dates in Chinese characters?

a Christmas Day (25 December)

b International Women's Day (8 March) (see cartoon at the end of this unit)

c Your birthday (you might not fill all the squares in!)

d Your father's birthday

e Your mother's birthday

How to write the years

This is dead easy! Revise what you learnt on p. 50.

1945 is 一九四五 **nián** (*year*)

Nián is written:

Practice

7 Write down the years represented by the Chinese characters in the spaces provided:

e.g. 一九一四年 ___1914___

a 二〇*八年 _____

b 一九三七年 _____

c 一九四九年 _____

d 一八八五年 _____

e 一六四二年 _____

* 〇 is used for 'zero' in the People's Republic of China while the traditional character 零 **líng** is still widely used in Hong Kong and Taiwan.

How to write the time

For this you will need to learn to write the character for *minute* **fēn** 分 and the characters for *o'clock* **diǎn** (**zhōng**). Before you do this, revise how to tell the time on pp. 49–50. Now let's look at the two characters **diǎn** and **zhōng**.

点
diǎn

is made up of the radical for *fire* **huǒ** 灬 (also written 火) and the phonetic element 占 **zhàn**. Whoops! This one has moved a long way from its original pronunciation. **Diǎn** is written as follows:

| 丨 | 上 | 上 | 占 | 占 | 点 | 点 | 点 | 点 | **diǎn** |

钟
zhōng

is made up of the radical for *metal* **jīn** 钅 (also written 金) and the phonetic element 中 **zhōng**. Whew! This character is pronounced **zhōng** too! **Zhōng** is written as follows:

| 丿 | 上 | 上 | 牛 | 钅 | 钅 | 钊 | 钊 | 钟 | **zhōng** |

So 3.20 is 三点二十分 and 5.00 is 五点钟

i By the way, you should never give a Chinese person a clock for a present, as the character for 'clock' has exactly the same sound and tone (**zhōng**) as the character in classical Chinese meaning 'the end' or 'death'. So giving somebody a clock might send the wrong message!

You will also need to know the characters for *quarter* **kè**, for *half* **bàn**, and for *minus* or *to lack* **chà**.

刻
kè

is made up of the radical for *knife* **dāo** 刂 (also written 刀) and the phonetic element 亥 **hài**. **Kè** is written as follows:

| 丶 | 二 | 亠 | 歺 | 亥 | 亥 | 刻 | 刻 | **kè** |

半
bàn

is made up of the vertical line radical 丨 and the phonetic element 八 **bā** (often written ⸌ as here), plus two horizontal lines. **Bàn** is written as follows:

| 丶 | 丷 | 丷 | 半 | 半 | | **bàn** |

差

chà

is made up of the radical for *sheep* **yáng** 羊 (slanted here) and the phonetic element 工 **gōng**. No help here for pronunciation, unfortunately. **Chà** is written as follows:

`	``	丷	半	兰	羊	差	差	差

chà

Practice

8 What time is it?

a 九点一刻   *9.15*
b 十二点二十五分
c 六点半
d 差十分四点
e 八点差一刻

Can you write out the following times in Chinese characters? (One square represents one Chinese character, but there are alternatives.)

a 6.20 ⬜⬜⬜⬜⬜

b 11.45 ⬜⬜⬜⬜⬜

c 10.10 ⬜⬜⬜

d 4.48 ⬜⬜⬜⬜⬜

e 7.30 ⬜⬜⬜

Congratulations! If you have got this far you obviously have an aptitude for writing and recognizing Chinese characters. You will be able to build on your knowledge in the second half of the book. Hopefully some of the signs in the first half of the book will also make a bit more sense to you.

The different style of writing Chinese characters is an art form known as calligraphy, which is highly valued by the Chinese. You have just had a little taste of it!

12

zài lǚguǎn
at the hotel

In this unit you will learn
- how to check into a hotel
- how to say if something is wrong
- how to make requests
- how to make complaints

Revise before you start

The numbers in brackets refer to the unit in which the item first appears.

- use of possessive **de** (3)
- measure words (4)(7)
- making comparisons (6)(7)
- room numbers (3)
- new situation **le** (5)
- verb endings (10)
- helping verbs (6)
- how long (9)
- when . . . (6)
- **tài . . . le** (7)
- not any more (10)
- to do something for somebody (6)
- to be in the middle of doing something (6)

长城饭店	和平宾馆	东风旅馆
CHÁNGCHÉNG FÀNDIÀN	**HÉPÍNG BĪNGUĂN**	**DŌNGFĒNG LǓGUĂN**

In Chinese, there are several words for something that has just one word in English. Read the following passage and find out what those words are and what they mean. Furthermore, if you go to China as a foreigner can you stay in just any hotel so long as you can afford it? (Words in *italics* are explained in the box below the passage.)

Fàndiàn *Hotel*

Xuǎnzé lǚguǎn *Choosing a hotel*

Hotel zhèi gè *cí* de Zhōngwén kěyǐ shì *bīnguǎn*、*fàndiàn*、*lǚguǎn* hé *lǚdiàn*. Fàndiàn hé bīnguǎn *yìbān* hěn dà, lǚguǎn hé lǚdiàn yìbān bú dà. *Guǎn* hé *diàn* dōu shì 'house' de yìsi. *Bīn* de yìsi shì 'guest', *lǚ* de yìsi shì 'travel'. *Fàn* shì 'food' de yìsi.

Dà fàndiàn、bīnguǎn de *tiáojiàn* bǐ lǚguǎn、lǚdiàn de tiáojiàn hǎo duōle. Dāngrán tāmen yě bǐ lǚguǎn、lǚdiàn guì duōle.

bīnguǎn/fàndiàn/lǔguǎn/lǔdiàn	hotel
cí	word
fàn	food; meal
tiáojiàn	condition
wèishénme?	why?
xuǎnzé	to choose
yìbān	usually

Exercise 1 Read the opening passage twice. Then answer the following questions in Chinese. You may need to read the passage a few more times to answer all the questions.

a What are some of the Chinese words for *hotel*?
b What do they mean?
c Can foreigners stay in any hotel in China?
d Does the passage tell you why this is the case?
e What is the position for Chinese people themselves?

Key words and phrases

ānjìng	quiet
Bāo zǎocān ma?	Is breakfast included?
-zǎocān/zǎofàn	breakfast
biǎo	form
biéde	other
bǐjiào	relatively
búguò	but, however
cèsuǒ	toilet
chǎo	noisy
cì	time, occasion
dǎ diànhuà	to telephone
dānrén/shuāngrén fángjiān	single / double room
. . . de shíhou	time when (not used in question)
diànshì	television
fúwù	service
fúwùtái	reception (lit. service platform)
gàosu	to tell
hái yǒu	another thing (lit. still have)
huán	to return something to
hùzhào	passport
jiān	(measure word for rooms)
jīnglǐ	manager

línyù	*shower*
měiyuán	*US dollar*
néng	*to be able to, can*
rúguǒ	*if*
shénme shíhou?	*when? / what time?*
shuǐ	*water*
tián	*to fill in* (a form)
wǎnfàn	*dinner, supper*
xiǎng yào	*would like*
xiǎoshí	*hour*
xǐzǎojiān	*bathroom*
xiū	*to repair*
yàoshi	*key*
yídìng	*certainly, definitely*
yǒu wèntí	*to have problems*
zhǎo	*to ask for, to want to see*
zhèngzài	*at this moment*
zǒu	*to leave, to walk*

Dialogues

▶ Dialogue 1

Frank is checking into a hotel. Listen to or read the dialogue between Frank and the **fúwùyuán** (*attendant*), and then do Exercise 2.

Fúwùyuán	Nín hǎo!
Frank	Nǐ hǎo! Wǒ xiǎng yào yì jiān dānrén fángjiān.
Fúwùyuán	Nín yùdìng le ma?
Frank	Méi yǒu.
Fúwùyuán	Nín yào zhù jǐ tiān?
Frank	Sān、sì tiān. Wǒ míngtiān gàosu nǐ wǒ shénme shíhou zǒu, kěyǐ ma?
Fúwùyuán	Kěyǐ.
Frank	Yì tiān duōshao qián?
Fúwùyuán	Dānrén fángjiān měi tiān wǔshí měiyuán.
Frank	Bāo zǎocān ma?
Fúwùyuán	Dāngrán bāo.
Frank	Yǒu xǐzǎojiān ma?
Fúwùyuán	Yǒu. Búguò zhǐ yǒu línyù hé cèsuǒ.
Frank	Hǎo ba.

Fúwùyuán	Qǐng xiān tián **yíxiàr** zhèi zhāng biǎo. . . . Qǐng gěi wǒ nínde hùzhào. Nín zǒu de shíhòu huán gěi nín.
Frank	Zhè shì wǒde hùzhào.
Fúwùyuán	Nínde fángjiān shì èr-líng-yāo, zài èr lóu. Zhè shì yàoshi.
Frank	Xièxie.
Fúwùyuán	Rúguǒ nín yǒu wèntí, qǐng gěi fúwùtái dǎ diànhuà.
Frank	Bú huì yǒu wèntí ba.

Yíxià(r) placed after the verb softens the meaning; it is often used after instructions or advice as in the example above.

Exercise 2 Are these statements about **Dialogue 1 duì** or **bú duì**?

		duì	bú duì?
a	The price does not include breakfast.	☐	☐
b	The guest can take a bath in his room.	☐	☐
c	The hotel keeps the guest's passport during his stay.	☐	☐
d	The guest's room is on the first floor.	☐	☐
e	The guest is asked to ring reception if he has any problems.	☐	☐

Fúwùtái

服务台

Reception

▶ Dialogue 2

Frank is ringing reception from his hotel room to make some complaints. What are his complaints and how are they resolved?

Fúwùyuán	Nín hǎo. Fúwùtái.
Frank	Wǒshì(zhù) èr-líng-yāo fángjiān de Frank. Wǒde fángjiān tài chǎo le. Néng bu néng huàn yì jiān ānjìng yìdiǎnr de?
Fúwùyuán	Duìbuqǐ, méi yǒu biéde dānrén fángjiān le. Zhǐ yǒu shuāngrén fángjiān.
Frank	Shuāngrén fángjiān yì wǎnshang duōshao qián?
Fúwùyuán	**Bǐ** dānrén fángjiān **guì èrshí měiyuán**.

Frank	Tài guì le.
Fúwùyuán	Rúguǒ míngtiān wǒmen yǒu biéde dānrén fángjiān, yídìng gěi nín huàn.
Frank	Hǎo ba. Ò, hái yǒu, wǒde línyù zěnme méi yǒu rè shuǐ?
Fúwùyuán	Duìbuqǐ, xiànzài zhèngzài xiū. Wǔ ge xiǎoshí yǐhòu jiù yǒu le.
Frank	Wǔ ge xiǎoshí yǐhòu? Bù xíng. Wǒ yào zhǎo nǐmende jīnglǐ.

You know how to say A is much more expensive than B:

A bǐ B guì deduō/duōle.

If you want to say exactly by how much A is more expensive than B, you use:

A bǐ B guì + (*by how much*)

Shuāngrén fángjiān **bǐ** dānrén fángjiān **guì** èrshí měiyuán.	*A double room is US$20 more expensive than a single.*

Exercise 3 You are staying in a hotel in China. The following dialogue is between you and the hotel *receptionist* (**fúwùyuán**). You are ringing to complain:

Fúwùyuán	Nín hǎo. Fúwùtái.
a **You**	*(Say your name and that you are in room 301 and your room is too small. Ask if it is possible to change to a bigger one.)*
Fúwùyuán	Duìbuqǐ, méi yǒu biéde dānrén fángjiān le. Zhǐ yǒu shuāngrén fángjiān.
b **You**	*(Ask how much a double room costs.)*
Fúwùyuán	Bǐ dānrén fángjiān guì èrshí měiyuán.
c **You**	*(Say that's too much. Another thing. Ask why there is no television in your room.)*
Fúwùyuán	Duìbuqǐ, diànshì xiànzài zhèngzài xiū. Liǎng ge bàn xiǎoshí yǐhòu jiù xiū-hǎo le.
d **You**	*(Say the football match will be starting in half an hour!) (Use after half an hour)*

Key words and phrases

cāntīng	restaurant, canteen
jiā	to add
jiàoxǐng	to (call to) wake up
máfan	(to) trouble
qǐ	to get up

shénme yàng de?	*what kind?*
sòng lái	*to send over* (to the speaker)
sòng qù	*to send over* (away from the speaker)
Wǎn'ān!	*Good night!*
xiànzài	*now*
yìhuǐ(r)	*a short while*
chī de	*something to eat*
hē de	*something to drink*
huǒtuǐ	*ham*
jīròu	*chicken* (meat)
kāfēi	*coffee*
nǎi	*milk*
nǎilào	*cheese*
niúròu	*beef*
sānmíngzhì	*sandwich*
táng	*sugar*
yǐnliào	*drink(s)*

Dialogue 3

Frank gets back to his hotel very late and finds the bar (**jiǔbā**) closed. Read the dialogue and find out why.

Fúwùyuán Nín hǎo. Fúwùtái.

Frank Wǒ shì èr-líng-yāo fángjiān de Frank. Néng bu néng máfan nǐmen gěi wǒ sòng **lái** yìdiǎnr chī de? Wǒ è le.

Fúwùyuán Duìbuqǐ, cāntīng xiànzài guān mén le. Wǒmen zhǐ yǒu sānmíngzhì hé yǐnliào.

Frank Kěyǐ. Nǐmen yǒu shénme yàng de sānmíngzhì?

Fúwùyuán Wǒmen yǒu nǎilào de、huǒtuǐ de、jīròu de hé niúròu de.

Frank Wǒ yào yí ge nǎilào de、yí gè niúròu de、hé yì bēi kāfēi.

Fúwùyuán Hǎo de. Kāfēi yào jiā nǎi, jiā táng ma?

Frank Yào jiā nǎi, bù jiā táng.

Fúwùyuán Xíng. Wǒmen yìhuǐr jiù sòng **qù**.

Frank Hái yǒu. Míngtiān zǎoshang wǒ yào qǐ-de hěn zǎo. Nǐmen néng bu néng dǎ diànhuà jiàoxǐng wǒ?

Fúwùyuán Kěyǐ. Jǐ diǎn?

Frank Qī diǎn bàn.

Fúwùyuán Méi wèntí.

Frank Xièxie nǐ. Wǎn'ān.

Fúwùyuán Wǎn'ān.

Jiǔbā

The Chinese language is much more specific about the direction in which things are said or done by the speaker than English. This means that you will often find the little words **qù** (*go*) or **lái** (*come*) at the end of a sentence: **qù** indicates *away* from the speaker and **lái** indicates *towards* the speaker:

Néng bu néng máfan nǐmen gěi
  wǒ sòng **lái** yìdiǎnr chī de?
Wǒmen yìhuǐr jiù sòng **qù**.

*Could I trouble you to send
me up something to eat?
We'll send it up as soon as
we can (lit. in a moment).*

Qǐng wù dǎrǎo!   *Do not disturb!*

ℹ Rooms in small hotels in China are usually equipped with thermos flasks containing hot water for you to make tea. These are emptied and refilled every morning often quite early so if you don't want to be disturbed at say 7am, remember to put the 'Don't disturb' notice on your door. When you leave your room, you can put the thermos flask(s) outside your door so that they can be refilled before your return.

Exercise 4   Make the following requests in Chinese using the pattern: **Néng bu néng gěi wǒ . . . ?**. If you want to be more polite, you can say **néng bu néng máfan nǐ(men) gěi wǒ . . . ?**. The measure word for each object is written in brackets after it.

a Can you send me up something to eat?
               something to drink?
               a cup of tea, with milk but no sugar?
               two sandwiches, one cheese, and
               one ham?

tǎnzi (tiáo) **wèishēngzhǐ** (juǎn) **xiāngzào** (kuài) **rèshuǐpíng** (gè)

b Can you give me a wake-up call?
            give me a phone call?
            buy me a bottle (**píng**) of wine?
            give me another blanket/roll of toilet paper?
            give me a bigger piece of soap?
            give me a thermos flask (of hot water)?

▶ **Exercise 5** Listen to the recording and fill in the following blanks. You need to remember the words **fúwù** (*service*) and **lǐmào** (*to be polite/courteous*). If you haven't got the recording, read the dialogue which comes after this exercise and then fill in the blanks.

a Frank now stays at _____ Hotel.
b The conditions in the hotel are _____ .
c The service there is _____ .
d The staff are _____ .
e He has changed his hotel _____ .

Lìli	Nǐ xiànzài zhù zài nǎr?
Frank	Dōngfāng Bīnguǎn.
Lìli	Tiáojiàn zěnmeyàng?
Frank	Tiáojiàn búcuò, kěshì fúwù bù zěnmeyàng.
Lìli	Fúwù zěnme bù hǎo?
Frank	Fúwùyuán bú tài lǐmào.
Lìli	Wèishénme bú huàn yí ge dìfang?
Frank	Wǒ yǐjing huàn le liǎng **cì**. Zhè shì dì sān **cì** le.

Cì (*time(s)*) is like **tiān** (*day*) and **nián** (*year*) in that it acts as both a measure word and a noun. *Once* is **yí cì**, *twice* is **liǎng cì** (note that it is **liǎng** and not **èr**), *three times* is **sān cì**, and so on. To say the first time, the second time, and so on all you have to do is put the little word **dì** in front. Note, however, that the second time is **dì-èr cì** and not **dì liǎng cì**.

Exercise 6 The receptionist at a hotel is asking you a few questions. How would you respond?

Fúwùyuán	Nǐ yùdìng le ma?
a **You**	(*No. I hope (xīwàng) you've still got rooms.*)
Fúwùyuán	Wǒmen hái yǒu jǐ jiān. Nǐ yào shénme fángjiān?
b **You**	(*A double room and a single room.*)
Fúwùyuán	Nǐmen dǎsuàn zhù jǐ tiān?
c **You**	(*Three or four days. We'll tell you tomorrow when we'll be leaving. Is that OK?*)
Fúwùyuán	Xíng. Jīntiān wǎnshang zài bīnguǎn chī wǎnfàn ma?
d **You**	(*No thank you, we've already eaten.*)

▶ Quick review

You are checking into a hotel. Ask the following questions in Chinese.

a Is breakfast included?
b When is lunch (**wǔfàn**)?
c Is there a television in the room?
d Have you got a bigger single room?
e How much is it per night?

13
huǒchē, piào hé chūzūchē
trains, tickets and taxis

In this unit you will learn
- how to ask for and understand information about trains
- how to understand train announcements
- how to buy train tickets
- many useful time expressions

Revise before you start

- yāo (*one*) (3)
- numbers over 100 (7)
- measure words (4)(7)
- use of **de** (3)(5)
- making comparisons (6)(7)
- **tài . . . le** (7)
- noun + **on** (5)

- **duō** + verb (10)
- how long (9)
- first . . . then . . . (9)
- use of **háishi** (6)
- use of **ba** (3)
- when . . . (10)

ℹ️ Trains in China

In China all trains are numbered. For example, train number 21 is called **èrshíyī cì**. Train number 161 is either **yāo-liù-yāo cì** or **yìbǎi liùshíyī cì**. The route of these numbered trains is fixed. **Èrshíyī cì** goes from Beijing to Shanghai, and **èrshíjiǔ cì** is the train from Beijing to Hangzhou. In general, the smaller the number of the train the faster it is.

There are three types of train: special express (**tèkuài**), express (**zhíkuài** or **kuàichē**) and normal (**pǔtōng kèchē**). The general word for train in Chinese is **huǒchē** for which the literal translation is *fire vehicle*.

In China they don't have first-class tickets (**tóuděng piào**) and second-class tickets (**èrděng piào**). But they do have four types of tickets: **ruǎnwò, ruǎnzuò, yìngwò** and **yìngzuò**. **Ruǎnwò** is really a first-class sleeper. **Ruǎnzuò** is just first class. **Yìngwò** is second class sleeper and **yìngzuò** is second class. As you may have noticed, these Chinese words involve different combinations of four characters: **ruǎn** meaning *soft*, **yìng** (*hard*), **wò** (*lying down*), and **zuò** (*seat*).

Note that train numbers use the word **cì** (p. 142, Unit 12) after the number:

train number 21 = **21 cì (èrshíyī cì)**
train number 161 = **161 cì (yìbǎi liùshíyī cì; yāo-liù-yāo cì)**

Train numbers of three digits can either be broken down into single digits or said as one number. **Yāo** is used instead of **yī** to avoid any confusion (see Unit 3, p. 27).

When train announcements are made, the sequence is different from the one you are used to in English. The order is normally **kāi wǎng** (drive towards) + destination + number (of train). The time is not usually mentioned. Do note that your ticket is only valid for a particular time.

Kāi wǎng Tiāntán *To Tiantan* (Temple of Heaven)

Exercise 1 What is the Chinese for these phrases?

a 'soft' sleeper
b 'hard' seat
c 'soft' seat
d 'hard' sleeper
e first class
f second class

What is the English for these Chinese words?

g kèchē
h tèkuài
i huǒchē
j kuàichē
k zhíkuài

Key words and phrases

cì	(number of trains)
dàgài	*approximately*
děi	*to need, must*
děng	*to wait*
hòutiān	*the day after tomorrow*
kāi	*to drive*
míngbai	*to understand* (colloquial)
něi zhǒng?	*which kind?*
rénmínbì	*Chinese currency*
shàng	*to board* (vehicle)
shuì	*to sleep*
suǒyǐ	*so, therefore*
ya	(end particle indicating surprise)
Yōnghé Gōng	*the Lama Temple* (in Beijing)

yǒu shénme . . . ?	in what ways . . . ? (lit. has what)
Yǒu shénme bù yíyàng?	In what ways are they different?
zhǎo (qián)	to give change

Travelling by train

èrděng	second-class (ticket)
ruǎnwò	'soft' sleeper
ruǎnzuò	'soft' seat
tèkuài	special express
tóuděng	first-class (ticket)
yìngwò	'hard' sleeper
yìngzuò	'hard' seat
zhíkuài	express (train)

Dialogues

▶ Dialogue 1

Frank is buying a train ticket from Běijīng to Shànghǎi. Listen to, or read, the dialogue and find out which trains go to Shànghǎi.

Frank	Wǒ xiǎng mǎi yì zhāng qù Shànghǎi de huǒchē piào.
Assistant	Něi tiān de?
Frank	Hòutiān de.
Assistant	Yào něi cì chē de?
Frank	Wǒ bù míngbai nǐde yìsi.
Assistant	Qù Shànghǎi de huǒchē yǒu shísān cì、èrshíyī cì hé yāo-liù-yāo cì.
Frank	Tāmen yǒu shénme bù yíyàng?
Assistant	Shísān cì hé èrshíyī cì shì tèkuài, yìbǎi liùshíyī cì shì zhíkuài.
Frank	Shénme shì tèkuài hé zhíkuài?
Assistant	Tèkuài jiù shì fēicháng kuài de yìsi. Shísān cì tèkuài bǐ yāo-liù-yāo cì zhíkuài **kuài sì、wǔ ge xiǎoshí**.
Frank	Shì bu shì tèkuài de piào yě bǐ zhíkuài de piào guì?
Assistant	Nà dāngrán le.

Note that if you want to say that train no. 13 is four hours quicker than train no. 161 you say:

13 cì bǐ 161 cì **kuài** (*quick*) + *by how much*
13 cì bǐ 161 cì **kuài sì ge xiǎoshí**

There is another example using **màn** *slow* in **Dialogue 2**. Look out for it!

This is the same pattern as you used in Unit 12 (p. 138), only here you are talking about a difference in time rather than money.

Shì bu shì can also be put at the beginning or in the middle of a sentence as well as at the end (see Unit 3). It conveys the idea that the speaker is confident that what she says is correct but wishes to soften the tone. You might have noticed that there is no tone on the second **shi** when it occurs at the end of a sentence.

Exercise 2   Answer the following questions based on the opening passage and **Dialogue 1**.

a   Which trains go to Shanghai?
b   Which train is faster, **zhíkuài** or **tèkuài**?
c   Is it cheaper to buy a ticket for a **tèkuài** than for a **zhíkuài** train?
d   What are the two ways of saying train number 351 in Chinese?
e   Is train number 243 faster than train number 43?

▶ Dialogue 2

Ann is now at the Beijing Railway Station ticket office. What type of ticket does she want to buy and what ticket does she buy in the end?

Ann	Qǐng wèn, hái yǒu shíbā hào èrshíyī cì de piào ma?
Assistant	Yǒu. Nín yào něi zhǒng piào?
Ann	Wǒ yào sān zhāng yìngwò.
Assistant	Duìbuqǐ, yìngwò zhǐ yǒu yì zhāng le. Wǒmen hái yǒu ruǎnwò hé yìngzuò.
Ann	Ruǎnwò bǐ yìngwò guì duōshao?
Assistant	Yìbǎi bāshí kuài.
Ann	Nàme shíbā hào yāo-liù-yāo cì hái yǒu yìngwò ma?
Assistant	Yǒu.
Ann	Tài hǎo le! Wǒ mǎi sān zhāng shíbā hào yāo-liù-yāo cì de yìngwò piào.
Assistant	Yāo-liù-yāo cì bǐ èrshíyī cì màn sì ge xiǎoshí.
Ann	Méi guānxi. Wǒmen kěyǐ zài huǒchē shàng duō shuì sì ge xiǎoshí.

Ticket for the underground/subway

Train ticket

火车站	候车室
Huǒchēzhàn *Train station*	**Hòuchēshì** *Waiting room*

▶ Some useful time expressions

qiánnián	*the year before last*
qùnián	*last year*
jīnnián	*this year*
míngnián	*next year*
hòunián	*the year after next*

shàng shàng ge yuè	*the month before last*
shàng (ge) yuè	*last month*
zhè/zhèi (ge) yuè	*this month*
xià (ge) yuè	*next month*
xià xià ge yuè	*the month after next*

shàng shàng ge xīngqī	*the week before last*
shàng (ge) xīngqī	*last week*
zhè/zhèi (ge) xīngqī	*this week*
xià (ge) xīngqī	*next week*
xià xià ge xīngqī	*the week after next*

qiántiān	*the day before yesterday*
zuótiān	*yesterday*
jīntiān	*today*
míngtiān	*tomorrow*
hòutiān	*the day after tomorrow*

Exercise 3   In **Dialogue 2** there are two useful structures, or patterns, for buying tickets.

i   **Qǐng wèn, hái yǒu X ma?**   *Have you still got X?*
ii   **Wǒmen mǎi X zhāng**   *We would like to have X*
     (time) de (type/event) piào.   *number of Y tickets for Z (where Y is the type of ticket and Z is the time).*

Now here's some practice: You want to know if the following kinds of tickets are still available.

Example: tickets for next Tuesday's football match
            You ask: **Qǐng wèn, hái yǒu xià ge xīngqī'èr de zúqiú piào ma?**

a   tickets for tonight's film
b   tickets for the flight (use **fēijī**) on October 4th
c   tickets for train number 153
d   tickets for trains going to Tianjin

If the answer to your above questions is *yes*, you can simply say **Wǒ yào X zhāng.** If, however, you know the tickets you want to buy are available, you would use pattern **ii**.

Example: Two film tickets for 2 o'clock Sunday afternoon
You say: **Wǒ mǎi liǎng zhāng xīngqī'èr xiàwǔ liǎng diǎn de diànyǐng piào.**

e three tickets for tonight's film
f four tickets for the flight on October 4th
g five tickets for train number 153
h six tickets for trains going to Tianjin

Exercise 4 Can you tell your Chinese friends something about British trains in Chinese?

a There are two types of tickets: first class and second class.
b First-class tickets are more expensive than second-class tickets.
c Trains in Britain are both fast and comfortable.

If you are from **Fǎguó**, **Měiguó**, **Déguó**, **Yìdàlì** or other countries, say something similar to the above sentences in Chinese.

▶ Dialogue 3

Chūzū qìchēzhàn *Taxi rank*

The following dialogue is between a taxi driver (**sījī**) and his customer (**chèngkè**). Before you read the dialogue, listen to the recording and answer the following two questions:

1 How many places did the man plan to visit?
2 How much did the taxi-driver charge him in the end?

Now read the dialogue and see if you answered the questions correctly.

Sījī	Nín qù nǎr?
Chèngkè	Wǒ xiǎng xiān qù Yōnghé Gōng, zài qù Tiāntán.
Sījī	Qǐng shàng chē ba.
Chèngkè	Nǐ néng bu néng xiān gàosù wǒ qù zhè liǎng ge dìfang dàgài děi duōshao qián?
Sījī	Qù Yōnghé Gōng sìshíwǔ kuài, zài qù Tiāntán yě shì sìshíwǔ kuài.
Chèngkè	Shì rénmínbì háishì měiyuán?
Sījī	Rénmínbì.
Chèngkè	Hǎo ba.
	(*getting off at Tiāntán Park*)

Chèngkè	Xièxie nǐ. Zhè shì yìbǎi kuài. Bié zhǎo qián le.
Sījī	Duìbuqǐ. Yígòng yìbǎi jiǔshí kuài.
Chèngkè	Zěnme shì yìbǎi jiǔshí kuài?
Sījī	Nǐ qù Yōnghé Gōng de shíhou, wǒ děng le nǐ liǎng ge xiǎoshí. Děng yí ge xiǎoshí wǔshí kuài. Suǒyǐ yígòng yìbǎi jiǔshí kuài.
Chèngkè	Nǐ zěnme méi xiān gàosu wǒ?
Sījī	Nǐ méi wèn ya.

Line 4 in **Dialogue 3** is a long sentence. **Bié zháojí** (*don't worry*)! Try the following two exercises and you'll be able to say it fluently.

▶ **Exercise 5** This exercise is called 'back chaining'. You practise long sentences like these by reading them phrase by phrase (the whole gradually increasing in length), starting with the end of the sentence first.

yìngwò piào
yāo-liù-yāo cì de yìngwò piào
shíbā hào yāo-liù-yāo cì de yìngwò piào
Wǒ mǎi sān zhāng shíbā hào yāo-liù-yāo cì de yìngwò piào

I'll buy three second-class sleepers for train number 161 on the 18th.
(*lit.* I buy three measure word eighteen number one six one time hard sleeper ticket.)

duōshao qián?
dàgài děi duōshao qián?
qù zhèi liǎng ge dìfang dàgài děi duōshao qián?
xiān gàosu wǒ qù zhèi liǎng ge dìfang dàgài děi duōshao qián?
Nǐ néng bu néng xiān gàosu wǒ qù zhèi liǎng ge dìfang dàgài
děi duōshao qián?

Can you first tell me roughly how much it costs to go to these two places?
(*lit.* you can not can first tell me go these two places roughly need how much money?)

Exercise 6 The long sentence you have just practised has two parts.

The main part is:

Nǐ néng bu néng gàosu wǒ 'X'. *Can you tell me 'X'?*

The second part can be an independent question such as *how old is he?* or *where does she live?*. In the dialogue the independent question is **qù zhè liǎng ge dìfang yào/děi duōshao qián?** (*how much does it cost to get to these two places?*).

Now request the following information starting with **nǐ néng bu néng gàosu wǒ**:

Example: How old is he?
         You ask: **Nǐ néng bu néng gàosu wǒ tā duō dà le?**

First try these independent questions and then combine each one with the main sentence.

a Where does she live?
b What is your telephone number?
c How old is his daughter?
d How long do they intend staying there?

Exercise 7 Put each group of phrases into the correct order to make complete questions in Chinese. (First say each phrase separately, then sort them into order.)

Example: How much, by train, go to Nanjing?
         You ask: **Zuò huǒchē qù Nánjīng děi duōshao qián?**

a How much / to go to Xī'ān / by train?
b To fly / how long / from London to Shànghǎi?
c To go to Hépíng Hotel / by taxi / how much?
d By ship (**chuán**) / how long / to go from Japan to China?

Quick review

Can you match the Chinese words on the left with their English equivalents on the right? There will be one word in the left-hand column that you will not recognize. Which one is it? What must it mean? (Notice that all the Chinese words have the character **chē** in them.)

a	zìxíngchē	i	coach
b	huǒchē	ii	express (train)
c	chūzū (qì)chē	iii	bicycle
d	gōnggòng qìchē	iv	train
e	kuàichē	v	taxi
f	chángtú qìchē	vi	normal (passenger) train
g	pǔtōng kèchē	vii	bus

Chūzū qìchē

14

yúlè huódòng
free time and entertainment

In this unit you will learn
- how to say what you like doing in your free time
- how to ask somebody what they would like to do
- about sports and hobbies
- about making arrangements
- about summer and winter, indoor and outdoor activities

Revise before you start

- use of **de** after verb (8)
- **zuì** (*most*) (7)
- **gèng** (*even more*) (8)
- use of **háishi** (6)
- both . . . and . . . (9)
- to be in the middle of doing something (6)
- making comparisons (6)(7)
- A is the same as B (6)

A park in Chinese is actually a public garden. Do you remember Frank in Unit 6? If you go to China, try to get up early at least one morning, say at 6 o'clock, and go to a local park. You too will be fascinated by what some of the Chinese do there. The following passage tells us a little bit more about what people do in a park.

▶ Qù gōngyuán *Going to the park*

Hěn duō Zhōngguó-rén qǐ-de hěn zǎo. Tāmen rènwéi zǎo shuì zǎo qǐ duì shēntǐ hǎo. Zǎoshang tāmen zuò shénme? Bù shǎo rén qù gōngyuán.

Zài gōngyuán lǐ, tāmen dǎ tàijíquán、zuò qìgōng、chàng gē、 tiào wǔ, děngděng. Yǒu de lǎo rén zài gōngyuán sànbù、xià qí、dǎ pái、chàng jīngjù.

Hěn duō gōngyuán dōu yǒu hú. Zài běifāng, xiàtiān kěyǐ zài hú lǐ yóuyǒng, dōngtiān kěyǐ zài hú shàng huá bīng.

Key words and phrases

běifāng	the north
chàng (gē)	to sing (song)
chàng jīngjù	to sing Peking opera
dǎ pái	to play cards
děngděng	etc. / and so on
dōngtiān	winter
gōngyuán	park
hú	lake
huá bīng	to skate
lǎo	old
lǎo rén	old person / people
qǐ	to get up
rènwéi	to think, to believe
sàn bù	to stroll
shǎo	few, less
bù shǎo	quite a lot
tiào wǔ	to dance
xià qí	to play chess
xiàtiān	summer
yóuyǒng	to swim
zài (hú) lǐ/shàng	in / on (the lake)
zǎo	early
zǎo shuì	early to bed
zǎo qǐ	early to rise

Exercise 1 When you have the opportunity, ask a Chinese person these questions:

a Do the Chinese get up very early?
b Where do you go in the morning?
c What do old people do in the park?
d Do you swim in the lake?

i There is a huge difference between the type of Chinese which is spoken and the type of Chinese which is written. Spoken Chinese is normally much more informal than written Chinese. Sometimes a different word is used in written Chinese to convey the same meaning as a simpler word in the spoken language. There is a good example of this in the passage above where **rènwéi** (*to be of the opinion that*) is used instead of **xiǎng** (*to think*).

This need not concern you very much on a practical level because you are concentrating on spoken Chinese. Unless, of course, you plan to get to grips with the Chinese writing system at some stage and therefore read material in Chinese characters. Why not go on to *Teach Yourself Chinese* once you've finished this book or to *Teach Yourself Beginner's Chinese Script* if you are especially interested in Chinese characters?

Key words and phrases

Àolínpǐkè	Olympic
bàn	to handle
bàng	excellent (colloquial)
biǎoyǎn	show, performance; to act, perform
dànyuànrúcǐ	I hope so
dào	to arrive
děng	to wait
fāngbiàn	convenient
gèng duō de	more (of something)
hǎo jiǔ bú jiàn	long time no see
hòu bàn (chǎng)	second half (of a show)
huódòng	activity
jīhuì	opportunity
juédìng	to decide
liànxí	to practise, exercise
lóushàng	upstairs
lǚxíng	to travel; travel
lǚxíngtuán	tourist group
niánqīng	young
pái	row (of seats)
X pái Y hào	number Y in row X
qiānzhèng	visa
qiūtiān	autumn
Shì nǐ ya!	It's you!
shòu	thin
shūfu	comfortable
tán	to talk, chat
tán liàn'ài	to be in love, go steady (lit. talk love)
tǐng	quite, fairly (colloquial)
wèizi	seat
xué-hǎo	to master (see Unit 10, p. 115)
yǎn	to act
yúlè	entertainment
yùndòng	sports, take exercises
yùndònghuì	sports meeting, games
zhǎo	to look for
zhěngtiān	all day
zìjǐ	oneself
zìyóu	freedom
zuìjìn	recent, recently

Nǐ xǐhuan shénme yùndòng?
What's your favourite sport/game?

dǎ	*to play . . .*	**(tī) zúqiú**	(play) *football*
dǎ pīngpāngqiú	. . . *pingpong*	**qí mǎ**	*horse riding*
dǎ lánqiú	. . . *basketball*		(lit. *to ride horse*)
dǎ yǔmáoqiú	. . . *badminton*	**huá xuě**	*skiing* (lit. *to slide*
dǎ qūgùnqiú	. . . *hockey*		*snow*)
dǎ wǎngqiú	. . . *tennis*	**(dǎ) Tàijíjiàn**	(do) *Tai Chi sword*

▶ Dialogue 1

Edward and Xiǎo Fù are talking about their favourite sports. Listen to the recording and make a note of what sports they each like before you read the dialogue.

Edward   Nǐ xǐhuan shénme yùndòng?
Xiǎo Fù   Wǒ zuì xǐhuan **wǎngqiú** (i) hé **yóuyǒng** (ii).
Edward   Wǒ yě xǐhuan **wǎngqiú** (i), kěshì gèng xǐhuan **zúqiú** (iv).
Xiǎo Fù   Nǐ xǐhuan **tī** (iii) **zúqiú** (iv) háishì kàn **zúqiú** (iv)?
Edward   Dōu xǐhuan.
Xiǎo Fù   Wǒ zhǐ xǐhuan kàn, bù xǐhuan **tī** (iii).

Exercise 2   Use the groups of words below to substitute for the sports in **Dialogue 1**. a under column i substitutes for (i) in the dialogue, i.e. **pīngpāngqiú** substitutes for **wǎngqiú**; a under column ii substitutes for (ii) in the dialogue and so on. Do the same with **b** to **e**. Each time you have completed one row of substitution read out the dialogue using the new words.

	i	ii	iii	iv
a	pīngpāngqiú	huá bīng	dǎ	lánqiú
b	lánqiú	xià qí	dǎ	yǔmáoqiú
c	yǔmáoqiú	qí mǎ	dǎ	qūgùnqiú
d	qūgùnqiú	huá xuě	dǎ	tàijíquán
e	tàijíquán	tàijíjiàn	dǎ	pái

Exercise 3   What do you like and dislike?

You are given three activities each time. Use **i** to show an ascending order of preference. Use **ii** to rank your dislikes. We have given you sample answers in the **Key to the exercises**.

i   Wǒ xǐhuan A, gèng xǐhuan B, zuì xǐhuan C.
ii   Wǒ bù xǐhuan A, gèng bù xǐhuan B, zuì bù xǐhuan C.

Example: diànyǐng, jīngjù, yīnyuèhuì

   i   Wǒ xǐhuan kàn jīngjù, gèng xǐhuan kàn diànyǐng, zuì xǐhuan tīng yīnyuèhuì.

   ii Wǒ bù xǐhuan tīng yīnyuèhuì, gèng bù xǐhuan kàn diànyǐng, zuì bù xǐhuan kàn jīngjù.

a   zuò fēijī, zuò chuán, zuò huǒchē

b   qí zìxíngchē, qí mǎ (*horse*), qí mótuōchē (*motorbike*)

c   zuò gōnggòng qìchē (*bus*), zuò dìtiě (*underground/subway*), zuò chūzū (qì)chē

d   kàn jīngjù, kàn diànshì, kàn diànyǐng

e   tīng gǔdiǎn (*classical*) yīnyuè, tīng xiàndài (*modern*) yīnyuè, tīng liúxíng (*pop*) yīnyuè

▶ Dialogue 2

Yáo Mínglì is asking Ann about her forthcoming holiday. Why has Ann not yet made up her mind?

Mínglì	Tīngshuō jīnnián qiūtiān nǐ yào qù Zhōngguó lǚxíng.
Ann	Duì. Kěshì wǒ hái méi juédìng zěnme qù.
Mínglì	Zěnme qù? Dāngrán zuò fēijī qù. Zuò huǒchē yòu màn yòu bù shūfu.
Ann	Wǒ bú shì nèi ge yìsi. Wǒ hái méi juédìng gēn lǚxíngtuán qù háishì zìjǐ qù.
Mínglì	Gēn lǚxíngtuán qù hěn fāngbiàn, kěshì yòu guì yòu bú zìyóu.
Ann	Zìjǐ qù yòu piányi yòu zìyóu, kěshì zhēn bù fāngbiàn.
Mínglì	Zěnme bù fāngbiàn?
Ann	Wǒ yào zìjǐ qù bàn qiānzhèng、dìng fēijī piào、zhǎo lǚguǎn, děngděng.
Mínglì	Kěshì zìjǐ qù kěyǐ yǒu gèng duō de jīhuì liànxí Zhōngwén.
Ann	Duì, wǒ yídìng yào xué-hǎo Zhōngwén, èr-líng-líng-bā nián qù Běijīng kàn Àolínpǐkè Yùndònghuì.

Note that if you want to say that something still hasn't happened, you put the word **hái** in front of **méi** (yǒu):

Kěshì wǒ **hái** méi juédìng zěnme qù.	*But I haven't yet decided how to go.*
Tā **hái** méi yǒu lái (ne).	*She still hasn't come.*

There is an optional **ne** at the end of such sentences.

Exercise 4   The following passage is based on **Dialogue 2**. Fill in the blanks (use one word per blank) according to the information given in the dialogue.

Ann jīnnián(**a**) dǎsuàn qù Zhōngguó (**b**). Kěshì tā (**c**) (**d**) juédìng gēn lǚxíngtuán qù (**e**) zìjǐ qù. Gēn lǚxíngtuán qù (**f**) guì (**g**) bú zìyóu. Zìjǐ qù yòu (**h**) yòu (**i**). Kěshì zìjǐ qù hěn (**j**) fāngbiàn. Tā yào zìjǐ qù (**k**) qiānzhèng, (**l**) fēijī piào, (**m**) lǚguǎn, děngděng.

Dialogue 3

Lǎo Qián and Xiǎo Zhào meet at the cinema entrance. Read the dialogue to find out what they have been doing lately.

Xiǎo Zhào	Lǎo Qián, hǎo jiǔ bú jiàn.
Lǎo Qián	Xiǎo Zhào, shì nǐ ya!
Xiǎo Zhào	Nín xiànzài zài zuò shénme?
Lǎo Qián	Gēn yǐqián yíyàng. Měi tiān dǎda pái、xiàxia qí、dǎda tàijíquán, tǐng yǒu yìsi.
Xiǎo Zhào	Nín bǐ yǐqián niánqīng duōle.
Lǎo Qián	Nǎli, nǎli. Lǎo duōle. Xiǎo Zhào, nǐ zuìjìn zài zuò shénme?
Xiǎo Zhào	Wǒ zhèngzài tán liàn'ài. Zhěngtiān mǎi dōngxi、kàn diànyǐng、tiào wǔ. Zhēn méi yìsi.
Lǎo Qián	Nǐ bǐ yǐqián shòu duōle.
Xiǎo Zhào	Tán liàn'ài yòu lèi yòu bú zìyóu.
Lǎo Qián	Nǐde nǚ péngyou ne?
Xiǎo Zhào	Tā hái méi lái ne. Wǒ zài děng tā.

电影院

diànyǐngyuàn   *cinema*

Tán liàn'ài
To be in love

Gāng jié hūn
Just married

Sān nián yǐhòu
Three years later

▶ **Exercise 5** You are having a conversation with a Chinese friend. You begin:

a **You**   (*Greet Xiǎo Wáng and say you haven't seen him for ages.*)
  Friend   Nǐ hǎo, Xiǎo Mǎ. Shì nǐ ya!
b **You**   (*Ask him what he is up to these days.*)
  Friend   Gēn yǐqián yíyàng. Hái zài xuéxiào (*school*) gōngzuò.
c **You**   (*Ask if he is married.*)
  Friend   Hái méi yǒu. Wǒmen míngnián jié hūn.
d **You**   (*Ask him who he is waiting for.*)
  Friend   Wǒ zài děng wǒ nǚ péngyou. Nǐ qù nǎr?
e **You**   (*Tell him that you are going swimming.*)
  Friend   Hǎo, zánmen yǐhòu zài tán.
f **You**   (*Say goodbye to him.*)
  Friend   Zàijiàn!

Dialogue 4

Edward and Xiǎo Fù ran into each other during the interval of a show. Where are they sitting and what do they think of the performance tonight?

Edward   Nǐ zuò nǎr?
Xiǎo Fù Wǔ pái sì hào.
Edward   Nǐ de wèizi zhēn hǎo.
Xiǎo Fù Nǐ zài nǎr?
Edward   Wǒ zài lóushàng shí pái
             sānshí hào.
Xiǎo Fù Nǐ juéde jīntiān de biǎoyǎn
             zěnmeyàng?
Edward   Tāmen chàng-de tǐng hǎo.
             Nǐ juéde ne?
Xiǎo Fù Wǒ juéde tāmen chàng-de
             hái bú cuò. Kěshì yǎn-de
             bù zěnmeyàng.
Edward   Tīngshuō hòumiàn de
             biǎoyǎn hěn bàng.
Xiǎo Fù Dànyuànrúcǐ.

楼上
Lóushàng
upstairs

楼下
Lóuxià
downstairs

Note that there are still a few traces of the classical Chinese language in use today. Classical Chinese was monosyllabic but it often put four characters together to express a particular idea. Many of these four-character phrases became set phrases and still appear in the language today. **Dànyuànrúcǐ** is an example of such a four character phrase. Other examples are:

Wànshì rúyì	(*lit.* 10,000 things like wish) *your heart's desire*
Yílù píng'ān	(*lit.* all road peace) *bon voyage*
Yílù shùnfēng	(*lit.* all road following wind) *bon voyage*

Such phrases are usually preceded by **zhù nǐ (men)** . . . (*wish you* . . .). This is sometimes omitted, especially in written Chinese.

i Seating in Chinese cinemas and theatres: as you can see in **Exercise 6** below, all the even seat numbers are grouped together on one side and all the uneven ones on the other. Only seat numbers 1 and 2 are next to each other sequentially. This means that when you go into a Chinese cinema you need to check whether your seat numbers are **shuānghào** (*even*) or **dānhào** (*odd*). If they are even, you will need to follow the sign for 双号 seats and if odd, the signs for 单号 seats. It is obviously important to understand the way the seating is organized if ever you are buying seats yourself.

Exercise 6 Three rows of seats are given in each section. Give the Chinese for the seat number ○ in each of the three sections A, B, C, below.

双号 *Example*: Row 14, No. 19, upstairs 单号
　　　 Lóushàng shísì pái shíjiǔ hào.

Shuānghào　　　　　　　　　　　　　　　　　　　　**Dānhào**

```
A 1   30 28 26 24 . . . . . . 8 6 4 2 1 3 5 7 . . . . . . 21 23 ○ 27
   2   30 28 26 24 . . . . . . 8 6 4 2 1 3○7 . . . . . . 21 23 25 27
   3   30 28 ○ 24 . . . . . . 8 6 4 2 1 3 5 7 . . . . . . 21 23 25 27
B 24  30 28 26 ○ . . . . . . 8 6 4 2 1 3 5 7 . . . . . . 21 23 25 27
   25  30 28 26 24 . . . . . . 8 6○2 1 3 5 7 . . . . . . 21 23 25 27
   26  30 28 26 24 . . . . . . 8 6 4 2 1 3 5 7 . . . . . . 21 ○ 25 27
C [Lóushàng]
   11  30 28 26 24 . . . . . . 8○4 2 1 3 5 7 . . . . . . 21 23 25 27
   12  30 ○ 26 24 . . . . . . 8 6 4 2 1 3 5 7 . . . . . . 21 23 25 27
   13  30 28 26 24 . . . . . . 8 6 4 2 1 3 5 7 . . . . . . ○ 23 25 27
```

Exercise 7 Tell your Chinese guests where their seats are.

a	b	c	d
Row A No. 12	Row J No. 37	Row F No. 40 upstairs	Row K No. 2

Exercise 8 Your Chinese guests are planning a night out. Tell them in Chinese the options they have in their local area, which are shown in the advertisements below.

bālái	ballet	**gējù**	opera
huàjù	play	**tiān'é**	swan

You also need to know the word **bàng**. This time it means *pound in weight* (see Exercise 2, Unit 7, where it means *pound in money*). You should not now be surprised to learn that the Chinese character for **bàng** (*pound*) in money is different from the character for **bàng** (*pound*) in weight. Here they are:

bàng

The right-hand side is exactly the same for both but a pound in money has metal or gold on the left-hand side and a pound in weight has stone or mineral.

bàng

Film: *Winter Time* 18.00, 20.00, 22.00 *Saturday, 25th October* *Tickets: £5, £6.50*	**Ballet:** *Swan Lake* Time: 19.30 **Sunday 26th October** *Tickets: £12, £18, £25*
Play: *When we were young* Time: 19.15 **Saturday 25th October** *Tickets: £10, £12.50*	**Opera:** *Carmen* Time: 20.00 Sunday 26th October *Tickets: £16, £24, £30*

▶ Quick review

Yán Lóngfēng and his girlfriend Liú Língmǐn are discussing how they are going to spend the evening. Listen to, or read, the dialogue and answer the questions after it.

Yán   Zánmen qù kàn diànyǐng ba.
Liú   Yǒu shénme hǎo diànyǐng?
Yán   Tīngshuō 《**Wǒmen niánqīng de shíhou**》 búcuò.
Liú   Wǒ kàn-guo le. Méi yìsi.

Yán	Nàme wǒmen qù tīng yīnyuèhuì ba.
Liú	Yǒu shénme yīnyuèhuì?
Yán	Nǐ xiǎng tīng Zhōngguó yīnyuè háishì Xīfāng yīnyuè?
Liú	Dōu bù xiǎng tīng.
Yán	Nàme nǐ xiǎng zuò shénme?
Liú	Wǒ xiǎng qù tiào wǔ.

a What did Yán Lóngfēng first suggest that they did?
b Did Liú Língmǐn accept his suggestion? Why or why not?
c What types of concert did Yán Lóngfēng ask his girlfriend to choose from?
d Was Liú Língmǐn interested?
e What did Liú Língmǐn want to do?

15

zài yóujú hé huàn qián

at a post office and changing money

In this unit you will learn
- how to buy stamps
- how to send (and collect) a parcel
- how to make a long distance call
- how to send a fax
- numbers above 1,000

Revise before you start

- from ... to ...   (9)
- measure words   (4)(7)
- money   (7)
- weights   (7)
- zuì (*most*)   (7)

- verb endings   (10)
- use of **háishi**   (6)
- use of **de**   (3)(5)
- **huì**   (9)
- foreign currency   (7)

The following passage tells you something about the **yóujú** (*post office*) in China. Are there things you can do in a Chinese **yóujú** that you don't normally do in a post office in Britain?

Yóujú   *The post office*

邮局

post office

Zhōngguó de yóujú gēn Yīngguó de yóujú chàbuduō. Zài yóujú nǐ kěyǐ jì xìn、jì qián、jì bāoguǒ, yě kěyǐ mǎi yóupiào、xìnfēng hé míngxìnpiàn, hái kěyǐ cún qián、qǔ qián hé fù zhàng. Zài Zhōngguó de yóujú nǐ hái kěyǐ dǎ chángtú diànhuà hé guójì diànhuà.

Yóujú de kāi mén shíjiān chángcháng bù yíyàng. Yǒude shàngwǔ bā diǎn kāi mén, yǒude bā diǎn bàn kāi mén. Yǒude xiàwǔ wǔ diǎn bàn guān mén, yǒude wǎnshang qī diǎn guān mén. Xīngqīliù、xīngqītiān dōu kāi mén.

Shùnbiàn shuō yíxià, Zhōngguó de xìntǒng shì lǜsè de, Yīngguó de xìntǒng shì hóngsè de.

Key words and phrases

bāoguǒ	*parcel*
chàbuduō	*similar* (lit. *lacking not much*)
X gēn Y chàbuduō	*X is not much different to Y*
chángtú	*long distance*
dǎ chángtú diànhuà	*to make a long distance / national call*
cún qián	*to deposit money*
fù zhàng	*to pay bills*
guójì	*international*
jì	*to post*
míngxìnpiàn	*postcard*
qǔ qián	*withdraw money*
shùnbiàn shuō yíxià	*by the way* (when speaking)

shùnbiàn wèn yíxià	*by the way* (when asking a question)
yǒude	*some*
yóujú	*post office*
yóupiào	*stamp*
xìn	*letter*
xìnfēng	*envelope*
xìntǒng	*postbox, mailbox*

Exercise 1 Now would you like to tell the Chinese something about post offices in Britain?

a You can deposit and withdraw money in a post office.
b Post offices in Britain do not usually open on Saturday afternoons and Sundays.
c Postboxes in Britain are red, not green.
d In Britain, you can't make long distance calls in a post office.

Chinese stamps

Key words and phrases

chá	*to look up* (something)
chāo zhòng le	*to have exceeded the weight limit*
chèng	*scales*
chuánzhēn	*fax*
dào	*to go to; to*
diànzǐ yóujiàn	*e-mail (electronic mail)*
dìqū	*district*
fā	*to send* (a fax, e-mail, etc.)
fā-wán le	*have sent* (a fax) *through*
fàng	*to put*
fēng	*(measure word for letters)*
guāngpán	*compact disk (CD)*
hǎiyùn	*(to post) by sea*
hángkōng	*(to post) by air*

hǎokàn	*nice-looking*
jì dào	*to post to*
nèibiān	*over there*
shàng wǎng	*to use the internet* (lit. *on net*)
shōujù	*receipt*
shū	*book*
tào	*set* (stamps)
yè	*page*
yuànyì	*would like to, to be willing to*
zhàn xiàn	*(line) engaged*
zhuǎn	*to change to* (extension)

▶ Dialogue 1

Ann is now at a post office in China. At the end of the dialogue she will have done three things. What are they?

Ann   Qǐng wèn, zhèi fēng xìn jì dào Yīngguó, duōshao qián?

Assistant Qǐng fàng zài chèng shàng. . . . Chāo zhòng le. Sān kuài
              jiǔ.

Ann   Jǐ tiān néng dào?

Assistant Bù yídìng. Yìbān wǔ、liù tiān. Zhè shì nínde yóupiào.

Ann   Zhèi zhāng yóupiào zhēn hǎokàn. Wǒ néng mǎi yí
              tào ma?

Assistant Dāngrán kěyǐ. Yí tào liù kuài qī.

Ann   Wǒ hái xiǎng jì yí ge bāoguǒ.

Assistant Shì shénme dōngxi?

Ann   Dōu shì shū hé guāngpán.

Assistant Yě qǐng fàng zài chèng shàng. . . . Liǎng gōngjīn. Nín jì
              hángkōng háishi hǎiyùn?

Ann   Hángkōng.

ℹ In China, only standardized envelopes with boxes for postcodes may be used (see envelope on previous page). The top left-hand corner is for the addressee's postcode and the bottom right-hand corner for the sender's.

▶ **Exercise 2** You are now in a post office talking to the assistant. You begin:

a **You** (*Say this parcel is for America.*)
  Assistant Shì shénme dōngxi?
b **You** (*Say they are all books.*)
  Assistant Qǐng fàng zài chèng shàng. . . . Yìbǎi wǔshísān kuài.
c **You** (*Ask how many days it takes (to get to America).*)
  Assistant Bù yídìng. Yìbān sì、wǔ tiān.
d **You** (*Say you would like to buy postcards and ask how much it is for a set.*)
  Assistant Zhèi tào dà de shíliù kuài. Nèi tào xiǎo de shísì kuài wǔ.
e **You** (*Say you'll have a set of the big ones, and two sets of the small ones.*)
  Assistant Bāoguǒ yìbǎi wǔshísān kuài, yí tào dà de míngxìnpiàn shíliù kuài, liǎng tào xiǎo de èrshíjiǔ kuài, yígòng yìbǎi jiǔshíbā kuài.
f **You** (*Say here are 200 kuài.*)
  Assistant Zhǎo nín liǎng kuài.
g **You** (*Say thank you and goodbye.*)
  Assistant Zàijiàn!

Dialogue 2

Colin zài **shāngwù zhōngxīn** fā chuánzhēn. (*Colin is sending a fax at a business centre.*)

Colin Xiǎojie, qǐng wèn, kěyǐ zài zhèr fā **(yí) ge** chuánzhēn ma?
Assistant Kěyǐ. Fā-dào nǎr?
Colin Déguó.
Assistant Yígòng jǐ yè?
Colin Liǎng yè.
Assistant Hǎo de. Qǐng gěi wǒ chuánzhēn hàomǎ.
Colin Zhè shì chuánzhēn hàomǎ.
Assistant Qǐng děngyiděng. . . . Fā-wán le. Zhè shì shōujù.
Colin Duōshǎo qián?
Assistant Sìshí kuài. Qǐng dào nèibiān fù qián.
Colin Xièxie nǐ. Shùnbiàn wèn yíxià, kěyǐ zài zhèr shàng wǎng hé fā diànzǐ yóujiàn ma?
Assistant Dāngrán kěyǐ.

商务中心
Shāngwù zhōngxīn
Business centre

Note that in spoken Chinese, when **yī** (*one*) occurs with a measure word the **yī** is often omitted.

▶ **Exercise 3** You will find it useful to be able to ask and understand the following questions and instructions in Chinese. Look carefully at the example given in each section and then have a go at translating the English sentences which follow it into Chinese.

a Asking for services:

Example: **Qǐng wèn kěyǐ zài zhèr fā ge chuánzhēn mā?**

Can I make a phone call here?
Can I send a parcel here?
Can I send an e-mail here?

b Asking for items:

Example: **Qǐng gěi wǒ tāde chuánzhēn hào(mǎ).**

Can I have your telephone number?
Can I have their website address (**wǎngzhǐ**)?
Can I have your passport?
Can I have their address (**dìzhǐ**)?

c Giving instructions/directions:

Example: **Qǐng dào nèibiān fù qián.**

Please change money over there.
Please make the phone call outside (**wàibiān**).

Qǐng dào hòubiān pái duì (*Please queue at the back*) is another useful instruction you may wish to learn.

Dialogue 3

Xiè Qúnyì is making a long-distance call.

Operator	Nín hǎo. Nánfāng Dàxué.
Xiè	**Qǐng zhuǎn** sì-èr-qī fēnjī.
Operator	Duìbuqǐ, sì-èr-qī zhàn xiàn. Nín yuànyì děngyiděng háishì yìhuǐr zài dǎ **lái**?
Xiè	Wǒ zhè shì guójì diànhuà. Nín néng bu néng jiào sì-èr-qī de Wáng Bǎopíng gěi wǒ dǎ ge diànhuà?
Operator	Nínde hàomǎ shì duōshao?
Xiè	Yīngguó Lúndūn shì sì-sì-èr-líng-qī. Wǒde diànhuà shì èr-yāo-liù qī-qī-jiǔ-èr.
Operator	Nín guì xìng?
Xiè	Wǒ jiào Xiè Qúnyì.
Operator	Méi wèntí.
Xiè	Xièxie nín.

You learnt about straightforward telephone numbers in Unit 3, p. 27. If, having got through to the main switchboard, you need to ask for an extension number, such as 473, you say:

Qǐng zhuǎn sì-qī-sān (**fēnjī**).   *Extension 473 please.* (*lit.* invite transfer 4–7–3 branch machine)

Note the little word **lái** at the end of the operator's second speech in **Dialogue 3**:

Nǐ yuànyì děngyīděng háishi yìhuǐr zài dǎ **lái**?   *Do you wish to wait or phone again in a little while?* (*lit.* you wish wait a little while again hit [the electric speech] come?)

This use of **lái** indicates direction towards the speaker (see also Unit 12, p. 140).

Exercise 4   Read the dialogue and answer the following questions in English.

a   Where is the caller phoning?
b   Who does the caller want to speak to?
c   Why couldn't the operator connect the caller to the extension he gave her?
d   What seemed to be the mistake?

▶ A telephone conversation

Operator	Nín hǎo, Hépíng Bīnguǎn.
Mark	Qǐng zhuǎn wǔ-bā-sì fēnjī.
Operator	Duìbuqǐ, wǒmen méi yǒu wǔ-bā-sì fēnjī.
Mark	Shénme? Méi yǒu wǔ-bā-sì fēnjī?!
Operator	Nín yào zhǎo shéi?
Mark	Wǒ zhǎo cóng Měiguó lái de Bái Huá xiānsheng.
Operator	Tā zhù nǎ ge fángjiān?
Mark	Duìbuqǐ, wǒ bu zhīdào.
Operator	Qǐng děngyīděng. Wǒ chá yíxià. A, Bái Huá xiānsheng. Tā zhù wǔ-sì-bā fángjiān. Tā de fēnjī yě shì wǔ-sì-bā.
Mark	Duìbuqǐ. Nàme qǐng gěi wǒ zhuǎn yíxià.

公用电话

Gōngyòng diànhuà
Public telephone

It is not difficult to change money in big cities, but it can be difficult in small cities and towns. The following passage tells us one of the reasons.

BANK OF CHINA
中國銀行

Huàn qián *Changing money*

(Words in *italics* are explained in the box below.)

Zài Zhōngguó huàn qián yìbān zhǐ néng zài dà yínháng de *fēnháng* huàn, *duìhuànlǜ* dōu chàbuduō. Yǒude dà fàndiàn hé dà shāngdiàn yě yǒu huàn qián de dìfang. Yínháng de kāi mén shíjiān gēn pǔtōng de shāngdiàn bù yíyàng, bǐ shāngdiàn kāi mén shíjiān wǎn yìdiǎn, guān mén shíjiān zǎo yìdiǎn. Kěshi, zài dà fàndiàn lǐ de huàn qián de dìfang, kāi mén shíjiān bǐjiào *línghuó*, *kěnéng* huì kāi-dào hěn wǎn. *Jiānglái*, *qǔkuǎnjī* duō le, qǔ qián gèng fāngbiàn le, jiù bú yòng qù yínháng huàn qián le.

diǎn	*to count (e.g. money)*
duìhuànlǜ	*exchange rate*
fēnháng	*branch* (of a bank)
jiānglái	*in the future*
kěnéng	*possible, possibly*
línghuó	*flexible*
qǔkuǎnjī	*ATM (automatic teller machine)*
zhènghǎo	*just right* (amount)

Exercise 5 Respond with **duì** or **bú duì** to the following statements about the passage above.

		duì	**bú duì**
a	One can change money at any bank in China.	☐	☐
b	You can change money in some big hotels.	☐	☐
c	The opening hours of banks in China are different from those of ordinary shops.	☐	☐
d	The opening hours of Bureaux de Change in big hotels are the same as at banks in the high street.	☐	☐

If you have enjoyed learning something about Chinese characters, why not go on to *Teach Yourself Beginner's Chinese Script*, which will allow you to explore the Chinese script even more?

International Women's Day (8th March) and the day after . . .

měiyuán	*US dollar*	**yīngbàng**	*UK pound*
rìyuán	*Japanese yen*	**gǎngbì**	*HK dollar*
ōuyuán	*euro*	**rénmínbì**	*Chinese yuan*

Numbers above 1,000

1,000	**yìqiān**	100,000	**shíwàn** (ten wàns)
10,000	**yíwàn**	480,000	**sìshíbā wàn**
20,000	**èr/liǎng wàn**	1,000,000	**yìbǎi wàn**
35,000	**sānwàn wǔqiān**		(100 wàns)

$9 \times 1,000 = $ jiǔqiān
but $10 \times 1,000 = $ yíwàn

There is no specific word for one million. It is *100 wàns*! Two million is therefore *200 wàns*, and so on.

▶ Dialogue 4

The customer in the dialogue below wants to change some money. First he will have to fill out a **duìhuàndān** (*exchange memo*). Figures can be difficult to understand, so listen to the dialogue a few times and concentrate on the figures. What currency does the customer wish to exchange for **rénmínbì**? What is the exchange rate? How much does he want to change?

Customer	Qǐng wèn, jīntiān měiyuán hé rénmínbì de duìhuànlǜ shì duōshao?
Teller	Yī bǐ bā diǎnr jiǔ.
Customer	Yì měiyuán huàn bā kuài jiǔ, duì ma?
Teller	Duì.
Customer	Wǒ xiǎng huàn liǎngbǎi měiyuán de rénmínbì.
Teller	Qǐng xiān tián zhèi zhāng duìhuàndān.
Customer	. . . Tián-hǎo le. Zhè shì liǎngbǎi měiyuán.
Teller	Qǐng děngyiděng. . . . Zhè shì yìqiān qībǎi bāshí kuài. Qǐng diǎnyidiǎn.
Customer	(*Counting money*) Zhènghǎo. Xièxie nǐ.
Teller	Bú kèqi.

Exercise 6 How would you ask for the exchange rate of the following currency against **rénmínbì yuán**?

Example: (Jīntiān) rìyuán hé rénmínbì de duìhuànlǜ shì duōshao?

a £

b US $

c HK $

d € (euro)

Exercise 7 Now ask again for the exchange rates in **Exercise 6** and this time give the answer according to the table below. Try to use both expressions used in **Dialogue 4** for talking about the rates. (Leave out this exercise if you don't like working with figures.)

Example: 10,000 (Japanese) yen
     i Yíwàn (rìyuán) bǐ qībǎi bāshí'èr (kuài rénmínbì)
    ii Yíwàn rìyuán huàn qībǎi bāshí'èr kuài rénmínbì.

Foreign currencies			Rénmínbì (yuán)
US	$	100.00	850.00
HK	$	100.00	108.00
	£	100.00	1320.00
euro	€	100.00	910.00

Exercise 8 You want to change the following amount of currency into **RMB yuán**. What would you say?

Example: 75,000 rìyuán
      Wǒ xiǎng huàn qīwàn wǔqiān rìyuán de rénmínbì.

a £100
b US $200
c HK $500

d 60,000 yen
e €400

▶ Quick review

How do you ask or say the following?

a How much is it to post this postcard to Britain?
b I want to buy a set of stamps.
c What's the exchange rate between sterling and RMB today?
d I want to change £150 for RMB.
e My extension is 2115.

16

zuò kè

being a guest

In this unit you will learn
- how to make a toast
- how to make appropriate remarks and responses during a meal

Revise before you start

- when ... (10)
- cái (7)
- measure words (4)(7)
- polite talk (4)(8)
- tài ... le (7)
- use of háishi (6)
- verb endings (10)
- duō + verb (10)
- use of de after verb (8)
- yǐjīng (*already*) + le (10)
- not any more (10)
- gěi (*for*) (6)
- verb + guo (9)

No doubt you have eaten Chinese meals. But where? At a Chinese home or in a Chinese restaurant? Or both? Have you noticed some of the differences in the way Westerners and Chinese eat their meals? Now read the following passage which sums up some of the differences in simple Chinese.

Chī Zhōngguó fàn *Eating Chinese food*

Zhōngguó-rén chángcháng wèi kèrén zuò hěn duō cài. Tāmen xīwàng kèrén duō hē jiǔ, duō chī cài.

Zhōngguó-rén hé Xīfāng-rén chī fàn de xíguàn bù yíyàng. Zhōngguó-rén chī fàn yòng wǎn hé kuàizi; Xīfāng-rén chī fàn yòng pánzi hé dāochā. Dàbùfen Zhōngguó-rén yìbān xiān chī fàn, hòu hē tāng. Zài Xīfāng, rénmen yìbān xiān hē tāng, hòu chī fàn. Zhōngguó-rén chángcháng xiān hē jiǔ, chī liáng cài, ránhòu chī rè fàn、rè cài, zuìhòu chī shuǐguǒ. Xīfāng-rén xiān chī tóupán, ránhòu chī zhèngcān, zuìhòu chī tiánshí huò shuǐguǒ.

Zhōngguó-rén zài jiā lǐ chī fàn hé zài fànguǎn chī fàn chàbuduō, dàjiā yìqǐ chī suǒyǒude cài. Xīfāng-rén zài fànguǎn zìjǐ chī zìjǐ de cài. Zài jiā chī fàn de shíhou, bùtóng de cài xiān fàng zài zìjǐ de pán lǐ, ránhòu cái chī.

Key words and phrases

bùtóng de	*different*
chángcháng	*often*
dàbùfen	*majority*
dàjiā	*everyone*
dāochā (i.e. dāozi, chāzi)	*knife* (and) *fork*
hòu	*later*
huò(zhě)	*or* (used in statements)
jiǔ	*alcohol*

liáng	*cold, cool*
rénmen	*people* (in general)
shuǐguǒ	*fruit*
suǒyǒude	*all*
tiánshí	*dessert*
tóupán	*starter*
wèi	*for* (formal)
Xīfāng	*West*
xíguàn	*habit, customs*
xīwàng	*to hope; hope*
zhèngcān	*main course*
zìjǐ chī zìjǐ de	*to eat one's own*
zuìhòu	*last*

We mentioned the enormous difference between spoken and written Chinese in Unit 14, p. 155 and there are further examples of this in the passage above. **Wèi** is used instead of **gěi** in the first sentence, **hòu** is used instead of **ránhòu** in the fourth sentence (p. 175) and **huò** is used instead of **huòzhě** in the seventh sentence (p. 175). Using one-syllable words instead of two, or using a more 'ancient' word (**wèi** instead of **gěi**) gives a more formal feel to the language.

Note that **dōu** (*all*) can only be used in front of a verb. So, for example, when you want to say *all people* you have to use another word for *all* which is **suǒyǒude**:

Tā xǐhuan **suǒyǒude** rén.	*She likes everybody* (*lit.* all people).
Dàjiā yìqǐ chī **suǒyǒude** cài.	*Everybody shares all the dishes* (*lit.* big family together eat all dish).

Exercise 1 Choose the most appropriate words from the ones given in brackets to fill the blanks in the sentences below. You will be able to use all the words given in **a** and **b** but you will have to make a choice in **c**, **d** and **e**.

a Zhōngguó-rén yìbān xiān _____, ránhòu _____, zuìhòu _____.
(hē tāng, chī rè fàn、rè cài, hē jiǔ)

b Xīfāng-rén yìbān xiān _____, ránhòu _____, zuìhòu _____.
(chī shuǐguǒ, hē tāng, chī zhèngcān)

c Zhōngguó-rén chī fàn yòng ___ hé ___.
(dāozi, kuàizi, chāzi, pánzi, wǎn)

d Xīfāng-rén chī fàn yòng ___ gēn ___.
  (dāochā, kuàizi, pánzi, wǎn)

e ___ zài fànguǎnr chī fàn hé zài jiā lǐ chī fàn xíguàn yíyàng.
  (Zhōngguó-rén; Xīfāng-rén)

Key words and phrases

ài	to love, to like very much; love
báijiǔ	strong alcohol
chá	tea
chī-bu-xià le	to be unable to eat any more
chúfáng	kitchen
Gān bēi!	Cheers!
gān yì bēi	to have a drink
hǎochī (de)	delicious (food), tasty
hé	box
hē-bu-liǎo	to be unable to drink
hē-bu-xià le	to be unable to drink any more
huānyíng	to welcome; welcome
huí qù	to go back
jiācháng biànfàn	simple home meal
kètīng	sitting room
kètīng lǐ zuò ba	come and sit in the sitting room
màn zǒu	take care (as in goodbye; lit. *walk slowly*)
píjiǔ	beer
qiǎokèlì	chocolates
shìqing	matter, thing
shūshu	uncle (on father's side or someone of his generation)
tián (de)	sweet
wàiguó	foreign country
wàiguó-rén	foreigner
xiàndàihuà (de)	modern
xiāng	fragrant
zuò kè	to be a guest
zuǒshǒu	left hand
gōngzuò shùnlì	lit. *work smooth*
Lùshàng xiǎoxīn.	Have a safe journey (lit. *on the road (be) careful*)
quánjiā xìngfú	lit. *whole family happy*
shēnghuó yúkuài	lit. *life pleasant*
wànshì rúyì	lit. *ten thousand things as you wish*

Gěi nǐ(men) tiān máfan le.	*Sorry to have troubled you.*
Nà jiù bù liú nǐ le.	*I won't keep you then.*
Nǐ tài kèqi le.	*You are being too polite.*
Wèi . . . gān bēi!	*To . . . (used as a toast).*
Wǒ chī/hē-bu-xià le.	*I can't eat / drink any more.*
Wǒ gāi huí qù le.	*I must be off now.*
Wǒ sòngsong nǐ.	*I'll see you out.*
Wǒ zìjǐ lái.	*I'll help myself.*

Dialogues

Dialogue 1

Mr White, who is called Lǎo Bái by his Chinese friends, is invited to dinner at the Yuáns' home. Read the dialogue and note how Mr White presents his gifts to the family.

Mr Yuán	Lǎo Bái, huānyíng, huānyíng.
Lǎo Bái	Lǎo Yuán, nǐ hǎo. Wǒ zhīdao nǐ ài hē jiǔ. Zhè shì gěi nǐde jiǔ.
Mr Yuán	Fǎguó pútáojiǔ! Nǐ tài kèqi le.
Lǎo Bái	Zhèi hé qiǎokèlì shì gěi nǐmen nǚ'ér de.
Mr Yuán	Zhēn Zhēn, kuài xièxie Bái shūshu.
Zhēn Zhēn	Xièxie Bái shūshu.
Lǎo Bái	Bú yòng xiè. . . . Zhēn xiāng a! Yuán tàitai, zuò shénme hǎochī de ne?
Mrs Yuán	Méi shénme hǎochī de. Dōu shì jiācháng biànfàn.
Lǎo Bái	Nǐmen de chúfáng tǐng xiàndàihuà de.
Mrs Yuán	Kěxī tài xiǎo le.
Mr Yuán	Lǎo Bái, kètīng lǐ zuò ba.
Lǎo Bái	Hǎo, hǎo. Nǐmen de kètīng zhēn piàoliang.
Mr Yuán	Nǎli, nǎli. Lǎo Bái, nǐ xiǎng hē diǎnr shénme?
Lǎo Bái	Hē diǎnr chá ba.

Note the various examples of **kèqi huà** (*polite talk*), which was referred to in Unit 8, p. 90, in the dialogue above and in **Dialogues 2** and **3**.

i It is quite usual to take off your shoes when going into other people's houses or flats and your host will usually provide some **tuōxié** (slip-ons, *lit.* drag shoes) for you.

Exercise 2 The two patterns overleaf are often used when giving something to somebody. You will need a *measure word* (MW) in pattern ii:

i Zhè shì gěi nǐ de X.   *This is an X for you.*
ii Zhè MW X shì gěi nǐ de.   *This MW X is for you.*

You have brought with you the following things as presents when invited to dinner with a Chinese family. How would you present them? Try to use both **i** and **ii** patterns.

Example: Zhè shì gěi nǐ de huà.
            Zhè fú huà shì gěi nǐ de.

(hé)   (hé)   (běn)

(píng)   (zhāng)   (fú)

Exercise 3 Now use the presents and the patterns in **Exercise 2**, but this time you've bought them for different people.

Example: my father, painting
            Zhè shì gěi wǒ bàba de huà.
            Zhè fú huà shì gěi wǒ bàba de.

a my elder sister, chocolates
b his wife, a tin of green tea
c her uncle, a book
d her boyfriend, a bottle of wine
e their company (**gōngsī**), a painting
f your (pl) friends, two film tickets

四海为家

Chinese proverb: **Sì hǎi wéi jiā**
(*lit*. Four seas like home)

▶ Dialogue 2

The following dialogue is between Mr White and his Chinese hosts, Mr and Mrs Yuán, during a meal. Listen out for the **kèqi huà**.

Mr Yuán	Lǎo Bái, zánmen xiān hē yì bēi.
Lǎo Bái	Hǎo a.
Mr Yuán	Nǐ hē píjiǔ、pútáojiǔ háishi lái diǎnr báijiǔ.
Lǎo Bái	Báijiǔ wǒ hē-bu-liǎo. Hē diǎnr pútáojiǔ ba.
Mr Yuán	Bái de háishi hóng de?
Lǎo Bái	Hóng de ba.
Mr Yuán	Zhèi zhǒng jiǔ bù tián. Wǒ zhīdao wàiguó-rén yìbān bù xǐhuān hē tián de jiǔ.
Lǎo Bái	Shì, wǒ bù xǐhuan hē tián de jiǔ.
Mr Yuán	Zánmen xiān gān yì bēi. Zhù nǐ gōngzuò shùnlì, shēnghuó yúkuài!
Lǎo Bái	Zhù nǐmen quánjiā xìngfú, wànshì rúyì!
Mr Yuán	Gān bēi!
Lǎo Bái	Gān bēi!
Mrs Yuán	Bié kèqi, duō chī diǎnr.
Lǎo Bái	Hǎo, hǎo, wǒ zìjǐ lái.
Lǎo Bái	Cài dōu fēicháng hǎochī.
Mr Yuán	Zài duō chī diǎnr.
Lǎo Bái	Wǒ yǐjīng chī-bǎo le.
Mrs Yuán	Nǐ chī-de tài shǎo le.
Lǎo Bái	Wǒ zhēnde chī-bu-xià le.
Mr Yuán	Nǐ tài kèqi le.
Lǎo Bái	Wǒ méi kèqi.

(More examples of useful four-character phrases can be found in Unit 14, pp. 160–1).

Zhù nǐ(men) {	gōngzuò shùnlì!	*May your work go smoothly!*
	shēnghuó yúkuài!	*May your life be happy!*
	quánjiā xìngfú!	*May your whole family be blessed!*

i **Gān bēi** (*Drain your glass*) does not have to be taken literally, particularly in the case of 70 per cent proof **máotái** which is often used for toasts at banquets!

▶ **Exercise 4** The following are some useful expressions which might come in handy when you are having dinner with a Chinese family. Do you know how to say them in Chinese?

a Cheers!
b I really can't eat any more.
c It smells nice.
d I'll help myself.
e Wishing you every happiness.

▶ Dialogue 3

Read the dialogue and note carefully the exchanges between the guest and his hosts.

Lǎo Bái	Wǒ kěyǐ yòng yíxià nǐmende cèsuǒ ma?
Mr Yuán	Zuǒshǒu dì-èr jiān jiù shì.
Lǎo Bái	Oh, yǐjīng jiǔ diǎn duō le. Wǒ gāi huí qù le.
Mr Yuán	Hái zǎo ne. Zài zuò yìhuǐr ba.
Lǎo Bái	Bú zuò le. Míngtiān zǎoshang wǒ hái yǒu shìqing.
Mr Yuán	Hǎo ba. Nà jiù bù liú nǐ le.
Lǎo Bái	Gěi nǐmen tiān máfan le.
Mr Yuán	Méi shénme. Huānyíng nǐ zài lái.
Lǎo Bái	Yídìng, yídìng.
Mr Yuán	Wǒ sòngsong nǐ.
Lǎo Bái	Bú yòng le. Qǐng huí qù ba.
Mr Yuán	Màn zǒu.
Mrs Yuán	Lùshàng xiǎoxīn.
Lǎo Bái	Méi wèntí. Zàijiàn!
Mr & Mrs Yuán	Zàijiàn!

Exercise 5 What do you say?

a What do you say when you think it's time to leave?
b How might your host respond if he/she doesn't want you to leave yet?
c How do you thank your host for all the trouble s/he has taken?
d What's your host's response to c?
e What do you say when your host suggests seeing you off?
f How do you tell somebody to take care driving or cycling?
g What's the common parting remark made by the host to his/her guest?

▶ Dialogue 4

The following is a dialogue between a Chinese managing director, his wife and his foreign counterpart of a joint venture. They are at a banquet. Listen to the recording, and try to answer the following questions before you read the dialogue. Or read the dialogue and then answer the questions. This time the new words and expressions come after the dialogue, and we've given you the English translation of the questions.

Questions

a Bái xiānsheng kuàizi yòng-de zěnmeyàng?
Does Mr White use chopsticks very well?

b Tā shuō tā fàn zuò-de hǎo bu hǎo?
How well does he say he cooks?

c Tā chángcháng qù nǎr chī Zhōngguó fàn?
Where does he often go for Chinese meals?

d Duìhuà (*dialogue*) lǐ shuō Bái xiānsheng chī-guo/hē-guo shénme?
  i yànwō tāng
  ii Máotáijiǔ
  iii fèngzhǎo

According to the dialogue which of the following has Mr White ever eaten/drunk?
  i *birds' nest soup*
  ii *Máotái*
  iii *chicken feet*

Dǒngshìzhǎng	Bái xiānsheng, nín kuàizi yòng-de zhēn hǎo.
Mr White	Wǒ chángcháng chī Zhōngguó fàn.
Fūren	Nín zìjǐ zuò fàn ma?
Mr White	Wǒ zuò-de bù hǎo. Wǒ cháng qù Zhōngguóchéng de fànguǎnr chī fàn.
Dǒngshìzhǎng	Lái, xiān hē yì bēi. Zhè shì Máotáijiǔ. Nín hē-guo ma?
Mr White	Hē-guo liǎng cì.
Dǒngshìzhǎng	Wèi wǒmen liǎng ge gōngsī de chénggōng hézuò gān bēi!
Mr White	Wèi Dǒngshìzhǎng hé Dǒngshìzhǎng fūren de jiànkāng gān bēi!
Fūren	Zhè shì yànwō tāng, fēicháng yǒu yíngyǎng.
Mr White	Wǒ tīngshuō-guo, kěshì méi hē-guo.
Dǒngshìzhǎng	Zhè shì fèngzhǎo, bù zhīdao nín chī-guo ma?
Mr White	Kàn-jiàn-guo, hái méi chī-guo.
Fūren	Zhènghǎo, qǐng chángchang ba.
Fūren	Duō chī diǎnr cài.
Dǒngshìzhǎng	Zài hē yì bēi.
Mr White	Wǒ chī-bu-xià le, yě hē-bu-xià le.
Dǒngshìzhǎng	Zài hē zuìhòu yì bēi. Wèi Zhōng-Yīng liǎng guó rénmín de yǒuyì gān bēi!
Mr White	Gān bēi! Xīwàng nǐmen yǒu jīhuì qù Yīngguó fǎngwèn.

Key words and phrases

cháng (chang)	to taste
chángcháng	often
chénggōng	successful
dǒngshìzhǎng	managing director
fǎngwèn	visit (formal)
fèngzhǎo	chicken feet
fūren	wife (formal), madam
gōngsī	company
hézuò	co-operation, co-operate
jiànkāng	health, healthy
jīhuì	opportunity
kàn-jiàn	to see
Máotái(jiǔ)	Maotai (a very strong Chinese spirit)
yànwō	birds' nest
yǒu yíngyǎng	nutritious
Zhōngguóchéng	Chinatown
Zhōng-Yīng liǎng guó rénmín de yǒuyì	The friendship between the Chinese and British peoples
liǎng guó	two countries
rénmín	the people (of a country)
yǒuyì	friendship
zuò (fàn)	to cook

Exercise 6 Look at the Chinese words in the left-hand column and pair each of them with one in the right-hand column.

a	fǎngwèn	i	co-operate, co-operation
b	hézuò	ii	managing director
c	jīhuì	iii	to visit, visit (*formal*)
d	dǒngshìzhǎng	iv	success, successful
e	gōngsī	v	opportunity
f	chénggōng	vi	company

Exercise 7 The words in **Exercise 6** are some of the words you might need in formal business encounters.

Now cover up the Chinese and just look at the English. Can you remember how to say them in Chinese?

You met **zhè/zhèi** (*this*) and **nà/nèi** (*that*) in Unit 2 and **nǎ/něi** (*which?*) in Unit 7. They are normally followed by a measure word (see Unit 7). By putting the collective measure word **xiē** after **zhè/zhèi**, **nà/nèi** and **nǎ/něi** you have **zhèxiē/zhèixiē** (*these*), **nàxiē/nèixiē** (*those*) and **nǎxiē/něixiē** (*which?* plural):

zhèxiē (shū)	*these (books)*
nàxiē (cài)	*those (dishes)*
nǎxiē (jīhuì)	*which (opportunities)?*

Polite forms of address

The formal way of addressing a married woman in Chinese is **fūren** and not **tàitai**. Chinese speakers often translate **fūren** as *madam*:

Chén **fūren**   *Madam Chen*

When writing in English, a Chinese speaker may well address his or her letter to Madam Jones which seems rather strange to most English speakers. **Fūren** can also be put after titles which carry a certain status such as manager or headmaster and can refer to female postholders' or to male postholders' *wives*:

Dǒngshìzhǎng **fūren**   *Madam Manager* (used in Mr White's toast)

Xiàozhǎng **fūren**   *Madam Headmaster*

▶ Quick review

When you hear these toasts, do you know what they mean?

a Zhù nǐ shēntǐ jiànkāng!
b Zhù nǐ shēnghuó yúkuài!
c Zhù nǐ wànshì rúyì!
d Zhù nǐ gōngzuò shùnlì!
e Zhù nǐ chénggōng!
f Wèi wǒmen de yǒuyì gān bēi!
g Wèi wǒmen de hézuò gān bēi!

17

kàn yīshēng
seeing a doctor

In this unit you will learn
- how to describe symptoms to the doctor or the pharmacist
- to understand the instructions on the medicine bottle
- about acupuncture, Chinese herbal medicine, tàijíquán and qìgōng

Revise before you start

- measure words   (4)(7)
- both ... and ...   (9)
- yǒu yìdiǎnr (*a bit*)   (8)
- sentences ending in le   (4)
- verb + le   (9)
- shì bu shi   (3)
- use of háishi   (6)

- verb + **guo**   (9)
- use of **ba**   (3)
- on + noun   (5)
- when ...   (10)
- bié (*don't*)   (10)
- gěi (*for*)   (6)

Zhōngguó de *Yīliáo*   Medical care in China

The Chinese medical system is not the same as in Britain. The following passage tells us a little about some of the differences. (Words in *italics* are explained in the box below.)

Zài Zhōngguó, hěn duō *dānwèi* yǒu zìjǐ de *yīwùsuǒ*. Xiǎo de yīwùsuǒ zhǐ yǒu yí gè *yīshēng*, dà de kěyǐ yǒu *jǐ* ge yīshēng hé *hùshi*. Rúguǒ nǐ yǒu *bìng*, nǐ kěyǐ qù dānwèi de yīwùsuǒ, yě kěyǐ *zhíjiē* qù *yīyuàn*.

Zhōngguó de yīyuàn yìbān *fēnchéng* bùtóng de *kē*. Yǒude yīyuàn shì *zhuānkē* yīyuàn, zhǐ *kàn* yì、liǎng *zhǒng bìng*. Dà de yīyuàn yìbān yòu yǒu *Zhōngyī*, yòu yǒu *Xīyī*. Nǐ kěyǐ kàn Zhōngyī, yě kěyǐ kàn Xīyī.

bìng	*illness*
bìngrén	*patient*
dānwèi	*work unit*
fēnchéng	*to divide / to be divided into*
hùshi	*nurse*
jǐ	*several, a few*
kàn bìng	*to see a doctor* (to have the illness looked at)
kē	*department* (in a hospital)
Xīyī	*Western medical (doctor); Western medicine*
yīliáo	*medical care*
yīshēng	*doctor*
yīwùsuǒ	*clinic* (attached to a work unit)
yīyuàn	*hospital*
zhíjiē	*direct(ly)*
zhǒng	*kind, sort (measure word)*
Zhōngyī	*Chinese medical (doctor); Chinese medicine*
zhuānkē	*specialized; speciality ...*

Exercise 1 According to the above passage, are the following statements **duì** or **bú duì**?

	duì	**bú duì**
a Yǒude dānwèi méi yǒu yīwùsuǒ.	☐	☐
b Zài dà de yīyuàn, Zhōngyī、Xīyī dōu yǒu.	☐	☐
c Yǒude yīwùsuǒ méi yǒu hùshi.	☐	☐
d Bìngrén bù kěyǐ zhíjiē qù yīyuàn.	☐	☐

Key words and phrases

bú (yòng) xiè	*not at all*
cānjiā	*to attend*
chī (yào)	*to take* (medicine)
dùzi	*stomach, tummy*
lā dùzi	*to have diarrhoea*
fàn hòu	*after meals*
fàn qián	*before meals*
fúyòng fāngfǎ	*instructions* (for taking medicine)
gǎnmào	*to have a cold*
Hànzì	*Chinese characters*
kāfēi	*coffee*
kāishuǐ	*boiled water*
késou	*cough*
kǔ	*bitter*
lì	*pill; MW for pill-sized pieces, e.g. grain*
ná	*to take, fetch*
nèixiē	*those*
piàn(r)	*tablet; MW for small slices, e.g. snowflakes*
píngzi	*bottle*
téng	*painful; pain, ache*
tóuténg	*headache*
wán(r)	*(Chinese medicine) ball*
wēn	*warm*
Xīyào	*Western medicine*
yànhuì	*banquet*
yào	*medicine*
yàofāng	*prescription*
yàofáng	*pharmacy*
yìxiē	*some*
yǒu shíhou	*sometimes*
yǒu xiào	*effective*
zhā	*to pierce, to put in a needle, to do acupuncture*

zhēnjiǔ	acupuncture
zhěnsuǒ	clinic (open to the general public)
zhèyàng/zhèiyàng	like this, in this way
Zhōngyào	Chinese medicine
Wǒ bù shūfu.	I don't feel well.
Wǒ . . . téng.	My . . . hurts.
Wǒde tiān a!	Good heavens! (lit. my heaven)

Dialogues

▶ Dialogue 1

Mr White is not feeling at all well. He decides to go to the company's clinic. Listen to the dialogue and try to find out what's wrong with him. What does he think has caused the problem, and what does the doctor think the cause is? What medicine does the doctor prescribe?

Yīshēng	Nǐ nǎr bù shūfu?
Bái	Wǒ dùzi bù shūfu.
Yīshēng	Lā dùzi ma?
Bái	Yǒu yìdiǎnr.
Yīshēng	Nǐ zuótiān chī shénme le?
Bái	Wǒ cānjiā le yí ge yànhuì, chī le fèngzhǎo, hē le yànwō tāng.
Yīshēng	Nèixiē dōu shì hǎo dōngxi, duì nǐ shēntǐ hǎo.
Bái	Wǒ kěnéng chī-de tài duō le.
Yīshēng	Nǐ hē le hěn duō jiǔ, shì bu shi?
Bái	Bù duō, zhǐ hē le bā bēi.
Yīshēng	Wǒ míngbai le. Wǒ gěi nǐ yìxiē yào. Nǐ yuànyì shìshi Zhōngyào ma?
Bái	Wǒ méi chī-guo Zhōngyào. Tīngshuō Zhōngyào hěn kǔ, shì ma?
Yīshēng	Yǒude kǔ, yǒude bù kǔ. Wǒ gěi nǐ de yào bù kǔ.
Bái	Nà wǒ shìshi ba.
Yīshēng	Zhè shì yàofāng. Qǐng dào yàofáng qù ná yào.
Bái	Yīshēng, xièxie nín.
Yīshēng	Bú yòng xiè.

首都医院
Shǒudū yīyuàn
Capital hospital

急诊室
Jízhěnshì
Emergency room

▶ **Exercise 2** You have a cold, which is a common illness in China as well, and you're seeing a Chinese doctor. Complete the following dialogue.

	Yīshēng	Nǐ zěnme le?
a	**You**	(*Tell her that you have a headache.*)
	Yīshēng	Hái yǒu nǎr bù shūfu?
b	**You**	(*Say you cough a bit.*)
	Yīshēng	Wǒ xiǎng nǐ yǒu yìdiǎnr gǎnmào.
c	**You**	(*Say you also feel it's a cold.*)
	Yīshēng	Wǒ gěi nǐ diǎnr yào. Nǐ chī Zhōngyào ma?
d	**You**	(*Say you've never taken it before and ask the doctor if Chinese medicine is effective.*)
	Yīshēng	Yídìng yǒu xiào.
e	**You**	(*Say it's OK and you will give it a try.*)

▶ Dialogue 2

Mr White is at the pharmacy.

药房

Yàofáng   *Pharmacy*

Pharmacist	Zhè shì nínde yào.
Mr White	Zěnme chī ya?
Pharmacist	Píngzi shàng yǒu fúyòng fāngfǎ.
Mr White	Duìbuqǐ, wǒ hái bú rènshi Hànzì.
Pharmacist	O. Duìbuqǐ. Wǒ gàosu nǐ. Yì tiān chī sān cì, yí cì chī èrshí lì.
Mr White	Shénme? Yì tiān chī liùshí lì?!
Pharmacist	Duì.
Mr White	Wǒde tiān a!
Pharmacist	Chī yào de shíhou bú yào hē kāfēi、chá hé jiǔ. Yīnggāi hē wēn kāishuǐ.
Mr White	Wèishénme?
Pharmacist	Chī yào dōu yīnggāi zhèyàng.
Mr White	Wǒde yào fàn qián chī háishì fàn hòu chī?
Pharmacist	Dōu kéyǐ.
Mr White	Xièxie nín.
Pharmacist	Bú xiè.

You have seen that '**time when**' expressions such as *Tuesday, 9 o'clock*, come before the verb (Unit 1, p. 8) and that '**time during which**' expressions such as how long you do something for, come after the verb (Unit 9, p. 102).

Time *within* which something happens comes *before* the verb:

Wǒ yì tiān chī liǎng cì.	*I eat twice (in) a day.*
Yì tiān yào chī liùshí lì.	*(You) have to take (lit. eat) 60 pills (in) a day.*

Fàn qián is a more formal way of saying **chī fàn yǐqián** (*before a meal – lit.* eat cooked rice before) and **fàn hòu** of saying **chī fàn yǐhòu** (*after a meal – lit.* eat cooked rice after). Note that **(yǐ)qián** and **(yǐ)hòu** go after the noun in Chinese, the reverse of the English word order.

Instructions for taking Chinese medicine are given in the reverse of the way they are usually given in English-speaking countries. The normal word order in Chinese is:

fàn qián/hòu	*meal before/after*
yì tiān	*per day*
jǐ cì	*how many times*
yí cì chī X lì/piàn/wán(r)	*every time eat X pills/tablets/balls*

Chinese medicine sometimes comes in the form of small balls which you have to chew. This is not all unpleasant (they are often flavoured with liquorice), but this form of medicine is not so commonly found in Chinese herbal medicine shops in the West catering for Westerners. The Chinese seem to believe that Westerners prefer to take pills!

Exercise 3 Read the instructions about taking the following medicines. Indicate whether each medicine is to be taken before or after meals and fill in the gaps (two per line).

a	before/after meal; ____ times a day; take ____ every time
b	before/after meal; ____ times a day; take ____ every time
c	before/after meal; ____ times a day; take ____ every time
d	before/after meal; ____ times a day; take ____ every time

1 Zhèi zhǒng Zhōngyào fàn qián chī, yì tiān liǎng cì, yí cì yì wánr.
2 Zhèi ge yào fàn hòu chī, yì tiān chī sì cì, yí cì chī sān piànr.
3 Nèi ge yào bú yào fàn qián chī. Fàn hòu yí ge xiǎoshí zài chī. Yì tiān chī sān cì, yí cì hē yì sháo (*tablespoon*).
4 Zhè ge yào zǎoshang chī yí cì, wǎnshang chī yí cì. Yí cì chī liǎng, sān piàn.

服用方法

Fúyòng fāngfǎ
Instructions for taking (the) medicine

▶ Dialogue 3

The following dialogue is between a Westerner visiting a Chinese clinic and a Chinese doctor working at the clinic. Before reading the dialogue, listen to the recording and try **Exercise 4** first. You can then check your answers when you read it.

Visitor   Nǐmen zhěnsuǒ bìngrén duō ma?
Doctor   Bù shǎo.
Visitor   Nǐmen dōu kàn shénme bìng?
Doctor   Gèzhǒng gèyàng de bìng. Nǐ kàn, zhèi ge bìngrén chángcháng tóu téng. Tā kàn-guo Xīyī, chī-guo Xīyào, kěshì hái bù hǎo. Wǒmen gěi tā zhā le zhēnjiǔ, xiànzài tā hǎo duōle.
Visitor   Zhēnde? Wǒ yě yǒu shíhou tóu téng. Tā zhā le jǐ cì le?
Doctor   Sì cì le.
Visitor   Zhēnjiǔ shì bu shì hěn téng?
Doctor   Zhēnjiǔ shì bù shūfu, kěshì chángcháng hěn yǒu xiào.
Visitor   Zhēnde ma?
Doctor   Nǐ yǒu shénme bìng? Wǒ kěyǐ gěi nǐ zhā.
Visitor   Bú yòng、bú yòng, wǒ méi bìng. Wǒde shēntǐ hěn hǎo. Xièxie nín.

Exercise 4   Select the correct answer to complete the statements which are based on **Dialogue 3**.

a   There are ____ patients visiting the clinic.   (*a lot*, *quite a few*, *few*)
b   The clinic treats ____ illnesses.   (*all sorts of*, *some*, *one or two kinds of*)
c   The patient being treated in the clinic often has ____.   (*diarrhoea*, *headaches*, *stomach ache*)
d   The visitor declined the offer of acupuncture because he ____.   (*was scared*, *had no illness*, *did not have the time*)

仰卧位
Supine posture

仰靠坐位
Sitting with supine posture

俯卧位
Prone posture

俯伏坐位
Sitting with curved posture

When two 'le's occur in the same sentence, as in the visitor's 3rd line in **Dialogue 3,** one after the verb and one at the end of the sentence, they convey the idea that the action of the verb is still going on:

(Nǐ gěi) tā zhā **le** jǐ cì (zhēnjiǔ) **le**?

How many times have you given her acupuncture (so far)?

Tā zài Lúndūn zhù **le** sān nián **le**.

He's been living in London for three years (and still is).

By putting **shì** in front of a verb or adjective you emphasize it:

Zhēnjiǔ **shì** bu shūfu.

Acupuncture is uncomfortable.

Xiě Hànzì **shì** hěn nán.

Writing Chinese characters is difficult.

i To the Chinese way of thinking, each individual (and on a much larger scale the universe) is made up of **yīn** (*the female or passive/negative principle*) and **yáng** (*the male or active/positive principle*). To enjoy good health your **yīn** and **yáng** must be in balance. Chinese medicine seeks to redress any imbalance that exists.

Exercise 5 When a part of your body aches, you say **Wǒ(de) ____ téng.**

If you feel uncomfortable somewhere, you may say **Wǒ(de) ____ bù shūfu.**

If you don't know the Chinese word for the part of body you want to refer to, you can simply point at the place and say **Wǒ zhèr** (*here*) **téng**, or **Wǒ zhèr bù shūfu.**

Now practise these two patterns using the different parts of the body in turn (the Chinese for them is given in the drawing). You are answering the doctor's question **Nǐ nǎr bù shūfu?** So for the back you would say:

Wǒ yāo téng, *or*
Wǒ yāo bù shūfu.

i Acupuncture is an ancient Chinese method of treating disease. It is based on the theory that the human body has a whole series of meridians up and down it through which your **qì** (sometimes written **ch'i** in the West) (*vital energy*) flows.

Having made his/her diagnosis, the acupuncturist inserts fine needles at various points (which all have different names) in your meridians to clear any blockages to your **qì**.

Some conditions seem to respond particularly well to acupuncture – rheumatoid-arthritis, gynaecological problems and the after-effects of strokes to mention just a few.

Why not be brave and try acupuncture treatment yourself if you suffer from a long-standing condition that has not improved with conventional methods? But be sure to go to a reputable acupuncturist who is accredited or better still ask your GP or enquire at your local health shop to see if they can recommend someone.

Exercise 6 Find the Chinese equivalents in Section B to match the English sentences in Section A. Then put the Chinese sentences in the same order as the English sentences and you'll see a short passage about **qìgōng** in Chinese.

Section A:
a There are all kinds of qigong.
b Many people believe that qigong can cure all sorts of illness
c Qigong is very popular nowadays in China.   4)
d It's good for your health to do qigong very often.
e Both Tai Chi and qigong are slow forms of exercise.
f Some forms (of qigong) are not difficult (to practise); son.
   are not easy.

Section B:
  i Xiànzài zài Zhōngguó, zuò qìgōng hěn liúxíng.
 ii Yǒude qìgōng bù nán, yǒude hěn bù róngyì.
iii Chángcháng zuò qìgōng duì shēntǐ hǎo.
 iv Qìgōng yǒu gèzhǒng gèyàng de.
  v Hěn duō rén rènwéi qìgōng kěyǐ zhì gèzhǒng gèyàng de bìng.
 vi Qìgōng gēn tàijíquǎn dōu shì hěn màn de yùndòng.

▶ Quick review

a You see your Chinese friend looking unwell. Ask what's wrong with her (*lit.* where she is not comfortable).
b Say you want to try acupuncture.
c Say you think you have a cold.
d Tell the doctor that you have never taken Chinese medicine.
e Tell the doctor that you sometimes have a headache.

jiāotōng	transport, traffic
lìng yí gè	another; another one
lù shàng	on the road
Ōuzhōu (dàlù)	(continental) Europe
shìjiè (shàng)	(in the) world
yàoshi	if
yīnwei/yīnwéi	because
yòu	right
yòubiān	right side
zǒu lù de yòubiān	to drive / cycle on the right
zìxíngchē dào	bicycle lane
zǒngshì	always
zū	to hire, rent
zuǒ	left (opposite of right)

Exercise 1 How do you say the following in Chinese about traffic in the West?

At first sight the sentences may seem to be difficult. But if you model them on the sentences in the passage above you should find them quite manageable.

a In Britain driving and cycling are on the left-hand side of the road.
b This is the same as in Japan and Ireland but not the same as on the Continent.
c America is the country that has the most cars in the world.
d In the West it's not difficult to hire a car.

Key words and phrases

bāo	bag
qiánbāo	purse / wallet
biérén	other / another person
chēdài	tyre
bǔ chēdài	to mend a tyre
chéng lǐ	in the city, in urban areas
cuò	fault, mistake
dàshǐguǎn	embassy
dēng	lights
diū	to lose
duō yuǎn?	how far?

Hái yǒu duō yuǎn?	How far is it still to . . . ?
gāoxìng	happy
guǎi	to turn
hǎoxiàng	to seem
hòulái	later
huài	broken, not working; bad
jǐngchá	police officer
jǐn(yì)jǐn	to tighten
lǐ	inside
liàng	(measure word for vehicles including bicycles)
líng	(for brakes) to work well
mǎshàng	at once
shāndìchē	mountain bike
shéide?	whose?
shēnfènzhèng	identity card
shīfu	title used when addressing a skilled worker (lit. master)
shǒu	hand
shuāi le yì jiāo	to have had a fall
tōngzhī	to inform
xiāoxi	news, information
yī . . . jiù	no sooner . . . than . . . , as soon as
yòng-bu-zháo	not necessary
zěnme huí shì?	what's the matter?
zhá	brakes
zhàoxiàngjī	camera
zhuàng	to collide
zhuàng-huài (le)	damage(d) (lit. collide broken)
Zhēn dǎoméi!	How unfortunate! Bad luck!

Placewords such as **lǐ** (*inside*) as in **chéng lǐ** can also have a longer form, so you will sometimes see **lǐmiàn(r)** (*lit.* in surface) or **lǐbiān(r)** (*lit.* in side) instead of just **lǐ**. There is no difference in meaning, however. This also applies to words like **shàng** (*on* or *on top of*), **xià** (*underneath*) and **wài** (*outside*).

Note that **shìjiè shàng** does not mean *on top of the world* but *in the world*. **Lǐ** is only used when you can actually get inside something, such as a shop, or when referring to money *in* a purse.

Dialogues

▶ Dialogue 1

When visiting a Chinese city, it is worth hiring a bicycle to explore the local area. It's economical too! This is what Ann and her friend are trying to do when they visit Nanjing. Listen to, or read, the dialogue and find out what kind of bicycle is available and how much they cost.

Ann	Wǒ xiǎng zū liǎng liàng zìxíngchē.
Shopkeeper	Yǒu shēnfènzhèng ma?
Ann	Yǒu. Zhè shì wǒde hùzhào.
Shopkeeper	Hǎo. Nín zū něi zhǒng chē?
Ann	Wǒ yào yí liàng xiǎo de. Wǒde péngyou yào yí liàng dà de.
Shopkeeper	Nǐmen zū jǐ tiān?
Ann	Yì tiān.
Shopkeeper	Nèi liǎng liàng shāndìchē búcuò. Nǐmen shìshi ba.

Ann and her friend try the bikes.

Ann	Zhèi liàng chē de zhá hǎoxiàng bú tài líng.
Shopkeeper	Shì ma? Wǒ gěi nǐ jǐnyijǐn.
Ann	Zhèi xiē chē zěnme dōu méi yǒu dēng?
Shopkeeper	Zài chéng lǐ yòng-bu-zháo dēng.
Ann	Hǎo ba. Wǒ zū zhèi liǎng liàng. Duōshǎo qián?
Shopkeeper	Zhèi liàng dà de yì tiān shíbā kuài. Nà liàng xiǎo de yì tiān shíwǔ kuài. Yígòng sānshísān kuài.
Ann	Gěi nín sìshí kuài.
Shopkeeper	Zhǎo nín qī kuài.

ℹ️ Bicycle parking lots (**Cúnchēchù**) abound in Chinese cities. For a very modest charge you can leave your bicycle there. It will be much safer.

Cúnchēchù

▶ **Exercise 2** Now you are visiting Taiwan and you want to hire a car. Complete the dialogue below. **Dialogue 1** should help you.

a	**You**	*(Say you would like to hire a car.)*
	Clerk	Nín yǒu jiàzhào *(driving licence)* ma?
b	**You**	*(Say yes and yours is a British one.)*
	Clerk	Nín yào něi zhǒng chē?
c	**You**	*(Say you'd like to have a small one.)*
	Clerk	Zhèi liàng kěyǐ ma?

d	**You**	(*Say it's fine.*)
	Clerk	Nín zū jǐ tiān?
e	**You**	(*Say two days.*)
	Clerk	Qǐng dào nèibiān fù qián.
f	**You**	(*Ask if they take credit cards.*)
	Clerk	Shōu.

Dialogue 2

Unfortunately Ann has got a flat tyre on her bike. She sees a bike repair man by the side of the road and walks over for help.

Ann	Shīfu, wǒde chēdài huài le, nín néng bāng wǒ xiūxiu ma?
Shīfu	Méi wèntí.
Ann	Děi duō cháng shíjiān?
Shīfu	Yìhuǐr jiù xíng.
Ann	Shīfu, chōu zhī yān ba.
Shīfu	Hǎo, hǎo. Xièxie, xièxie.
Ann	Shīfu, qù Xiāngshān hái yǒu duō yuǎn?
Shīfu	Wǎng běi qí èrshí fēnzhōng, zài wǎng xī guǎi jiù dào le.

* * *

Shīfu	Xiū-hǎo le.
Ann	Zhēn kuài. Xièxie nín. Zhèi liàng chē de zhá bú tài líng, nín néng kànkan ma?
Shīfu	Kěyǐ. Wǒ gěi nín jǐnjin. . . . Xíng le.
Ann	Xièxie nín. Yígòng duōshao qián?
Shīfu	Bǔ chēdài liǎng kuài wǔ. Jǐn zhá jiù bù shōu nǐ qián le.
Ann	Xièxie shīfu. Nín zài chōu zhī yān ba.

雪中送碳

Chinese proverb: **Xuě zhōng sòng tàn**
Send charcoal in snowy weather – provide timely help

Exercise 3 In **Dialogue 2**, you saw several noun phrases consisting of a verb and an object, such as: **bǔ chēdài, jǐn zhá** and **qù Xiāngshān**.

These phrases can be used at the beginning of a sentence as a kind of topic – the opposite of the word order in English. You can see this clearly from the example:

**Kāi chē shàng bān děi
duō cháng shíjiān?**   *How long does it take **to drive
to work?***

Now try the same thing with the sentences below when you put
them into Chinese.

a It takes an hour *to drive to work.*
b How much does it cost *to have the tyre mended?*
c How do I *get to the Fragrant Hills by bus?*
d It costs 30 yuan *to hire a bike.*

▶ Dialogue 3

Ānyīn notices that her friend Ben is looking rather unhappy.
Listen to, or read, the dialogue and find out what happened
to Ben.

Ānyīn	Nǐ hǎoxiàng yǒu diǎnr bù gāoxìng.
Ben	Méi shénme.
Ānyīn	Nǐde shǒu zěnme le?
Ben	O, wǒ shuāi le yì jiāo.
Ānyīn	Zěnme huí shì?
Ben	Zhēn dǎoméi! Wǒ gēn biérén zhuàng chē le.
Ānyīn	Shì shéide cuò?
Ben	Wǒ shuō shì tāde cuò, tā shuō shì wǒde cuò.
Ānyīn	Chē zhuàng-huài le ma?
Ben	Zhuàng-huài le.
Ānyīn	Nǐmen zhǎo jǐngchá le ma?
Ben	Zhǎo le. Jǐngchá shuō wǒmen dōu yǒu cuò.
Ānyīn	Hòulái ne?
Ben	Hòulái, wǒmen dōu qù xiū zìjǐ de chē le.

ⓘ In China you can turn right at a red light (**hóng dēng**) so be very
alert when you see a red traffic light whether you are driving a car
or riding a bicycle. **Hónglǜdēng** means *traffic lights* (*lit.* red green
light).

▶ **Exercise 4** Say whether the following statements are **duì** or **bú duì** (true or false).

	duì	bú duì
a Ānyīn hěn bù gāoxìng.	☐	☐
b Ben gēn biérén zhuàng chē le.	☐	☐
c Nà ge rén shuō shì Ben de cuò.	☐	☐
d Zhuàng chē yǐhòu, Ben zhǎo le jǐngchá.	☐	☐
e Ben de chē zhuàng-huài le.	☐	☐
f Jǐngchá shuō shì Ben de cuò.	☐	☐
g Ben qù xiū Ānyīn de chē le.	☐	☐

▶ **Dialogue 4**

Ben is now at a local police station. He really has had bad luck. Read the dialogue, and find out what his problem is and what he is advised to do.

Jǐngchá	Nín yǒu shénme shì?
Ben	Wǒde bāo diū le.
Jǐngchá	Bāo lǐmiàn yǒu shénme?
Ben	Yǒu wǒde hùzhào hé qiánbāo. Qiánbāo lǐ yǒu wǒde xìnyòng kǎ、sìbǎi duō rénmínbì hé liǎngbǎi měiyuán. O, hái yǒu yí ge xiǎo zhàoxiàngjī.
Jǐngchá	Nín diū le hùzhào, yīnggāi tōngzhī nǐmen guójiā de dàshǐguǎn.
Ben	Wǒ gěi dàshǐguǎn dǎ diànhuà le.
	(The policewoman takes down the details of the incident.)
Jǐngchá	Nín xiànzài zhù zài nǎr?
Ben	Yùlóng Fàndiàn sān-líng-yāo fángjiān.
Jǐngchá	Qǐng nín xiān huí qù. Wǒmen **yī** yǒu xiāoxi **jiù** mǎshàng tōngzhī nín.

Linking words (also known as conjunctions) often come in pairs in Chinese so it is good to memorize them as such. There are two examples in this unit.

yīnwei . . . suǒyǐ . . .	because . . . therefore . . .
. . . yī + verb¹ jiù + verb²	as soon as verb¹ happens, then verb² will happen (**Dialogue 4**)

Exercise 5 Now you have listened to, or read, **Dialogue 4** answer the following questions.

a What was Ben's problem?
b What was in the bag?
c How much money had he taken with him?
d Where was Ben staying?
e What was he advised to do about the loss of the passport?
f What did the police say they would do?

Exercise 6 Make at least one statement about the problems in the following pictures.

Nǐ zuò-cuò chē le.   *You've taken the wrong bus.*

▶ Quick review

You happen to have run into a problem:

a How would you say 'What bad luck!'?
b Say that it's not your fault.
c Say that you think they should go to the police.
d Say that you've lost your credit card.
e Something has gone wrong with your bike (or anything), ask if someone can have a look at it.

19

xuéxí
Zhōngwén
learning Chinese

In this unit you will learn
- the basic vocabulary to describe the characteristics of a language
- how to talk about your future plans
- how to respond to compliments or forthright remarks

Revise before you start

- use of **háishi** (6)
- **gēn . . . yíyàng** (6)
- use of **de** after verbs (8)
- **tài . . . le** (7)
- helping verbs (6)

- be in the middle of doing something (6)
- **gèng** (*even more*) (8)
- verb endings (10)
- **zuì** (*most*) (7)
- **duō** + verb (10)

Zhōngwén háishi Hànyǔ?   *The Chinese for 'Chinese'!*

Which Chinese word describes the language you have been learning in this book? Is it **Hànyǔ**, **Zhōngwén**, **Pǔtōnghuà**, **Guóyǔ** or **Huáyǔ**? Read the passage below and find out.

Zhōngwén yìbān zhǐ Hànyǔ. *Zhōngwén de zhōng* **shì Zhōngguó** de *zhōng*. **Wén shì** *writing* **huòzhě** *language* **de yìsi. Hànyǔ de** **hàn shì Hànzú de hàn. Yǔ shi** *yǔyán* **de** *yǔ*, **yě shì** *language* **de** **yìsi. Hànyǔ jiù shì Hànzú-rén de yǔyán. Zhōngguó de hěn duō** **shǎoshù mínzú dōu yǒu zìjǐ de yǔyán.**

Hànyǔ yǒu hěn duō zhǒng fāngyán. Shànghǎihuà shì yì zhǒng **fāngyán. Shànghǎi-rén shuō Shànghǎihuà. Guǎngdōnghuà yě** **shì yì zhǒng fāngyán. Guǎngdōng-rén hé Xiānggǎng-rén shuō** **Guǎngdōnghuà.**

Wǒmen xuéxí de Zhōngwén shì Pǔtōnghuà. Pǔtōnghuà bú **shì fāngyán, shì guānfāng yǔyán. Táiwān-rén jiào tā Guóyǔ,** **Dōngnányà de Huá-rén jiào tā Huáyǔ. Guóyǔ hé Huáyǔ jiù** **shì Pǔtōnghuà. Pǔtōnghuà bú shì Běijīnghuà. Běijīnghuà hé** **Pǔtōnghuà chàbuduō. Hěn duō Běijīng-rén shuō de Pǔtōnghuà** **yǒu Běijīng kǒuyīn.**

Key words and phrases

Dōngnányà	South-East Asia
fāngyán	dialect
guānfāng	official
Guóyǔ	national language
Hànzú	Han nationality
Hànzú-rén	the Han people
Huá	another word for China
Huá-rén	overseas Chinese people
kǒuyīn	accent
Pǔtōnghuà	Chinese (Mandarin) (lit. common language)
shǎoshù mínzú	national minority
wén	language, writing
yǔ (yán)	language
zhǐ	to refer to

Exercise 1 There are several language terms in the passage on the previous page. You will find them very useful. Without referring to the vocabulary list, can you match the words with their correct meanings?

a	Pǔtōnghuà	i	Cantonese
b	Guóyǔ	ii	Chinese (spoken by overseas Chinese)
c	Guǎngdōnghuà	iii	Chinese language
d	fāngyán	iv	Chinese (spoken in Mainland China)
e	Zhōngwén	v	accent
f	kǒuyīn	vi	Chinese (spoken in Taiwan)
g	Huáyǔ	vii	dialect

Exercise 2 Fill in the blanks with suitable words. You will find it useful to go back to the passage on the previous page.

a Dàbùfen Zhōngguó-rén shì _____ rén. Tāmen shuō _____.
b Sìchuānhuà bú shì Pǔtōnghuà, shì yì zhǒng _____. Yǒude Sìchuān-rén shuō de Pǔtōnghuà yǒu Sìchuān _____.
c Pǔtōnghuà zài Táiwān jiào _____, zài Dōngnányà jiào _____.
d Zài Zhōngguó, hěn duō shǎoshù mínzú de rén huì shuō tāmen zìjǐ de _____, yě huì shuō _____.

bù xíng	*not that good*	
cōngming	*clever*	
dàjiā	*everyone*	
dāng	*to be; to work / act as*	
duì . . . yǒu / gǎn xìngqu	*to be interested in*	
duō tīng/shuō/dú/xiě	*to listen / speak / read / write more*	
Éguó-rén	*Russian (person)*	
èrhú	*a two-stringed musical instrument*	
fāngfǎ	*method*	
fānyì	*interpreter, translator; to translate*	
guòjiǎng	*to exaggerate, to flatter*	
Hánguó-rén	*Korean (person)*	
jiǎndān	*simple*	
jièshào	*to introduce; introduction*	
jīngjì	*economy*	
jìzhě	*journalist*	
Kǒngzǐ	*Confucius*	
Lǎozǐ	*an ancient philosopher*	
Lǐ Bái	*an ancient poet*	
lìshǐ	*history*	
liúlì	*fluent*	
pípa	*a musical instrument*	
qiānxū	*modest*	
shēng	*tone (e.g. **dì-yī/èr shēng** = the lst / 2nd tone)*	
shēngdiào	*tones*	
wénxué	*literature*	
xiānsheng	*husband*	
xiě	*to write*	
xìngqu	*interest*	
xuésheng	*student*	
yánjiū	*to study, to research*	
yǔfǎ	*grammar*	
yǔyīn	*pronunciation*	
zhéxué	*philosophy*	
zhǐyào . . . jiù . . .	*so long as . . . then . . .*	
Zhuāngzǐ	*an ancient philosopher*	

Dialogues

▶ Dialogue 1

Lányīn, a student of Chinese, is talking to Huáyàn, a Chinese student of English, about learning foreign languages. Listen to, or read, the dialogue and find out the secret of Lányīn's success in learning Chinese.

Huáyàn	Nǐde Zhōngwén zhēn bàng, shuō-de zhēn liúlì.
Lányīn	Nǎli, nǎli, shuō-de bù hǎo.
Huáyàn	Nǐde yǔyīn, shēngdiào dōu fēicháng hǎo.
Lányīn	Bù xíng, bù xíng, hái chà-de hěn yuǎn.
Huáyàn	Nǐ xué le jǐ nián le?
Lányīn	Sān nián le.
Huáyàn	Shénme? Zhǐ yǒu sān nián?! Nǐ tài cōngming le.
Lányīn	Nǐ guòjiǎng le.
Huáyàn	Wǒ xué le liù nián Yīngyǔ le, kěshì shuō-de hái hěn chà.
Lányīn	Nǐ zhēn qiānxū.
Huáyàn	Nǐ yídìng yào gàosu wǒ nǐde xuéxí fāngfǎ.
Lányīn	Hěn jiǎndān. Wǒ xiānsheng shì Zhōngguó-rén.

Exercise 3   Answer the following questions in Chinese based on **Dialogue 1**.

a   In what aspects is Lányīn's Chinese good?
b   How long has Lányīn been learning Chinese?
c   How good is Huáyàn's English?
d   How long has Huáyàn been learning English?
e   What does Huáyàn want to know from Lányīn?
f   Who does Lányīn think she owes her success to?

Key words and phrases

The following table lists the degrees of goodness you have met in descending order.

zuì hǎo	*the best*
fēicháng hǎo	*extremely good / well*
búcuò	*pretty good / well*
(hěn) hǎo	*(very) good / well*
bú tài hǎo	*not very good / well*
bù hǎo	*not good / well*
hěn bù hǎo/hěn chà	*very poor / badly*

Note that **hǎo** translates as *good* or *well* depending on whether it is being used as an adjective/verb, when it means *good*, or as an adverb, when it means *well*.

Tā shuǒ de hěn **hǎo**.	*He speaks very well.*
Tāde Yīngwén hěn **hǎo**.	*Her English is very good.*

Dialogue 2

On the first day of a Chinese summer course the students introduce themselves and talk about their reasons for studying Chinese. Read the dialogue to find out where they are from and why they want to learn Chinese.

Lǎoshī   Nǐmen hǎo. Wǒ xìng Táng, shì nǐmen de lǎoshī. Nǐmen kěyǐ jiào wǒ Táng lǎoshī. Wǒ hái bú rènshi nǐmen. Xiān qǐng dàjiā jièshào yíxiàr zìjǐ.

Wèimín   Wǒ shì Éguó-rén. Wǒ jiào Bái Wèimín. Bái shì Lǐ Bái de Bái. Wǒ hěn xǐhuan Zhōngguó wénxué. Jiānglái wǒ xiǎng dāng fānyì.

Ānfāng   Wǒ xìng Cuī, jiào Cuī Ānfāng. Wǒ shì Hánguó-rén. Wǒ duì Zhōngguó yīnyuè hěn yǒu xìngqu. Wǒ xiànzài zài xuéxí èrhú hé pípa.

Wénzhé   Wǒ shì Měiguó-rén. Wǒ de Zhōngwén míngzi jiào Shǐ Wénzhé. Shǐ shì lìshǐ de shǐ, wén shì wénxué de wén, zhé shì zhéxué de zhé. Wǒ yě xǐhuan Zhōngguó wénxué. Wǒ gèng xǐhuan Zhōngguó zhéxué. Wǒ yào yánjiū Kǒngzǐ、Lǎozǐ hé Zhuāngzǐ.

Lányīn   Wǒ shì Yīngguó-rén. Wǒ duì Zhōngguó de shǎoshù mínzú hěn yǒu xìngqu. Wǒ jiānglái xiǎng yánjiū tāmen de lìshǐ hé yǔyán.

Lǎoshī   Nǐ jiào shénme míngzi?

Lányīn   O, duìbuqǐ. Wǒ jiào Lányīn. Wǒ hái bù zhīdao jiānglái zuò shénme, kěnéng dāng jìzhě.

Shānběn   Wǒ jiào Shānběn, shì Rìběn-rén. Wǒ xiànzài zài yánjiū Zhōngguó jīngjì.

Lǎoshī   Xièxie dàjiā de jièshào.

Exercise 4   Refer to **Dialogue 2** and fill in the blanks in the sentences below saying who is who and who is doing what.

a   _____ xuésheng Cuī Ānfāng zài xuéxí _____ hé _____.

b   Lányīn shì _____ -rén. Tā xiǎng yánjiū _____ de yǔyán hé lìshǐ.

c   Nà ge _____ xuésheng jiào Shānběn. Tā duì _____ yǒu xìngqu.

d   Bái Wèimín xiǎng dāng _____. Lányīn xiǎng dāng _____.

e   Wénzhé de wén shì _____ de wén, zhé shì _____ de zhé. Tā shuō tā duì _____ yǒu xìngqu, duì _____ gèng yǒu xìngqu.

Exercise 5 Imagine that you are one of the students in the class (in **Dialogue 2**) and try to introduce your teacher and fellow students in Chinese. You could use some of the sentences in **Exercise 4**.

▶ Dialogue 3

Is Chinese difficult? Let's hear what the students in **Dialogue 2** have to say.

Lǎoshī	Nǐmen juéde Zhōngwén nán bu nán?
Shānběn	Hànzì bù nán, yǔyīn hěn nán.
Lányīn	Yīnwei nǐ shì Rìběn-rén, huì xiě Hànzì, suǒyǐ nǐ juéde Hànzì bù nán. Wǒ juéde Hànzì tài nán le.
Wénzhé	Hànzì bù róngyì, kěshì yǔfǎ gèng nán. Wǒ zǒngshì bù zhīdao shénme shíhou yòng **le**, shénme shíhou bú yòng **le**.
Wèimín	Hànyǔ yǔfǎ bú tài nán, shēngdiào zhēn bù róngyì. Wǒ chángcháng shuō-bu-hǎo dì-èr shēng hé dì-sì shēng.
Ānfāng	Wǒ juéde dì-sān shēng zuì nán.
Lǎoshī	Zhōngwén bù róngyì, kěshì **zhǐyào** wǒmen duō tīng、duō shuō、duō dú、duō xiě, wǒmen **jiù** yídìng kěyǐ xué-hǎo.

This is a good time to go back over the **Pronunciation guide** and to practise your tones. If you have the recording, go right back to the beginning again and repeat all the sounds and tones. Hopefully this will now seem very easy!

Here's another pair of linking words to add to the ones you met in Unit 18, p. 202.

Zhǐyào . . . jiù . . .   *if only / as long as . . . then . . .*

He can read when it suits him!

No spitting

No smoking

No photography

Danger: electric shock

Exercise 6   Do you speak other languages? What would you say about them in terms of pronunciation and grammar? How well do you speak them? Do you speak them with an accent or not? Try to use some of the sentences in **Dialogue 3**. (We have provided sample answers in the **Key to the exercises**.)

Here are some phrases you might find useful:

bàng	fēicháng hǎo	hěn hǎo/liúlì
búcuò	tǐng hǎo	hái kěyǐ
bú (tài) hǎo/liúlì	hěn bù hǎo/liúlì	hěn chà

a   Wǒ huì shuō ____ (hé ____).
b   Wǒde ____ búcuò. *or* Wǒde ____ shuō-de ____.
c   Wǒ huì shuō yìdiǎnr ____.
d   Wǒ shuō____ (shuō-de) yǒu (yìdiǎnr) ____ kǒuyīn.
e   ____ (a language) de yǔyīn ____.

▶ Quick review

How do you say/ask the following in Chinese?

a   Do you find English pronunciation difficult?
b   I can only write a few Chinese characters.
c   I speak a little Chinese but I find tones difficult.
d   You are modest.
e   I find it difficult to understand her accent.
f   Your English/French/German is pretty good.
g   You are flattering me.

20

lǚxíng hé tiānqì

travel and weather

In this unit you will learn
- (revise) how to get somewhere
- about Chinese festivals
- about regional differences
- how to talk about the weather

Revise before you start

- making comparisons (6)(7)
- cóng ... dào (9)
- zuì (*most*) (7)
- new situation le (5)
- zěnmeyàng (8)
- gēn ... yíyàng (6)
- tài ... le (7)
- helping verbs (5)

- ... de shíhou (10)
- A lí B yuǎn/jìn (7)
- xiān ... zài (9)
- ... yǐhòu (10)
- verb + de (8)
- yǒu diǎnr (8)
- yòu ... yòu (9)

▶ Qìhòu hé tiānqi *Climate and weather*

The passage below, together with the dialogues later in this unit, will help you talk in Chinese about the weather, a topic for all seasons! Can you work out from this passage which seasons Chinese people prefer and why?

Zhōngguó hěn dà, dōng、xī、nán、běi de *qìhòu* chángcháng hěn bù yíyàng. *Yìbānláishuō*, *nánfāng* de xiàtiān bǐ běifāng de rè, běifāng de dōngtiān bǐ nánfāng de *lěng*.

Zài Zhōngguó, dàbùfen dìfang yǒu sì ge *jìjié*: chūn、xià、qiū、dōng. *Chūntiān* cóng sānyuè dào wǔyuè. Liùyuè、qīyuè、bāyuè shì xiàtiān. *Qiūtiān* shì jiǔ、shí hé shíyīyuè. Shí'èryuè dào èryuè shì dōngtiān. Yìbān qī、bāyuè zuì rè; yī、èryuè zuì lěng. Zhōngguó-rén *bǐjiào xǐhuan* chūntiān hé qiūtiān, yīnwéi chūntiān hé qiūtiān bù lěng yě bú rè.

bǐjiào xǐhuan	to prefer
chūn(tiān)	spring
jìjié	seasons
lěng	cold
nánfāng	the south
qìhòu	climate
qiū(tiān)	autumn
yìbānláishuō	generally speaking

Exercise 1   Follow the sentences in paragraph two in the passage and talk about the seasons in your part of the world or a country or region that you know well. We have given sample answers for Europe in the **Key to the exercises**.

a Chūntiān cóng ____ dào ____.
b ____、 ____、 ____ shì xiàtiān.
c Qiūtiān shì ____、 ____、 ____.
d ____ dào ____ shì dōngtiān.

Exercise 2 How would you answer these questions that a Chinese person might ask you?

a Nǐmen guójiā yǒu jǐ ge jìjié?
b Nǎ ge yuè zuì rè? Nǎ ge yuè zuì lěng?
c Nǐ bǐjiào xǐhuan nǎ ge jìjié?
d Zài nǐmen guójiā běifāng shì bu shì bǐ nánfāng lěng?

Key words and phrases

ānpái	arrangement; to arrange
Wǒ lái ānpái ba.	I'll make the arrangements.
cónglái	ever
dàibiǎotuán	delegation
dù	degree (°C)
fādá	developed
fēngjǐng	scenery
gōngzuò	work; to work
hěn shǎo	seldom; (very) few
huí guó	return to one's own country
huí lái	to come back
jiàn miàn	to meet
kāi xué	start of term
měi	beautiful
qìwēn	(weather) temperature
tè	extremely (colloquial)
Wǔtái Shān	Mount Wutai (in Shānxī province)
xiǎng	to miss, long for
(tiānqi) yùbào	(weather) forecast
yúkuài	happy, pleasant

fēng	wind	guā fēng	windy (lit. blow wind)
yǔ	rain	xià yǔ	to rain (lit. descend rain)
xuě	snow	xià xuě	to snow (lit. descend snow)
nuǎn(huo)	warm	liáng(kuai)	cool

Dialogues

▶ Dialogue 1

Colin, who is studying in Tiānjīn, is ringing his Chinese friend, Sūlán, in Kūnmíng, Yúnnán Province to arrange a meeting between them during the winter vacation.

Colin	Zhè jǐ tiān Tiānjīn tè lěng, kěshì fēngjǐng zhēn měi. Zuótiān xià xuě le.
Sūlán	Xuě dà ma?
Colin	Bù xiǎo. Tiānqi yùbào shuō, míngtiān hái yào xià xuě.
Sūlán	Kūnmíng cónglái bú xià xuě. Wǒ zhēn xiǎng qù Tiānjīn kàn xuě.
Colin	Nǐ nàr tiānqi zěnmeyàng?
Sūlán	Bù nuǎnhuo. Jīntiān de qìwēn shì shíwǔ dù.
Colin	Shénme? Shíwǔ dù? Gēn Tiānjīn de chūntiān yíyàng nuǎnhuo.
Sūlán	Kěshì wǒ juéde lěng. Jīntiān shàngwǔ xià le xiǎo yǔ.
Colin	Wǒ zuì xǐhuan xiǎo yǔ. Kěshì Tiānjīn dōngtiān hěn shǎo xià yǔ.
Sūlán	Nǐ lái Kūnmíng kàn yǔ, wǒ qù Tiānjīn kàn xuě, zěnmeyàng?
Colin	Zhēn shì ge hǎo zhǔyì! Wǒ lái ānpái ba.
Sūlán	Děngyiděng! Nàme wǒmen zài nǎr jiàn miàn ne?

Exercise 3 Are these statements about **Dialogue 1 duì** or **bú duì**?

		duì	bú duì
a	Tiānjīn zuótiān xià le xiǎo xuě.	☐	☐
b	Kūnmíng jīntiān xià le xiǎo yǔ.	☐	☐
c	Sūlán bù xǐhuan kàn xuě.	☐	☐
d	Kūnmíng tiānqi bù lěng, kěshì Sūlán juéde leng.	☐	☐
e	Colin rènwéi tāmen yīnggāi zài Kūnmíng jiàn miàn.	☐	☐

Exercise 4 Zhèi liǎng tiān tiānqi zěnmeyàng? *What's the weather been like the last two days?*

Read the following statements, and decide whether each is true. If not, negate it.

Example: Zuótiān xià yǔ le.
- Duì. (*i.e.* Zuótiān xià yǔ le.)
- Bú duì. Zuótiān méi xià yǔ.

a Jīntiān tiānqi hěn nuǎnhuo.
b Jīntiān zǎoshang guā fēng le.
c Jīntiān wǎnshang yǒu dà yǔ.
d Jīntiān èrshí dù.
e Zuótiān tiānqi tè rè.
f Zuótiān shàngwǔ xià le xiǎo xuě.
g Zuótiān xiàwǔ fēng bú dà.

▶ Dialogue 2

The students from Unit 19 are discussing where they plan to go during the holiday.

Lǎoshī	Jiàqī nǐmen dǎsuàn qù nǎr?
Shānběn	Wǒ xǐhuan dà chéngshì. Wǒ xiān qù Shànghǎi, ránhòu qù Guǎngzhōu. Shànghǎi hé Guǎngzhōu de jīngjì zuì fādá.
Lányīn	Wǒ bù xǐhuan dà chéngshì. Wǒ yào qù Yúnnán hé Guìzhōu. Nàr yǒu hěn duō shǎoshù mínzú.
Wénzhé	Yúnnán hé Guìzhōu dōu zài Zhōngguó de nánfāng, xiàtiān yídìng hěn rè. Wǒ qù Shānxī de Wǔtái Shān. Nàr yídìng hěn liángkuai.
Wèimín	Zhè ge jiàqī wǒ yǒu gōngzuò. Wǒ qù Tiānjīn gěi yí ge dàibiǎotuán dāng fānyì.
Lǎoshī	Ānfāng, nǐ ne?
Ānfāng	Wǒ zhēn xiànmù nǐmen. Kěshì wǒ yào huí Hánguó. Wǒ tài xiǎng wǒ bàba、māma le. Kāi xué de shíhou wǒ zài huí lái.

ℹ The Chinese calendar

In China there are two different calendars in use. One is identical to our Western calendar and the other is the traditional or lunar calendar. Chinese calendars include both! In the example below, the lunar calendar is written in small print. As you may have guessed, 廿 is the shortened form of 二十. On which date does Chinese New Year begin?

星期日	星期一	星期二	星期三	星期四	星期五	星期六
	1 元旦 7	2 初八 8	3 初九 9	4 初十 10	5 小寒 11	6 十二 12
7 十三 13	8 十四 14	9 十五 15	10 十六 16	11 十七 17	12 十八 18	13 十九 19
14 二十 20	15 廿一 21	16 廿二 22	17 廿三 23	18 廿四 24	19 廿五 25	20 大寒 26
21 廿七 27	22 廿八 28	23 廿九 29	24 正月 1/1	25 初二 2	26 初三 3	27 初四 4
28 初五 5	29 初六 6	30 初七 7	31 初八 8			

The Chinese New Year starts on 24 January in this particular year.

❶ Major Chinese festivals

The most important Chinese festival is **Chūnjié** the *Spring Festival* or the *Chinese Lunar New Year*, which falls on the first day of the first lunar month. The Lunar New Year itself may occur as early as January 21st and as late as February 21st. It is the major festival in China (rather like Christmas in the West) and most people try to get home to celebrate it with their families even if it means travelling long distances.

Firecrackers are set off on New Year's Eve and New Year's Day to warn off evil spirits even though many Chinese have probably forgotten the origin of this custom.

Other major festivals are the *Lantern Festival*, the *Pure Brightness* or *Grave Sweeping Festival*, the *Dragon Boat Festival* and the *Mid-Autumn Festival*, which was originally to pay homage to the full moon.

You could visit your local library to find out more about these festivals: what their origins are, when they occur and how they are celebrated. Most overseas Chinese communities observe these festivals too. You could learn a lot about Chinese traditions. It would also give you an insight into the traditional Chinese way of life which has helped to shape their language.

Exercise 5 Match the sentences in Column A with their English equivalents in Column B.

Column A

a Nàr xiàtiān yídìng hěn liángkuai.

b Dà chéngshì de jīngjì hěn fādá.

c Nàr yǒu hěn duō shǎoshù mínzú.

d Jiàqī wǒ dǎsuàn qù lǚxíng.

e Kāi xué de shíhou wǒ zài huí lái.

Column B

i During the holidays I plan to travel.

ii There are many minorities there.

iii I will come back again when term starts.

iv The economy in big cities is developed.

v It must be cool there in the summer.

Exercise 6 Now cover up Column B in **Exercise 5** and say what the sentences in Column A mean in English. Once you have done that, cover up Column A and say what the sentences in Column B mean in Chinese.

▶ Dialogue 3

Listen to the dialogue and find out how these students plan to travel to the places they are going to visit during the holiday. Go straight to **Exercise 7** without reading the dialogue below. If you haven't got the recording, read the dialogue, and then do **Exercise 7**.

Lǎoshī	Nǐmen zěnme qù?
Wèimín	Tiānjīn bù yuǎn. Wǒ zuò huǒchē qù. Liǎng、sān ge xiǎoshí jiù dào le.
Lányīn	Yúnnán lí Běijīng hěn yuǎn. Wǒ kěyǐ zuò huǒchē, yě kěyǐ zuò fēijī. Wǒ hái méi yǒu juédìng.
Lǎoshī	Fēijī bǐ huǒchē kuài duōle, kěshì yě guì duōle.
Wénzhé	Wǔtái Shān bù yuǎn yě bú jìn. Wǒ xiān zuò huǒchē, zài zuò chángtú qìchē.
Lǎoshī	Shānběn, nǐ yào qù liǎng ge dìfang. Nǐ zěnme qù?
Shānběn	Wǒ xiān zuò fēijī dào Shànghǎi, zài zuò huǒchē qù Guǎngzhōu.
Ānfāng	Wǒ bù xǐhuan zuò fēijī, kěshì wǒ zhǐ néng zuò fēijī huí guó.
Lǎoshī	Hǎo. Zhù dàjiā jiàqī yúkuài.

走马看花

Chinese proverb: **Zǒu mǎ kàn huā**
*Look at flowers while riding on horseback –
gain a superficial understanding*

Exercise 7 How will the students in **Dialogue 3** get to their destinations?

a Wèimín zuò _____ qù Tiānjīn.
b Lányīn zuò _____ huòzhě _____ qù Yúnnán.
c Wénzhé zuò _____ hé _____ qù Wǔtái Shān.
d Shānběn zuò _____ qù Shànghǎi, zuò _____ qù Guǎngzhōu.
e Ānfāng zuò _____ huí Hánguó.

Exercise 8 Make complete sentences with the words or phrases given. You will have to supply a missing word in each case. Pay attention to the word order.

Example: Lúndūn/ fēijī/ lái/ tā/ bù
　　　　　Tā bú zuò fēijī lái Lúndūn.

a tā/ qù/ Shànghǎi/ huǒchē/ míngtiān
b lái/ wǒde péngyou/ wǒ jiā/ gōnggòng qìchē
c qù gōngyuán/ zìxíngchē/ bù/ wǒ
d mǎi dōngxi/ chē/ tāmen/ chángcháng/ qù
e dìtiě/ huí jiā/ xiànzài/ wǒ

▶ **Exercise 9** Your Chinese friend, Yànmíng, is asking you about the holiday you plan to take.

	Yànmíng	Nǐ dǎsuàn qù shénme dìfang?
a	**You**	(Say you want to go to Hong Kong and Macao.)
	Yànmíng	Nǐ zěnme qù?
b	**You**	(Say you will fly to Hong Kong and then go to Macao by boat.)
	Yànmíng	Nàr de tiānqi zěnmeyàng?
c	**You**	(Say it's hot there in August.)
	Yànmíng	Xià bu xià yǔ?
d	**You**	(Say sometimes it rains.)
	Yànmíng	Nǐ qù jǐ tiān?
e	**You**	(Say you haven't decided yet.)

▶ **Exercise 10** Listen to the following passage and then answer the questions below.

Běijīng de Jìjié

Běijīng de dōngtiān yòu *cháng* yòu lěng; xiàtiān yòu cháng yòu rè. Běijīng de chūntiān hěn duǎn yě hěn nuǎnhuo, kěshì chángcháng guā fēng.

Běijīng zuì hǎo de jìjié shì qiūtiān. Qiūtiān bù lěng yě bú rè. *Báitiān* hěn nuǎnhuo, zǎoshang hé wǎnshang hěn liángkuai. Qiūtiān *qíngtiān* duō, *yīntiān* shǎo. Bù chángcháng guā fēng, yě hěn shǎo xià yǔ.

cháng	long	**qíngtiān**	sunny (day)
báitiān	daytime	**yīntiān**	cloudy (day)

a Běijīng de xiàtiān hěn duǎn, shì bu shì?
b Běijīng de dōngtiān shì bu shì hěn lěng?
c Běijīng de chūntiān zěnmeyàng?
d Běijīng de chūntiān shì zuì hǎo de jìjié ma?
e Wèishénme Běijīng-rén hěn xǐhuan qiūtiān?

▶ Quick review

The following pictures show what the weather was, is and will be like. Make two statements about each of them in relation to what time it is now. It's 10am Friday.

Example: Jīntiān zǎoshang xià dà yǔ le.
(Jīntiān zǎoshang) qìwēn (shì) qī dù.

a

20°c

xīngqīsì shàngwǔ

b

5°c

xīngqīsì wǎnshang

c

12°c

xīngqīwǔ shàngwǔ

d

18°c

xīngqīwǔ xiàwǔ

e

3°c

xīngqīliù

f

0°c

xià xīngqīyī

Bào shàng shuō jīntiān bú huì xià yǔ.
But the paper said it wouldn't rain today.

21

tán gǎnxiǎng

experiences, feelings and reflections

In this unit you will learn
- how to talk about things that happened in the past
- how to ask people about their impressions
- how to express regret
- how to express satisfaction
- how to write a thank you note

Revise before you start

- measure words (4)(7)
- numbers from 100 to 1,000 (7)
- verb + **guo** (9)
- helping verbs (6)
- **gèng** (*even more*) (8)
- verb + **de** (8)
- reduplicated verbs (5)
- **zuì** (*most*) (7)
- verb endings (10)
- . . . **de shíhou** (10)
- new situation **le** (5)
- **shì bu shì** (3)
- **tài . . . le** (7)
- sentence **le** (4)
- **gěi** (*for*) (6)

Qù Zhōngguó xuéxí, *lǚyóu* hé gōngzuò
Go to China to study, travel and work

With China opening up more and more, it attracts more and more visitors: students, tourists and business people. What do the students study? What are the tourists interested in? Why are business people going to China? Read the passage below to find out.

Měi nián yǒu hěn duō wàiguó-rén qù Zhōngguó xuéxí. Tāmen xuéxí Zhōngguó de yǔyán、wénxué、*wénhuà*、lìshǐ、*zōngjiào*, děngděng. Zài Zhōngguó de *jǐ bǎi duō suǒ dàxué* lǐ, yǒu jǐ *wàn* ge wàiguó *liúxuéshēng*.

Qù Zhōngguó lǚyóu de wàiguó-rén *yuè lái yuè* duō. *Tāmen hěn duō rén* duì Zhōngguó de wénhuà hé lìshǐ gǎn xìngqu. Hěn duō rén qù-guo Zhōngguó hěn duō cì.

Zhè jǐ nián qù Zhōngguó gōngzuò de wàiguó-rén yě yuè lái yuè duō. Zài Zhōngguó de *wàizī qǐyè* hé *hézī qǐyè* yě yuè lái yuè duō. Hěn duō gōngsī dōu xiǎng zài Zhōngguó kuòdà *shēngyi*.

dàxué	*university*
hézī qǐyè	*joint venture*
jǐ bǎi duō	lit. *several hundred more*
kuòdà	*to expand*
liúxuéshēng	*overseas student*
lǚyóu	*to travel*
shēngyi	*business*
suǒ	(measure word for schools, and so on)
tāmen hěn duō rén	*many of them* (lit. *they many people*)
yuè lái yuè . . .	*more and more . . .*
wàizī qǐyè	*foreign enterprise*
wàn	*ten thousand*
wénhuà	*culture*
zōngjiào	*religion*

Here's another pair of linking words to add to your list: **yuè lái … yuè …**

yuè lái yuè duō	*more and more*
yuè lái yuè hǎo	*better and better*
yuè lái yuè kuài	*quicker and quicker*

If you replace **lái** with another adjective/verb, you get:

yuè kuài **yuè** hǎo	*the quicker the better*
yuè duō **yuè** hǎo	*the more the better*

Exercise 1   How would you say the following?

a More and more Chinese come to Britain to study.
b Many of them are interested in the history and culture of Britain.
c Every year many foreign students come to Britain to study English.
d More and more European companies want to expand their business in China.

Key words and phrases

bāo	*to wrap; to make* (**jiǎozi**)
chángshòu (miàn)	*long life (noodles)*
chī-de-guàn	*to be used to the food*
chī-bu-guàn	*to be not used to the food*
dǒng	*to understand*
duì X yǒu shénme yìnxiàng?	*what is your impression of X?*
duì shénme (zuì) mǎnyì?	*(most) satisfied with what?*
fāzhǎn	*to develop*
jiàoxué	*teaching*
jiǎozi	*(Chinese) dumplings*
jiùshì	*it's just that*
kuàilè	*happy*
mǎnyì	*satisfied*
měi(-jíle)	*(extremely) beautiful*
nàli/nàr	*there*
nánshuō	*difficult to say*
qìngzhù	*to celebrate*
shān qū	*mountain(ous) area*
tán(yi)tán	*to talk (a bit) about*
tèsè	*feature, characteristics*
tīng-bu-dǒng	*to be unable to understand (verbal speech)*

tóngshì (men)	colleague(s)
tóngxué (men)	fellow student(s)
xià ge	next
xuéxiào	school
yìnxiàng	impression
yíqiè	everything
yìzhí	all the time
yǒuhǎo	friendly

Dialogues

▶ Dialogue 1

The group of students you met in Units 19 and 20 are now all safely back in college. What do they think of the places they have just visited? Let's find out.

Lǎoshī	Tóngxuémen, nǐmen jiàqī guò-de hǎo ma?
Xuésheng	Hěn hǎo.
(chorus)	Bú tài hǎo.
	Fēicháng hǎo.
	Hái kěyǐ.
Lǎoshī	Qǐng měi ge rén dōu tányitán, hǎo ma?
Wénzhé	Wǒ qù le Wǔtái Shān. Nàli yíqiè dōu hǎo, jiùshi fàn bù hǎo.
Lǎoshī	Fàn zěnme bù hǎo?
Wénzhé	Tāmen bù chī ròu. Kěshì wǒ zuì ài chī ròu, suǒyǐ wǒ chángcháng juéde è.
Wèimín	Nǐ yīnggāi gēn wǒ yìqǐ qù Tiānjīn. Wǒmen de dàibiǎotuán měi tiān dōu yǒu yànhuì.
Lǎoshī	Lányīn, shǎoshù mínzú de fàn nǐ chī-de-guàn ma?
Lányīn	Kāishǐ de shíhou chī-bu-guàn, hòulái jiù chī-de-guàn le. Nàxiē shǎoshù mínzú de rén zhēn yǒuhǎo.
Lǎoshī	Nàr shì bu shì hěn rè?
Lányīn	Wǒ qù de dìfang shì shān qū, suǒyǐ bú tài rè. Nàr de fēngjǐng měi-jíle.
Lǎoshī	Shānběn, nǐ duì Shànghǎi hé Guǎngzhōu yǒu shénme yìnxiàng?
Shānběn	Zhè liǎng ge chéngshì de jīngjì dōu fāzhǎn-de hěn kuài. Kěxī wǒ tīng-bu-dǒng Shànghǎihuà hé Guǎngdōnghuà.
Lǎoshī	Zhè liǎng zhǒng fāngyán dōu bù róngyì dǒng. Ānfāng, nǐ bàba、māma dōu hǎo ma?

Ānfāng	Tāmen dōu hěn hǎo, xièxie nín. Wǒ bàba, māma shuō xià ge jiàqī tāmen yào lái Zhōngguó. Wǒmen yìqǐ zài Zhōngguó lǚyóu.
Dàjiā	Nà tài hǎo le!

Learning tip

Keep reading all the dialogues in the book whenever you have a spare moment: better still listen to the recording whenever you can. Practise covering up the English words in the **Key words and phrases** and see how many of the Chinese words you know, then do the reverse. You can go back to the beginning of the book and do this right the way through for useful revision.

Exercise 2 Where did you go on your last holiday? Here are some questions a Chinese person might ask you:

a Nǐ de jiàqī guò-de hǎo bu hǎo?
b Nǐ qù le duō cháng shíjiān?
c Nàli de tiānqi zěnmeyàng?
d Nàli de fàn nǐ chī-de-guàn ma?
e Nàli de fēngjǐng měi bu měi?

Exercise 3 Nǐ duì shénme gǎn/yǒu xìngqu? *What are you interested in?*

State whether you are interested in the following things.

Example: Zhōngguó lìshǐ
       i Wǒ duì Zhōngguó lìshǐ gǎn/yǒu xìngqu.
      ii Wǒ duì Zhōngguó lìshǐ bù gǎn xìngqu *or*
     iii Wǒ duì Zhōngguó lìshǐ méi (yǒu) xìngqu.

a liúxíng (*popular*) yīnyuè   b Yìdàlì fàn
c dísīkē   d shōují (*collect*) yóupiào
e Déguó diànyǐng

Exercise 4 Are you used to the following food or drinks?

If you are, say **Wǒ chī/hē-de-guàn** X. If you are not, say **Wǒ chī/ hē-bu-guàn** Y. Remember you can also put the noun (the sort of thing) at the beginning of the sentence for emphasis.

tángcù yú   *sweet and sour fish*
 i Wǒ **chī-de-guàn** tángcù yú.
ii Tángcù yú wǒ **chī-bu-guàn**.

suānlà tāng   *hot and sour soup*
 i Suānlà tāng wǒ **hē-de-guàn**.
ii Wǒ **hē-bu-guàn** suānlà tāng.

Start with **tángcù yú** and **suānlà tāng**. And then:

a Yìndù (*Indian*) fàn?
b tián pútáojiǔ?
c dòufu (*tofu*)?
d Kěkǒukělè?
e mángguǒ (*mango*)?
f kāfēi?

▶ **Dialogue 2**

Mr Ford has lived and worked in China for nearly 12 years. He is interviewed by a Chinese journalist on his 60th birthday. What is he most satisfied and dissatisfied with?

Jìzhě	Fútè xiānsheng, zhù nín shēngrì kuàilè!
Ford	Xièxie, xièxie.
Jìzhě	Nín zài Zhōngguó jǐ nián le?
Ford	Chàbuduō shí'èr nián le.
Jìzhě	Nín yìzhí zài dàxué gōngzuò ma?
Ford	Duì. Wǒ fēicháng xǐhuan dāng lǎoshī.
Jìzhě	Zài Zhōngguó nín duì shénme zuì mǎnyì?
Ford	Dāngrán shì wǒde gōngzuò. Wǒmen xuéxiào de jiàoxué yuè lái yuè hǎo.
Jìzhě	Nàme nín duì shénme zuì bù mǎnyì?
Ford	Wǒ duì hěn duō shìqing bù mǎnyì. Kěshì hěn nánshuō duì shénme zuì bù mǎnyì.
Jìzhě	Nín dǎsuàn zěnme qìngzhù nínde shēngrì?
Ford	Zǎoshang wǒ tàitai gěi wǒ zuò le Zhōngguó de chángshòu miàn. Wǎnshang tóngshìmen lái wǒ jiā bāo jiǎozi.
Jìzhě	Nínde shēngrì guò-de zhēn yǒu Zhōngguó tèsè.
Ford	Wǒ xiànzài yǐjīng shì bàn ge Zhōngguó-rén le.

Do you remember meeting two phrases using **duì** in Unit 10?

A **duì** shēntǐ (bu) hǎo.	*A is (not) good for the health/body.*
Y **duì** X (bù) hǎo.	*Y is/(not) good to X.*

Here are some more useful phrases with **duì**:

Nǐ **duì** X yǒu shénme yìnxiàng?	*What impression have you of X?*
Wǒ **duì** X de yìnxiàng hěn hǎo.	*I have a very good impression of X.*
Nǐ **duì** shénme (zuì) bù mǎnyì?	*What are you (most) dissatisfied with?*

A **duì** B **bù mǎnyì.**　　*A is not satisfied with B.*
A **duì** B **zuì bù mǎnyì.**　*A is most dissatisfied with B.*

i It is very common for elderly people (the Chinese tend to regard people of 60 and over as elderly!) to eat 'long-life noodles' (**chángshòu miàn**) on their birthdays!

Miàntiáo
Noodles

Jiǎozi
Dumplings

On special occasions such as birthdays and the Chinese New Year the family (plus close friends or colleagues) might make Chinese dumplings (**bāo jiǎozi**) together. It is a very companionable activity which also requires some skill. Beginners can usually spot which **jiǎozi** are theirs when it comes to eating them as they tend to be the unsightly ones or the ones which have burst!

Exercise 5   Your Chinese friend is asking you about your visit to China. This passage is a brief account of your visit.

You visited China on a package tour for two weeks. You visited Beijing, Shanghai and Guilin. You liked all three places, but for different reasons. There were many parks in Beijing which you liked a lot. Shanghai was developing very fast, which impressed you. But there were too many people there and it was very crowded. The scenery at Guilin was extremely beautiful.

Now answer your friend's questions:

	Friend	Nǐ zài Zhōngguó duōshao tiān?
a	**You**	_____
	Friend	Nǐ qù le shénme dìfang?
b	**You**	_____
	Friend	Nǐ duì Shànghǎi yǒu shénme yìnxiàng?
c	**You**	_____
	Friend	Nàme Běijīng ne?
d	**You**	_____
	Friend	Nǐ duì Guìlín de yìnxiàng zěnmeyàng?
e	**You**	_____

▶ **Exercise 6** Listen to the thank-you message on Lányīn's answerphone. Then decide whether the statements below are **duì** or **bú duì**. Read the new words before you listen to the message.

bāngzhù	*help*	**gǎnxiè**	*to thank* (formal)
tèbié	*especially*	**wèn XX hǎo**	*say hello to XX*
dāngmiàn	*face to face*	**tiān**	*to add*

a Xiǎo Qīng jīntiān shàngwǔ qù Lányīn de xuéxiào le.
b Xiǎo Qīng dāngmiàn gēn Lányīn shuō le zàijiàn.
c Xiǎo Qīng qù-guo Lányīn de jiā.
d Xiǎo Qīng méi jiàn-guo Lányīn de bàba hé māma.

Lányīn,

Nǐ hǎo! Wǒ shì Xiǎo Qīng. Jīntiān xiàwǔ wǒ qù nǐde xuéxiào zhǎo nǐ, kěshì nǐ bú zài. Zhēn kěxī, wǒ bù néng dāngmiàn gēn nǐ shuō 'zàijiàn'.

Zhè cì lái Yīngguó fǎngwèn, wǒ guó-de zhēn yúkuài. Nǐ gěi le wǒ hěn duō bāngzhù. Wǒ fēicháng gǎnxiè nǐ. Tèbié gǎnxiè nǐ qǐng wǒ qù nǐde jiā chī fàn. Wǒ gěi nǐ hé nǐ bàba、màma tiān le hěn duō máfan.

Xīwàng nǐ jiānglái yǒu jīhuì yě qù Zhōngguó fǎngwèn. Zhù nǐ shēntǐ jiànkāng、shēnghuó yúkuài、gōngzuò shùnlì、wànshì rúyì!

Wèn nǐ bàba、māma hǎo! Zàijiàn!

Final review

1 Do you remember the opposites of these words? What is the opposite of:

a lěng	e piányi	i zǎo	m xià
b niánqīng	f ānquán	j yìng	n zuǒ
c shòu	g yuǎn	k hòu	o běi
d ānjìng	h liáng(kuai)	l yǐqián	p dōngnán

2 Can you find the Chinese equivalents in Section B to match the English sentences in Section A?

Section A

a Excuse me, is this seat taken?

b Could you please speak more slowly?

c Please come a little earlier tomorrow.

d Please tell the teacher I am not well today.

e Could you please say it again?

Section B

i Qǐng gàosu lǎoshī wǒ jīntiān bù shūfu.

ii Qǐng nǐ zài shuō yí biàn.

iii Qǐng nǐ shuō màn yìdiǎn.

iv Qǐng wèn, zhè ge wèizi yǒu rén zuò ma?

v Qǐng míngtiān zǎo yìdiǎnr lái.

3 We have given you the literal translations of some Chinese words in this book. Here are some new words with their literal translations. See if you can guess what they mean.

a shǒujī (*lit.* hand machine)

b diànnǎo (*lit.* electronic brain)

c guǎnggào (*lit.* extensive telling)

d lùxiàngjī (*lit.* record image machine)

e tiěfànwǎn (*lit.* iron rice bowl)

f nuǎnshuǐpíng (*lit.* warm water bottle)

g tiānxiàn (*lit.* sky thread)

▶4 Numbers are important. This listening exercise will give you some more practice. Listen to the message on the answerphone and fill in the missing information below. The only new word is **shǒujī** (*mobile phone*) which you've just met in the previous exercise. If you have not got the recording, the passage is included in the **Key to the exercises**.

a Time of arrival in Guangzhou is _____

b His room number is _____

c The hotel's number is _____

d His mobile number is _____

e Length of his stay in Guangzhou is _____

f Date of his departure is _____

g Time of the train is _____

h Stay in Shenzhen for _____ days.

i Date and time of flight back to the UK is _____

5 How do you say to or ask a Chinese person the following?

a Say you are not used to eating hot/spicy dishes.
b Ask her if she is interested in pop (**liúxíng**) music or classical (**gǔdiǎn**) music.
c Say there are more and more people going abroad for holidays.
d Ask her what is her impression of Britain (the US etc.).
e Ask her what she is (most) satisfied and/or not satisfied with.
f Wish her happy birthday!

有 志 者 ， 事 竟 成

Chinese proverb: **Yǒu zhì zhě, shì jìng chéng**
Where there's a will, there's a way.

Zhùhè nǐ! *Congratulations!*

You have completed *Teach Yourself Beginner's Chinese* and are now a competent speaker of basic Chinese. You should be able to handle most everyday situations on a visit to China and to communicate with Chinese people sufficiently to make friends. Should you wish to comment on any aspect of this book, you can contact us c/o Hodder and Stoughton Educational, 338 Euston Road, London NW1 3BH.

taking it further

If you would like to extend your ability so that you can develop your confidence, fluency and scope in the language, whether for social or business purposes, why not take your Chinese a step further with *Teach Yourself Mandarin Chinese*?

You could see if there are any Chinese language classes taking place in your area. Many big universities have Chinese departments or language centres which run courses in a number of foreign languages including Chinese. Large cities often have an annual publication listing all the courses taking place that year and where they are held.

You can also go online and look at the following websites, but do remember these are constantly changing and new ones are being added all the time.

http://www.zhongwen.com/
English and Chinese (full-form characters).
Brief introduction to Chinese language, writing, pinyin, etc.
Texts in Chinese (classical texts, and some modern texts).

http://www.chineseon.net/
English and Chinese (simplified characters).
Brief introduction to Chinese language, writing, pinyin, etc.
Illustration of stroke order.
For both Chinese language learners and teachers. Online course for beginners.
Texts in Chinese (classical texts and modern texts).

http://www.mandarintools.com/
Another site which has many links to China-related websites.
All the instructions are in English.
English and Chinese (simplified characters).

Online English–Chinese and Chinese–English dictionary.
Illustration of stroke order.
(You can get a Chinese name by typing in your English name.)

http://www.publicchinese.com/
Online tutorials available. You may find a language partner to practise your Chinese.

http://www.csulb.edu/~txie/online.htm
A comprehensive website with English and Chinese (in simplified and traditional scripts).

Chūkǒu *Exit*

Unit 1

1 a Nǐ hǎo! b Xièxie. c Bú yòng xiè.
2 a Nǐ hǎo! b Bú yòng xiè. c Xièxie. d Zàijiàn!
3 a Nǐ hǎo! b Lǐ tàitai hǎo ma? c Lǐ xiānsheng zài ma?
   d Xièxie (nǐ).
4 a Xièxie. b Bú yòng xiè. c Zàijiàn. d Míngtiān jiàn.
   e Qǐng jìn. f Qǐng zuò. g Wǒ/Tā hěn hǎo. h Nǐ/Tā hǎo ma?
5 a = iv, b = iii, c = ii, d = i.

Quick review

a Lǐ xiānsheng, nǐ hǎo! or, Nǐ hǎo, Lǐ xiānsheng!
b Nǐ tàitai hǎo ma? c Duìbuqǐ. d Xièxie nǐ.
e Bú yòng xiè. f Zàijiàn.

Unit 2

Let's try

a Qǐng jìn. b Nǐ hǎo. c Qǐng zuò. d Míngtiān jiàn.

1 a shénme; jiào. b huì; shuō. c shì; rènshi.
2 a Tāmen shì Lǐ xiānsheng、Yīng tàitai. b Tā jiào Lǐ Jīnshēng.
   c Duì. Tā xìng Yīng. d Bù. Tā xìng Lǐ. e Wǒ (bú) rènshi tāmen.
3 a Wáng. b Lányīng. c A little bit. / Huì yìdiǎn. d Chinese
   teacher. / Zhōngwén lǎoshī. e No, she doesn't. / Tā bú rènshi
   nǐ. f She's beautiful. / Tā hen piàoliang. g Yes. / Tā yǒu (nán
   péngyou).
4 a Tā jiào Zhào Huá. Tā shì jǐngchá. b Zhè shì Liú Guāng. Tā
   shì sījī. c Nà shì Guō Jié. Tā shì yīshēng. d Tā jiào Lǐ Mínglì.
   Tā shì lǎoshī. e Zhè shì Zhōu Jiābǎo. Tā shì xuésheng. f Nà
   shì Wú Zébì. Tā shì chūshī.
5 a bú duì, b bú duì, c bú duì, d bú duì, e bú duì, f duì.
6 a Nǐ huì shuō Yīngwén ma? Nǐ huì bu huì shuō Yīngwén?
   b Nǐmen shì lǎoshī ma? Nǐmen shì bu shì lǎoshī? c Xiǎo

Zhèng zài ma? Xiǎo Zhèng zài bu zài? d Lǐ xiānsheng jīntiān lái ma? Lǐ xiānsheng jīntiān lái bu lái? e Wáng Fāng yǒu Yīngwén míngzi ma? Wáng Fāng yǒu mei yǒu Yīngwén míngzi? f Lín lǎoshī jiào Lín Péng ma? Lín lǎoshī jiào bu jiào Lín Péng?

Quick review

a Nín guì xìng? Nǐ xìng shénme?   b Wǒ jiào xxx.
c Wǒ méi yǒu Zhōngwén míngzi.   d Wǒ bú rènshi tā.
e Méi guānxi.   f Wǒde péngyou bú shì lǎoshī.

Unit 3

Let's try

a Nǐ hǎo. Wǒ jiào X. Nǐ jiào shénme? or Nín guì xìng?
b Nǐ/Nín yǒu háizi ma? Nǐ/Nín yǒu mei yǒu háizi?

1 a shì/bú shì, b shì/bú shì, c shì/bú shì, d shì/bú shì, e shì/bù zhīdào, f shì/bù zhīdào.

2 *Speaker 1*: Nǐ hǎo! Wǒ jiào Chén Lìmǐn. Wǒ shì Xiānggǎng-rén. Wǒ zhù zài Xiānggǎng Lì Yè Lù 8 hào. Wǒde diànhuà hàomǎ shì 507 1293.
   Speaker 2: Nǐ hǎo! Wǒ jiào Wú Yìfēi. Wǒ shì Shànghǎi-rén. Wǒde diànhuà hàomǎ shì 874 3659. Wǒ zhù zài Shànghǎi Nánjīng Lù 9 hào.
   Speaker 3: Wǒ jiào Guō Wànjí. Wǒ shì Fǎguó-rén. Wǒ zhù zài Běijīng Hépíng Lù 6 hào. Wǒde diànhuà hàomǎ shì 724 6274.

4 a Běijīng Cháoyáng Lù èr hào, Lǐ Mínglì lǎoshī. b Sūzhōu Lónghǎi Lù jiǔ hào, Dōngfāng Fàndiàn sān-bā-sì fángjiān, Zhào Huá xiānsheng. c Nánjīng Xīchéng Qū Hépíng Lù wǔ hào, Zhào Jiābǎo xiǎojie.

5 a iii, b vii, c i, d v, e ii, f iv, g vi.

Quick review

a Tā shì shéi?   b Nǐ zhù (zài) nǎr?
c Wǒ bú zhù (zài) Lúndūn.
d Nǐde diànhuà hàomǎ shì duōshao?
e Diànhuà shì shénme yìsi?
f Zhè shì wǒde fēijī piào.

Unit 4

Let's try

a Nǐ zhù zài shénme fàndiàn? (Nǐ zhù zài) jǐ hào fángjiān?
b Zhè shì wǒde míngpiàn.

1 a èrshíjiǔ, b qīshíyī, c sānshí'èr.
2 a èrshíyī, b qīshí, c liùshíliù, d sìshíjiǔ e sānshí, f liùshí, g shíwǔ, h sānshísān.
3 Dīng Fèng is married. She's got two children, a son and a daughter. Her son is called Dīng Níng and is 12 this year. Her daughter's name is Dīng Yīng. She is 14 years old.
4 a Méi yǒu. b Méi yǒu. c Bú shì (Tā bú shì lǎoshī.) d Wǒ méi yǒu háizi. e Wǒ méi yǒu dìdi.
5 a Are you married? = iv b How old is she? = iii c What's Mr Wang, the teacher, called? = i d Have you any children? = v e Has Mrs Li a daughter? = ii
6 Wǒ jiào Mǎlì, jīnnián shíqī suì. Wǒ méi yǒu jiějie, méi yǒu mèimei. Wǒ yǒu yí ge gēge, yí ge dìdi. Wǒ gēge jiào Hēnglì. Tā èrshí suì. Wǒ dìdi jiào Bǐdé. Tā shíwǔ suì. Wǒmen dōu shì xuésheng.

Quick review

a Nǐ hǎo! b Nǐ jiào shénme (míngzi)? c Nǐ duō dà?
d Nǐ yǒu xiōngdì jiěmèi ma? e Xièxie (nǐ). f Zàijiàn!

Unit 5

Let's try

a Chén xiānsheng, nǐ hǎo ma? Nǐ jiào shénme míngzi? Nǐ huì bu huì shuō Yīngwén? Nǐ zhù zài nǎr? Nǐ jié hūn le ma? Nǐ yǒu háizi ma? Nǐ(de) háizi jǐ suì/duō dà? Nǐde diànhuà hàomǎ shì duōshao/shénme? Nǐ rènshi bu rènshi X? Nǐ shì Běijīng-/Shànghǎi-/Guǎngdōng-rén ma? Nǐ bàba\ māma dōu zài (Běijīng) ma?
b liùshísì, èrshíjiǔ, wǔshíqī, sānshíbā, shí'èr, jiǔshíwǔ, sìshí, èr, qīshísān, shí.
1 a yīyuè yī hào, b shí'èr yuè èrshíwǔ hào, c sānyuè bā hào, d shíyuè yī hào.
3 a September 9th b Sunday morning, c Thursday, November 28th, d 10.45am Saturday, e 3.30pm Friday, July 6th, f 11am Monday, December 31st.
4 a Wǔ diǎn yí kè; wǔ diǎn shíwǔ fēn. b Chà wǔ fēn wǔ diǎn; sì diǎn wǔshíwǔ fēn. c (Hái yǒu) sìshí fēnzhōng. d Zǎoshang wǔ diàn líng wǔ fēn. e Wǔ diǎn líng qī fēn.

Quick review

a Sānyuè sānshí hào. b Xīngqīsì. c Sì diǎn èrshíqī fēn.
d Sì diǎn sān kè **or** chà yí kè wǔ diǎn. Dī sān zhàntái.
e Sì diǎn wǔshí fēn **or** Wǔ diǎn chà shí fēn. Dì-yī zhàntái.

Unit 6

Let's try

1 Wǒ yào xīngqīsì shàngwu jiǔ diǎn bàn de huǒchē piào.

2 a yī-jiǔ-jiǔ-qī nián yīyuè liù hào b èr-líng-líng-líng nián sānyuè èrshíyī hào c yī-jiǔ-sì-sān nián bāyuè shíwǔ hào.

1 a Tā zài mǎi dōngxi. b Tāmen zài kàn zájì. c Tā zài huàn qián. d Tā zài dǎ tàijíquán. e Tāmen zài kàn diànyǐng. f Tā zài tīng yīnyuè.

3 a bù yíyàng (gāo), b yíyàng (dà), c bù yíyàng (zhòng), d bù yíyàng (gāo), e yíyàng (zhòng), f yíyàng (dà).

4 a Bú duì. Xǔ bǐ Hú gāo. b Bú duì. Hú bǐ Qū zhòng. c Bú duì. Tāmen yíyàng dà. d Duì. e Duì.

5 a Xīngqītiān, b xīngqīsì xiàwǔ, c xīngqīsān wǎnshang, d shàngwǔ, e xīngqīliù.

Quick review

a Nǐ míngtiān xiǎng zuò shénme?

b Xiǎo Mǎ gēn tā jiějie yíyàng gāo.

c Wǒ juéde zájì bǐ jīngjù yǒu yìsi.

d Xiǎo Zhào, jīntiān wǎnshang nǐ xiǎng qù nǎr?

e Lǐ xiǎojie, nǐ xiǎng qù kàn diànyǐng háishi tīng yīnyuèhuì?

Unit 7

Let's try

a Nǐmen xiǎng tīng yīnyuèhuì háishi kàn xì?

b Nǐmen xǐhuan (tīng) Xīfāng yīnyuè ma? Nǐmen xǐhuan bu xǐhuan (tīng) Xīfāng yīnyuè? c Zài Xīfāng dāngrán tīng Xīfāng yīnyuè.

1 a wǔ máo èr (fēn), b liǎng/èr kuài liǎng/èr máo wǔ, c shí'èr kuài qī máo liù, d jiǔshíjiǔ kuài jiǔ máo jiǔ, e èr/liǎngbǎi líng wǔ kuài wǔ máo sì. f bā kuài líng qī (fēn).

2 a Píngguǒ jiǔshí biànshì yì jīn. b Pútao yí bàng sì-jiǔ yì jīn. c Cǎoméi yí bàng qī-wǔ yì hé. d Xiāngjiāo wǔshíbā biànshì yì jīn.

3 a **Xīhóngshì zěnme** mài? b **Báicài yì jīn duōshao** qián? c **Tǔdòu duōshao** qián yì jīn?

4 **Recording: a** Yú zěnme mài? Qī kuài líng jiǔ yì jīn. b Cǎoméi duōshao qián yì hé? Qī kuài sì yì hé. c Báicài yì jīn duōshao qián? Yí kuài èr yì jīn. d Pútao guì bu guì? Bú guì. Yí kuài jiǔ yì jīn. e Wǒ mǎi liǎng jīn tǔdòu. Sān kuài èr.

5 a Tài dà le! b Tài rè le! c Tāde qián tài duōle! d (Piào) tài guì le! e Fǎwén tài nán le!
6 a Pútao bǐ píngguǒ guì (yìdiǎnr). b Xiǎo Wáng bǐ Lǎo Lǐ gāo yìdiǎnr. c Běijīng bǐ Lúndūn rè duōle. d Bái xiānsheng bǐ Bái tàitai dà deduō.
7 a jiù, b jiù, c cái, d jiù, e cái.

Quick review

a Zhǐ yào wǔ fēnzhōng jiù dào.
b Yào/děi wǔshí fēnzhōng cái dào.
c Zài wǒ jiā wǒ bàba zuì dà.
d Diànyǐngyuàn lí wǒ jiā bù yuǎn.
e Xiāngjiāo sìshíjiǔ biànshì yí bàng.

Unit 8

Let's try

1 No, she didn't. One was too big, one was too small, and one was too expensive.
2 He said his apples were a little bigger, his grapes were much sweeter, his strawberries were a lot fresher, and his things were the best.

1 a v, b vi, c iv, d i, e ii, f vii, g iii.
2 a yí jiàn bái chènyī, b yí jiàn huáng dàyī, c yì tào lán xīfú, d yì tiáo lǜ qúnzi, e yì shuāng hēi xié, f yì tiáo hóng kùzi.
3 Xiǎo Cài is wearing a white shirt, a blue skirt, and a pair of red leather shoes. Xiǎo Zhào is wearing a blue silk shirt, black trousers, and green cloth shoes. Lǎo Fāng is wearing a black suit, a white shirt, and a pair of black leather shoes.
4 a Lǎo Mǎ chuān yì shuāng hēi píxié、yí jiàn lán chènyī. b Xiǎo Qián chuān yí jiàn hóng chènyī、(yì tiáo) hēi kùzi、yì shuāng bùxié. c Liú xiānsheng chuān yí tào huī xīfú、huáng chènyī、zōng píxié.
5 a Lǐ xiānsheng Déwén (*German*) shuō-de fēicháng hǎo. b Zhāng tàitai jiàqī guò-de bú tài hǎo. c Cháo xiǎojie Yīngwén xué-de kuài-jíle. d Mǎlì yòng kuàizi yòng-de bù zěnmeyàng. e Hēnglì shuō Rìyǔ shuō-de hěn qīngchu.
6 a Zhāng Tóng de diànshì méi yǒu Mǎ Fēng de diànshì guì, yě méi yǒu Mǎ Fēng de diànshì dà. b Mǎ Fēng méi yǒu Zhāng Tóng gāo. Zhāng Tóng méi yǒu Mǎ Fēng dà, yě méi yǒu tā zhòng. c Mǎ Fēng de zì méi yǒu Zhāng Tóng de zì qīngchu.

Quick review

a Nǐde Yīngwén shuō-de zhēn hǎo.
b Zhè jiàn chènyī yǒu yìdiǎnr xiǎo.
c Nǐde jiàqī guò-de zěnmeyàng?
d Yīnggélán bǐ Ài'ěrlán dà.
e Déguó méi yǒu Fǎguó dà.

Unit 9

Let's try

1 a Jiǔshíjiǔ kuài. b Sān zhāng zúqiú piào.
2 a Fǎguó de dōngxi bǐ Yīngguó de (dōngxi) guì. Fǎguó de dōngxi méi yǒu Yīngguó de (dīngxi) guì. Fǎguó de dōngxi gēn Yīngguó de (dōngxi) yíyàng guì. b Nǎli, nǎli, shuō-de bù hǎo. (or Xièxie.)

2 **Recording:** First walk southwards. When you get to East Sea Road, turn east. Take the eastbound bus for two stops and you will find the cinema on the south side of the road opposite the department store. The answer is F.
3 (On foot) Wǎng xī zǒu, guò liǎng ge lùkǒu. Fàndiàn jiù zài lù de běibianr. (By bus) Zuò wàng xī kāi de chē. Zuò liǎng zhàn. Fàndiàn jiù zài lù de běibianr.
4 B = school; C = shop; D = Donghai Park; E = Bank of China.
8 a Fǎguó hé Yìdàlì. b Sì tiān. c Gēn tāde Fǎguó péngyou. Tāmen kāi chē qù. d Yí gè xīngqī. e Zuò fēijī. f Kāi chē. **Recording:** Mr White is going on holiday soon. He is going to two places. He'll first go from London to Paris by train. He plans to stay in Paris for four days. After that he and his French friend will drive to Italy. They will stay in Italy for a week. Lastly he will fly back to London from Italy. His friend will drive back to France.

Quick review

a Qù Zhōngguó Yínháng zěnme zǒu?
b Zuò shí lù (gōnggòng) qìchē. c Zuò wǔ zhàn.
d Wǒde péngyou méi (yǒu) qù-guo Zhōngguó.
e Kuài (yào) xià yǔ le.

Unit 10

Let's try

1 a Wǒ xiān zuò fēijī qù Xiānggǎng. Zài nàr zhù liǎng tiān. b Ránhòu (cóng Xiānggǎng) zuò huǒchē qù Shànghǎi. c Wǒ dǎsuàn bāyuè shí hào (cóng Shànghǎi) zuò fēijī qù Běijīng.
2 Nǐ qù-guo Shànghǎi ma? Nǐ qù-guo Shànghǎi méi you?

1 **Recording:** Mr. Jones ordered **yúxiāng ròusī** (fish flavoured shredded meat), **zhàcài tāng** (preserved vegetable soup) and **Wǔxīng píjiǔ** (Fivestar beer).

2 **a** yì wǎn chǎomiàn, **b** sì píng pútáojiǔ, **c** wǔ tīng kěkǒukělè, **d** liù zhī yān, **e** liǎng wǎn tāng, **f** sān zhāng piào.

4 **a** Fúwùyuán, qǐng jié zhàng. **b** Chī-hǎo le. Xièxie. **c** Nǐ suàn-cuò le ba. **d** Méi guānxi.

5 **a** bù, **b** méi, **c** méi, **d** bù.

Halfway review

1 1066, 1462, 1798, 1914, 1945, 2000, 2008.

2 **a** Tāmen shì bu shì jiěmèi? Tāmen shì jiěmèi ma? **b** Tāde chǎomiàn hǎochī bu hǎochī? Tāde chǎomiàn hǎochī ma? **c** Míngtiān tā tàitai qù bu qù mǎi dōngxi? Míngtiān tā tàitai qù mǎi dōngxi ma? **d** Nǐ rènshi bu rènshi tā? Nǐ bú rènshi tā ma? **e** Xiǎo Lǐ yǒu mei yǒu yì tiáo hóng kùzi? Xiǎo Lǐ yǒu yì tiáo hóng kùzi ma?

3 **a** Y, **b** X, **c** Y, **d** X.

4 **a** = v, **b** = i, **c** = ii, **d** = vi, **e** = iii, **f** = iv

5 **a** Méi qù-guo. **b** Qù Měiguó le. **c** Huì shuō. **d** Qù-guo. **e** Bù chōu le. **f** Chī-guo. **g** Qù Zhōngguó hé Rìběn.

Unit 11

1 **a** 2, **b** 6, **c** 10, **d** 5, **e** 11, **f** 24, **g** 83, **h** 69, **i** 57, **j** 36.

2 **a** 三 **b** 八 **c** 十 **d** 十五 **e** 四十二 **f** 九十八 **g** 六十七

3 **a** 天 **b** 三 **c** 六 **d** 四

4 **a** 天／日, **b** 期 **c** 期 **d** 星 **e** 星

5 **a** 3 November, **b** 16 June **c** 11 July **d** 14 October **e** 29 August

6 **a** 十二月二十五日 **b** 三月八日

7 **a** 2008, **b** 1937 **c** 1949 **d** 1995 **e** 1642

8 **a** 9:15, **b** 12:25, **c** 6:30 **d** 3:50, **e** 7:45

9 **a** 六点二十分, **b** 差一刻十二点, (十一点三刻, 十二点差一刻) **c** 十点十分, **d** 四点四十八分, **e** 七点半.

Unit 12

1 **a** lǚguǎn, lǚdiàn, fàndiàn, bīnguǎn. **b** Lǚ means *travel*. Diàn and **guǎn** both mean *house*. Fàn means *food*. Bīn means *guest*. **c** No. **d** It says there are all kinds of reasons. **e** Chinese people can stay in any hotel.

2 **a** Duì. **b** Bú duì. **c** Duì. **d** Duì (UK); Bú duì (USA). **e** Duì.

3 **a** Wǒ shì sān-líng-yāo fángjiān de (*your name*). Wǒde fángjiān tài xiǎo le. Néng bu néng huàn yì jiān dà yìdiǎn de?

b Shuāngrén fángjiān duōshao qián yì tiān? **c** Tài guì le. Hái yǒu, wǒde fángjiān lǐ zěnme méi yǒu diànshì? **d** Zúqiú sài bàn ge xiǎoshí yǐhòu jiù kāishǐ le!

4 **a** Nǐ néng bu néng gěi wǒ sòng lái yìdiǎnr chī de/ yìdiǎnr hē de/ yì bēi chá, jiā nǎi, bù jiā táng/ liǎng ge sānmíngzhì, yí ge nǎilào de, yí ge huǒtuǐ de? **b** Nǐ néng bu néng dǎ diànhuà jiàoxǐng wǒ/ gěi wǒ dǎ diànhuà/ gěi wǒ mǎi yì píng jiǔ/ zài gěi wǒ yì tiáo tǎnzi/ yì juǎn wèishēngzhǐ/ yí kuài dà yìdiǎnr de xiāngzào/ yí ge rèshuǐpíng?

5 **a** Dōngfāng, **b** pretty good, **c** not at all good, **d** not polite, **e** three times.

6 **a** Méi you. Wǒ xīwàng nǐmen hái yǒu fángjiān. **b** Yì jiān shuāngrén fángjiān, yì jiān dānrén fāngjiān. **c** Sān、 sì tiān. Wǒ míngtiān gàosu nǐ wǒmen shénme shíhou zǒu, kěyǐ ma? **d** Bù, wǒmen yǐjīng chī le.

Quick review

a Bāo zǎocān ma?
b Wǔfàn shì jǐ diǎn? Wǔfàn shì shénme shíhou?
c Fángjiān lǐ yǒu diànshì ma?
d Nǐmen yǒu méi yǒu (yì jiān) dà yìdiānr de dānrén fángjiān?
e Yì tiān/wǎnshang duōshao qián?

Unit 13

1 **a** ruǎnwò, **b** yìngzuò, **c** ruǎnzuò, **d** yìngwò, **e** tóuděng, **f** èrděng, **g** passenger train, **h** special express, **i** train, **j** express, **k** express.

2 **a** trains no. 13, no. 21 and no. 161. **b** tèkuài, **c** No. **d** sānbǎi wǔshíyī cì, *or* sān-wǔ-yāo cì, **e** No.

3 Qǐng wèn, hái yǒu: **a** jīntiān wǎnshang de diànyǐng piào, **b** shíyuè sì hào de fēijī piào, **c** yāo-wǔ-sān cì de huǒchē piào, **d** qù Tiānjīn de huǒchē piào. Wǒ mǎi: **e** sān zhāng jīntiān wǎnshang de diànyǐng piào, **f** sì zhāng shíyuè sì hào de fēijī piào, **g** wǔ zhāng yāo-wǔ-sān cì de huǒchē piào, **h** liù zhāng qù Tiānjīn de huǒchē piào.

4 **a** Yǒu liǎng zhǒng (huǒchē) piào: tóuděng hé èrděng. **b** Tóuděng piào bǐ èrděng piào guì. **c** Zài Yīngguó huǒchē yòu kuài yòu shūfu. or Yīngguó de huǒchē yòu kuài yòu shūfu.

6 **a** Nǐ néng bu néng gàosu wǒ tā zhù nǎr? **b** Nǐ néng bu néng gàosu wǒ nǐde diànhuà hàomǎ? **c** Nǐ néng bu néng gàosu wǒ tā nǚ'ér duō dà le? **d** Nǐ néng bu néng gàosu wǒ tāmen yào zhù duō cháng shíjiān?

7 a Zuò huǒchē qù Xī'ān duōshao qiān? b Cóng Lúndūn dào Shànghǎi zuò fēijī děi duō cháng shíjiān? c Zuò chūzūchē qù Hépíng Bīnguǎn děi duōshao qián? d Cóng Rìběn dào Zhōngguó zuò chuán yào/děi duō cháng shíjiān?

Quick review

a = iii, b = iv, c = v, d = vii, e = ii, f = i, g = vi.

The new word is **chángtú qìchē** (*coach*).

Unit 14

1 a Zhōngguó-rén qǐ-de hěn zǎo ma? b Zǎoshang nǐ qù nǎr? c Lǎo rén zài gōngyuán zuò shénme? d Nǐ(men) zài hú lǐ yóuyǒng ma?

3 a Wǒ xǐhuan zuò huǒchē, gèng xǐhuan zuò fēijī, zuì xǐhuan zuò chuán. b Wǒ bù xǐhuan qí mǎ, gèng bù xǐhuan qí zìxíngchē, zuì bu xǐhuan qí mótuóchē. c Wǒ bù xǐhuan zuò chūzūchē, gèng bù xǐhuan zuò dìtiě, zuì bù xǐhuan zuò gōnggòng qìchē. d Wǒ xǐhuan kàn jīngjù, gèng xǐhuan kàn diànshì, zuì xǐhuan kàn diànyǐng. e Wǒ xǐhuan tīng liúxíng yīnyuè, gèng xǐhuan tīng xiàndài yīnyuè, zuì xǐhuan tīng gǔdiǎn yīnyuè.

4 qiūtiān,/lǚxíng,/ hái,/ méi,/ háishi,/ yòu,/ yòu,/ piányi,/ zìyóu,/ bù,/ bàn,/ dìng/mǎi,/ zhǎo/ dìng.

5 a Xiǎo Wáng, hǎo jiǔ bú jiàn. b Nǐ zuìjìn zài zuò shénme? c Nǐ jié hūn le ma? d Nǐ zài děng shéi? e Wǒ qù yóuyǒng. f Zàijiàn!

6 A yì pái èrshíwǔ hào; èr pái wǔ hào; sān pái èrshíliù hào. B èrshísì pái èrshísì hào; èrshíwǔ pái sì hào; èrshíliù pái èrshísān hào. C Lóushàng shíyī pái liù hào; lóushàng shí'èr pái èrshíbā hào; lóushàng shísān pái èrshíyī hào.

7 a A pái shí'èr hào, b J pái sānshíqī hào, c lóushàng F pái sìshí hào, d K pái èr hào.

8 a Shíyuè èrshíwǔ hào xīngqīliù wǎnshang liù diǎn、bā diǎn hé shí diǎn. Diànyǐng jiào (is called) 《Dōngtiān》. Diànyǐng piào wǔ bàng、liù bàng wǔ yì zhāng. b Shíyuè èrshíwǔ hào xīngqīliù wǎnshang qī diǎn yí kè. Huàjù jiào 《Wǒmen niánqīng de shíhou》. Huàjù piào yì zhāng shí bàng、shí'èr bàng wǔ. c Shíyuè èrshíliù hào xīngqītiān wǎnshang qī diǎn bàn. Bāléi 《Tiān'é Hú》. Piào yì zhāng shí'èr bàng、shíbā bàng hé èrshíwǔ bàng. d Shíyuè èrshíliù hào xīngqīrì wǎnshang bā diǎn. Gējù 《Kǎmén》. Yì zhāng piào shíliù bàng、èrshísì bàng hé sānshí bàng.

Quick review

a Go to see a film. b No, because she had already seen it.
c Chinese music or Western music. d No.
e To go dancing.

Unit 15

1 a Nǐ kěyǐ zài yóujú cún qián、qǔ qián. b Yīngguó de yóujú
xīngqīliù xiàwǔ hé xīngqītiān yìbān bù kāi mén. c Zài
Yīngguó xìntǒng shì hóngsè de, bú shì lǜsè de. d Zài Yīngguó
bù kěyǐ zài yóujú dǎ chángtú diànhuà.
2 a Zhè ge bāoguǒ jì dào Měiguó. b Dōu shì shū. c Yào
duōshao/jǐ tiān? d Wǒ xiǎng mǎi míngxìnpiàn. Duōshao
qián yí tào? e Wǒ yào yí tào dà de, liǎng tào xiǎo de. f Gěi
nín liǎng/èr bǎi kuài. g Xièxie. Zàijiàn.
3 a Qǐng wèn, kěyǐ zài zhèr dǎ (ge) diànhuà ma? Qǐng wèn,
kěyǐ zài zhèr jì (ge) bāoguǒ ma? Qǐng wèn, kěyǐ zài zhèr fā
(ge) e-mail (diànzǐ yóujiàn) ma? b Qǐng gěi wǒ nǐde diànhuà
hàomǎ. Qǐng gěi wǒ tāmende wǎngzhǐ. Qǐng gěi wǒ nǐde
hùzhào. Qǐng gěi wǒ tāmende dìzhǐ. c Qǐng dào nèibiān
huàn qián. Qǐng dào wàibiān dǎ diànhuà.
4 a Hépíng Bīnguǎn. b Bái Huá xiānsheng. c There is no such
extension number. d The caller had got the number wrong.
5 a Bú duì. b Duì. c Duì. d Bú duì.
6 a Qǐng wèn, jīntiān yīngbàng hé rénmínbì de duìhuànlǜ
shì duōshao? b Qǐng wèn, jīntiān měiyuán hé rénmínbì de
duìhuànlǜ shì duōshao? c Qǐng wèn, jīntiān gǎngbì hé
rénmínbì de duìhuànlǜ shì duōshao? d Qǐng wèn, jīntiān
ōuyuán hé rénmínbì de duìhuànlǜ shì duōshao?
7 a yìbǎi bǐ bābǎi wǔshí; yìbǎi měiyuán huàn bābǎi wǔshí
yuán. b yìbǎi bǐ yìbǎi líng bā; yìbǎi gǎngbì huàn yìbǎi líng
bā yuán. c yìbǎi bǐ yìqiān sānbǎi èrshí; yìbǎi yīngbàng huàn
yìqiān sānbǎi èrshí yuán. d yìbǎi bǐ jiǔbǎi yīshí; yìbǎi ōuyuán
huàn jiǔbǎi yīshí yuán.
8 a Wǒ xiǎng huàn yìbǎi yīngbàng de rénmínbì. b Wǒ xiǎng
huàn èrbǎi měiyuán de rénmínbì. c Wǒ xiǎng huàn wǔbǎi
gǎngbì de rénmínbì. d Wǒ xiǎng huàn liùwàn rìyuán de
rénmínbì. e Wǒ xiǎng huàn sìbǎi ōuyuán de rénmínbì.

Quick review

a Zhèi zhāng míngxìnpiàn jì dào Yīngguó duōshao qián?
b Wǒ xiǎng mǎi yí tào yóupiào.
c Jīntiān yīngbàng hé rénmínbì de duìhuànlǜ shì duōshao?

d Wǒ xiǎng huàn yìbǎi wǔshí yīngbàng de rénmínbì.

e Wǒde fēnjī shì èr-yāo-yāo-wǔ.

Unit 16

1 **a** hē jiǔ, chī rè fàn、rè cài, hē tāng, **b** hē tāng, chī zhèngcān, chī shuǐguǒ, **c** wǎn/kuàizi, **d** dāochā/pánzi, **e** Zhōngguó-rén.

2 **a** Zhè shì gěi nǐ de (yì hé) qiǎokèlì. Zhè hé qiǎokèlì shì gěi nǐ de. **b** Zhè shì gěi nǐ de (yì píng) jiǔ. Zhè píng jiǔ shì gěi nǐ de. **c** Zhè shì gěi nǐ de (liǎng zhāng) diànyǐng piào. Zhè liǎng zhāng diànyǐng piào shì gěi nǐ de. **d** Zhè shì gěi nǐ de (yì hé) lǜ chá. Zhè hé lǜ chá shì gěi nǐ de. **e** Zhè shì gěi nǐ de (yì běn) shū. Zhè běn shū shì gěi nǐ de.

3 **a** Zhè shì gěi wǒ jiějie de (yì hé) qiǎokèlì. Zhè hé qiǎokèlì shì gěi wǒ jiějie de. **b** Zhè shì gěi tā tàitai de (yì hé) lǜ chá. Zhè hé lǜ chá shì gěi tā tàitai de. **c** Zhè shì gěi tā shūshu de (yì běn) shū. Zhè běn shū shì gěi tā shūshu de. **d** Zhè shì gěi tā nán péngyou de (yì píng) jiǔ. Zhè píng jiǔ shì gěi tā nán péngyou de. **e** Zhè shì gěi nǐmende péngyou de (liǎng zhāng) diànyǐng piào. Zhè liǎng zhāng diànyǐng piào shì gěi nǐmende péngyou de. **f** Zhè shì gěi tāmen gōngsī de (yì fú) huà. Zhè fú huà shì gěi tāmen gōngsī de.

4 **a** Gān bēi! **b** Wǒ chī-bu-xià le. **c** Zhēn xiāng a! **d** Wǒ zìjǐ lái. **e** Zhù nǐ wànshì rúyì!

5 **a** Wǒ gāi zǒu le. **b** Hái zǎo ne. Zài zuò yìhuǐr ba. **c** Gěi nǐmen tiān máfan le. **d** Méi shénme (máfan). **e** Bú yòng le. Qǐng huí qù ba. **f** Lùshang xiǎoxīn. **g** Màn zǒu. Màn zǒu.

6 **a** = iii, **b** = i, **c** = v, **d** = ii, **e** = vi, **f** = iv.

Quick review

a Wishing you good health! To your good health!

b Wishing you a happy life!

c Wishing you every happiness!

d May your work go smoothly/well!

e Wishing you success! To your success!

f To our friendship!

g To our co-operation!

Unit 17

1 **a** Duì. **b** Duì. **c** Duì. **d** Bú duì.

2 **a** Wǒ tóu téng. **b** Wǒ yǒu (yì) diǎnr késou. **c** Wǒ yě juéde shì gǎnmào. **d** Wǒ méi chī-guo Zhōngyào. Zhōngyào yǒu xiào ma? **e** Hǎo ba. (Xíng.) Wǒ shìshi ba.

3 **a** before/twice/one ball, **b** after/4 times/3 tablets, **c** one hour after meal/3 times/one spoonful, **d** twice (early morning and evening)/2–3 tablets.

4 **a** quite a few, **b** all sorts of, **c** headaches, **d** was scared.

6 **a** = iv, **b** = v, **c** = i, **d** = iii, **e** = vi, **f** = ii.

Quick review

a Nǐn nǎr bù shūfu?   **b** Wǒ xiǎng shìshi zhēnjiǔ.
c Wǒ juéde wǒ gǎnmào le.   **d** Wǒ méi chī-guo Zhōngyào.
e Wǒ yǒu shíhou tóu téng.

Unit 18

1 **a** Zài Yīngguó kāi chē hé qí zìxíngchē dōu zǒu lù de zuǒbiān.
b Zhè gēn zài Rìběn hé Ài'ěrlán yíyàng, gēn zài Ōuzhōu dàlù bù yíyàng. **c** Měiguó shì shìjiè shàng qìchē zuì duō de guójiā.
d Zài Xīfāng zū qìchē bù nán.

2 **a** Wǒ xiǎng zū yí liàng chē. **b** Yǒu. Shì Yīngguó de (jiàzhào).
c Wǒ xiǎng zū yí liàng xiǎo de (*or*) xiǎo chē. **d** Kěyǐ. **e** Liǎng tiān. **f** Nǐmen shōu bu shōu xìnyòng kǎ?

3 **a** Kāi chē shàng bān yào/děi yí ge xiǎoshí. **b** Bǔ chēdài yào/děi duōshao qián? **c** Zuò gōnggòng qìchē dào Xiāngshān zěnme qù? **d** Zū yí liàng zìxíngchē yào/děi sānshí kuài.

4 **a** Bú duì. **b** Duì. **c** Duì. **d** Duì. **e** Duì. **f** Bú duì. **g** Bú duì.

5 **a** He'd lost his bag. **b** His passport, wallet, credit card, some money, and a small camera. **c** More than 400 yuan and 200 US dollars. **d** Yulong Hotel. **e** Report its loss to his Embassy.
f Inform him once they'd got any news.

6 **a** Tāde chēdài huài le. **b** Tāde chē huài le. **c** Tāde bāo diū le. **d** Tāmen zhuàng chē le. **e** Tā tóu téng. **f** Tāde chē dēng huài le.

Quick review

a Zhēn dǎoméi!
b Bú shì wǒde cuò.
c Wǒ xiǎng tāmen yīnggāi qù zhǎo jǐngchá.
d Wǒde xìnyòng kǎ diū le.
e Wǒde zìxíngchē huài le. Nín néng bu néng bāng wǒ kàn(yi)kan?

Unit 19

1 **a** = iv, **b** = vi, **c** = i, **d** = vii, **e** = iii, **f** = v, **g** = ii.

2 **a** Hànzú, Hànyǔ; **b** fāngyán, kǒuyīn; **c** Guóyǔ, Huáyǔ;
d yǔyán, Hànyǔ.

3 **a** Fluent with good pronunciation and tones. **b** Three years.
   c Not good (according to himself). **d** Six years. **e** Her learning
   method(s). **f** Her husband.
4 **a** Hánguó, pípa, èrhú; **b** Yīngguó, shǎoshù mínzú; **c** Rìběn,
   Zhōngguó jīngjì; **d** fānyì, jìzhě; **e** wénxué, zhéxué, wénxué,
   zhéxué.
6 **a** Wǒ huì shuō **Déwén** (hé **Fǎwén**). **b** Wǒde Rìyǔ búcuò *or*
   Wǒde **Yìdàlìyǔ** shuō-de bú tài **liúlì**. **c** Wǒ huì shuō yìdiǎnr
   Éyǔ. **d** Wǒ shuō **Zhōngwén** (shuō-de) yǒu (yìdiǎnr) Měiguó
   kǒuyīn. **e** **Fǎyǔ** de yǔyīn hěn nán.

Quick review

a Nǐ juéde Yīngwén (de) yǔyīn nán ma?
b Wǒ zhǐ huì xiě jǐ ge/yìxiē Hànzì.
c Wǒ huì shuō yìdiǎnr Zhōngwén, kěshì wǒ juéde shēngdiào
     hěn nán.
d Nǐ hěn qiānxū. (Nǐ tài qiānxū le.)
e Wǒ juéde tāde kǒuyīn hěn nán dǒng.
f Nǐde Yīngyǔ/Fǎyǔ/Déyǔ búcuò.
g Nǐ guòjiǎng le.

Unit 20

1 **a** sānyuè, wǔyuè **b** liùyuè、qīyuè、bāyuè **c** jiǔyuè、shíyuè、
   shíyīyuè **d** shí'èryuè, èryuè.
3 **a** Bú duì. **b** Duì. **c** Bú duì. **d** Duì. **e** Bú duì.
5 **a** = v, **b** = iv, **c** = ii, **d** = i, **e** = iii.
7 **a** huǒchē; **b** huǒchē, fēijī; **c** huǒchē, chángtú qìchē; **d** fēijī,
   huǒchē; **e** fēijī.
8 **a** Tā míngtiān zuò huǒchē qù Shànghǎi. **b** Wǒde péngyou
   zuò gōnggòng qìchē lái wǒ jiā. **c** Wǒ bù qí zìxíngchē qù
   gōngyuán. **d** Tāmen chángcháng kāi/zuò chē qù mǎi dōngxi.
   e Wǒ xiànzài zuò dìtiě huí jiā.
9 **a** Wǒ xiǎng qù Xiānggǎng hé Àomén. **b** Wǒ (xiān) zuò fēijī
   qù Xiānggǎng, zài zuò chuán qù Àomén. **c** Nàr/nàli bāyuè
   hěn rè. **d** Yǒu shíhou xià yū. **e** Wǒ hái méi juédìng(ne).
10 **a** Bú shì. **b** Shì. **c** Hěn duǎn yě hěn nuǎnhuo, kěshì
   chángcháng guā fēng. **d** Bú shì. **e** Qiūtiān bù lěng yě bú rè.
   Qíngtiān duō, yīntiān shǎo. Bù cháng guā fēng, yě hěn shǎo
   xià yǔ.

Quick review

a Zuótiān shàngwǔ xià yǔ le, qìwēn èrshí dù.
b Zuótiān wǎnshang guā fēng le, qìwēn wǔ dù.

c Jīntiān shàngwǔ shì qíngtiān, qìwēn shí'èr dù.
d Jīntiān xiàwǔ yǒu xiǎo yǔ, qìwēn shíbā dù.
e Míngtiān yīntiān, qìwēn sān dù.
f Xià xīngqīyī yǒu/xià xuě, qìwēn líng dù.

Unit 21

1 a Yuè lái yuè duō de Zhōngguó-rén lái Yīngguó xuéxí.
b Tāmen hěn duō rén duì Yīngguó de lìshǐ hé wénhuà yǒu
xìngqu. c Měi nián hěn duō wàiguó xuésheng lái Yīngguó
xuéxí Yīngwén. d Yuè lái yuè duō de Ōuzhōu gōngsī xiǎng
zài Zhōngguó kuòdà shēngyi.
5 a Liǎng ge xīngqī. b Wǒ qù le Běijīng、Shànghǎi hé Guìlín.
c Shànghǎi fāzhǎn-de hěn kuài. d Běijīng yǒu hěn duō
gōngyuán. Wǒ hěn xǐhuan tāmen. e Guìlín de fēngjǐng měi-
jíle.
6 a Bú duì. b Bú duì. c Duì. d Bú duì.

Final review

1 a rè b lǎo c pàng d chǎo e guì f wēixiǎn g jìn h nuǎn(huo)
i wǎn j ruǎn k qián l yǐhòu m shàng n yòu o nán p xīběi.
2 a = iv, b = iii, c = v, d = i, e = ii.
3 a mobile, b computer, c advertise/advertisement, d video
recorder, e job guaranteed for life, f thermos flask, g aerial,
antenna.
4 a 8:30pm the day before yesterday b 1147 c 9764 3772
d 2437 8910 e About a week f Next Thursday g 12:15pm
i 7:10am on the 17th.
Recording: Ānní, wǒ shì Cài Míng. Wǒ yǐjing dào le
Guǎngzhōu. Wǒ shì qiántiān wǎnshang bā diǎn bàn dào
de. Wǒ xiànzài zhù zài Báiyún Bīnguǎn. Wǒ de fángjiān shì
yāo-yāo-sì-qī. Qǐng nǐ gěi wǒ dǎ ge diànhuà. Bīnguǎn de
diànhuà shì jiǔ-qī-liù-sì sān-qī-qī-èr. Yàoshi wǒ bú zài
fángjiān lǐ, qǐng nǐ dǎ wǒ de shǒujī. Wǒ de shǒujī hàomǎ shì
èr-sì-sān-qī bā-jiǔ-yāo-líng. Wǒ huì zài Guǎngzhōu zhù
chàbuduō yí ge xīngqī. Xià xīngqīsì zhōngwǔ shí'èr diǎn yí
kè zuò huǒchē qù Shēnzhèn. Wǒ zài Shēnzhèn zhù liǎng tiān,
ránhòu qù Xiānggǎng, shíqī hào zǎoshang qī diǎn shí fēn zuò
fēijī huí Lúndūn.
5 a Wǒ chī-bu-guàn là de (cài). b Nǐ duì gǔdiǎn yīnyuè háishi
duì liúxíng yīnyuè yǒu/gǎn xìngqu? c Yuè lái yuè duō de rén
qù wàiguó dù jià. d Nǐ duì Yīngguó de yìnxiàng zěnmeyàng?
e Nǐ duì shènme (zuì) mǎnyì, shénme (zuì) bù mǎnyì? f Zhù
nǐ shēngrì kuàilè!

vocabulary

Chinese–English

The number after each vocabulary item indicates the unit in which it first appears.

ài *love; to love, to like very much* **16**

Ài'ěrlán *Ireland* **3**

àiren (sometimes used in the People's Republic) *husband/wife* **10**

ānjìng *quiet* **12**

ānpái *arrangement, to arrange* **20**

ānquán *safe* **9**

Àolínpīkè *Olympic* **14**

Àolínpīkè *Olympic Games* **14** Yùndònghuì

Àomén *Macao* **9**

ba (particle indicating suggestion) **3**

bàba *dad, father* **4**

bǎi *hundred* **7**

báijiǔ *strong alcohol* **16**

bái(sè) (de) *white* **7**

báitiān *daytime* **20**

bàn *half* **5**

bàn *to handle* **14**

bāng *to help* **5**

bàng *excellent* **14**

bāo *bag* **18**

bāo *to include; to make (jiǎozi)* **21**

bāoguǒ *parcel* **15**

bēi *a cup of; cup* **10**

běi *north* **9**

běifāng *the north* **14**

bǐ *compared to* **6**

biān *side* **9**

biǎo *form* **12**

biǎoyǎn *show, performance; to act/to perform* **14**

bié *don't* **9**

biérén *other/another person* **18**

biéde *other* **12**

bǐjiào *relatively* **12**

bǐjiào xǐhuan *to prefer* **20**

bìng *illness* **17**

bīngqílín *ice-cream* **10**

bìngrén *patient* **17**

bù *not* **1**

bǔ chēdài *to mend a tyre* **18**

bú kèqi *you are welcome* **4**

bú xiàng *not look it* **4**

bú xiè *not at all* **17**

bù xíng *not that good* **19**

bú yòng xiè *not at all*
(lit. *no need thank*) **1**

bù zěnmeyàng *not so good* **8**

búcuò *pretty good, not bad* **7**

búguò *but, however* **12**

bùtóng de *different* **16**

cái *not . . . until, only then* **7**

cài *dish* **10**

càidān *menu* **10**

cānjiā *to attend* **17**

cāntīng *restaurant, canteen* **12**

cǎoméi *strawberry* **7**

cèsuǒ *toilet* **12**

chá *to look up (something)* **15**

chá *tea* **16**

chà *lacking, short of* **5**

chàbuduō *similar* (lit. *different not much*) **15**

cháng *long* **20**

chàng (gē) *to sing (a song)* **14**

chàng jīngjù *to sing Peking opera* **14**

cháng(chang) *to taste* **16**

chángcháng *often* **16**

Chángchéng *the Great Wall* **10**

chángshòu (miàn) *long life (noodles)* **21**

chángtú *long distance* **15**

chángtú qìchē *coach* **18**

chǎo *noisy* **12**

chǎomiàn *stir-fried noodles* **10**

chāozhòng le *exceeded the weight limit* **15**

chē *vehicle (bus, bike, car)* **6**

chēdài *tyre* **18**

chèng *scales* **15**

chéng lǐ *in the city, in urban areas* **18**

chénggōng *success, successful* **16**

chéngshì *city* **18**

chēzhàn *bus/train stop or station* **9**

chī *to eat* **10**

chī (yào) *to take (medicine)* **17**

chī-bǎo le *to eat one's fill* **10**

chī de *something to eat* **12**

chī fàn *to eat, eating* **16**

chī sù *to be vegetarian* **10**

chōu (yān) *to smoke (a cigarette)* **10**

chuán *ship, boat* **9**

chuánzhēn *fax* **15**

chúfáng *kitchen* **16**

chūntiān *spring* **20**

Chūnjié *the Spring Festival, Chinese New Year* **5**

chūzū (qì)chē *taxi* **13**

cí *word* **12**

cì *measure word for trains* **13**

cì *time, occasion* **12**

cóng *from* **9**

cónglái *ever* **20**

cōngming *clever* **19**

cún qián *to deposit money* **15**

cuò *fault* **18**

dà *big, old* **4**

dǎ diànhuà *to telephone* **12**

dǎ tàijíquán *to do Tai Chi* **6**

dàbùfen *majority* 16

dàgài *approximately* 13

dàibiǎotuán *delegation* 20

dàjiā *everyone* 16

dāng *to be; to work/to act as* 19

dāngrán *of course* 2

dānrén/shuāngrén fángjiān *single/double room* 12

dānwèi *work unit* 17

dànyuànrúcǐ *I hope so* (four-character phrase) 14

dào *to; to arrive, to go to* 5, 7

dāochā *knife and fork* 16

dǎ pái *to play cards* 14

dàshǐguǎn *embassy* 18

dǎsuàn *to plan* 9

dàxiǎo *size* 8

dàxué *university* 21

de *possessive indicator* 2

. . . de shíhou (*the time*) *when* . . . 12

. . . deduō *much (more)* . . . 7

Déguó *Germany* 3

děi *to need, must; it takes* 13

dēng *lights* 18

děng *to wait* 13

děngděng *etc.* 14

dì *for ordinal numbers* 5

diǎn *o'clock* 5

diǎn *to count* 15

diànchē *tram* (lit. *electric vehicle*) 18

diànhuà *telephone* 3

diànshì *television* 9

diànyǐng *film, movie* 6

diànzǐ yóujiàn *e-mail* (*electronic mail*) 15

dìdi *younger brother* 4

dìfang *place* 9

dìng *to book* (a ticket) 6

dìqū *district* 15

dìtiě *underground/ subway* 18

diū *to lose* 18

dōng *east* 9

dǒng *to understand* 21

Dōngnányà *South-East Asia* 19

dǒngshìzhǎng *managing director* 16

dōngtiān *winter* 14

dōngxi *thing, object* 6

dōu *all, both* 5

dòufu *beancurd, tofu* 10

dù *degree* (°C) 20

dǔ chē (*to be in a*) *traffic jam* 18

dù jià *to take a holiday* 9

duì *yes, correct* 3

duì *to, for* 10

duìbuqǐ *excuse me/I'm sorry* 1

duìfu *to cope with* 18

duìhuànlǜ *exchange rate* 15

duìmiàn *opposite* 9

duō *many, more* 10

. . . duōle *much (more)* 7

duōshao? *how much, how many, what's the number of?* 3

duō cháng? *how long?* 7

duō yuǎn? *how far?* 7

dùzi *tummy, stomach* 17

è *hungry* 10

Éguó-rén *Russian* (*person*) 19

èrděng *second-class* (ticket) 13

èrhú *a two-stringed musical instrument* 19

érzi *son* 4

fā *to send* (a fax, e-mail etc.) **15**
fā chuánzhēn *to send a fax* **15**
fā fēng *mad* **9**
fādá *developed* **20**
Fǎguó *France* **3**
fàn *food, meal* **12**
fàn hòu *after meals* **17**
fàn qián *before meals* **17**
fàndiàn *hotel* **3**
fàng *to put* **15**
fāngbiàn *convenient* **14**
fāngfǎ *method* **19**
fángjiān *room* **3**
fǎngwèn *visit; to visit* (formal) **16**
fāngyán *dialect* **19**
fānyì *interpreter, translator* **19**
fǎnzheng *no way, in any case* **9**
fāzhǎn *to develop* **21**
fēicháng *extremely* **8**
fēijī *plane* **3**
fēn(zhōng) *minute* **5**
fēnchéng *to divide/to be divided into* **17**
fēnháng *branch* (of a bank) **15**
fēng *measure word for letters* **15**
fēng *wind* **20**
fēngjǐng *scenery* **20**
fèngzhǎo *chicken feet* **16**
fù qián *pay (money)* **10**
fù zhàng *to pay bills* **15**
fūren *wife* (formal), *madam* **16**
fúwù *service* **12**
fúwùtái *reception* **12**
fúwùyuán *assistant, housestaff* **6**

fúyòng fāngfǎ *instruction* (for taking medicine) **17**

gān bēi! *cheers!* **16**
gānjìng *clean* **10**
gǎnmào *to have a cold* **17**
gàosu *to tell* **12**
gāoxìng *happy* **18**
gè *measure word* **4**
gēge *elder brother* **4**
gěi *for; to give* **6**
gēn *and, with, to follow* **6**
gèng *even more* **8**
gōnggòng qìchē *bus* (lit. *public together steam vehicle*) **18**
gōngjīn *kilogram* **7**
gōngsī *company* **16**
gōngyuán *park* **14**
gōngzuò *to work, work* **20**
guā fēng *windy* (lit. *blow wind*) **20**
guǎi *to turn* **18**
guān (mén) *to close* (door) **5**
guānfāng *official* **19**
Guǎngdōng *Canton* (province) **3**
guāngpán *CD* **15**
guì *expensive; honourable* **2**
guò *to pass, spend* (of time) **8**
-guo *have ever done* (verbal, suffix) **9**
guójì *international* **15**
guójiā *country* **18**
guòjiǎng *to exaggerate, to flatter* **19**
guóyǔ *national language* **19**

hái *still* 5

hái kěyǐ *just so so* 8

háishi *or* (used in question forms) 6

háishi *would be better* 9

hǎiyùn *(to post) by sea* 15

háizi *child/children* 2

hángkōng *(to post) by air* 15

Hánguó-rén *Korean (person)* 19

Hànzì *Chinese characters* 11, 17

Hànzú *Han nationality* 19

Hànzú-rén *the Han people* 19

hǎo *good, well* 1

hào *number* 3

hǎochī (de) *delicious, tasty* 10

hǎokàn *nice-looking* 15

hàomǎ *number* (often used for telephone, telex, fax numbers and car registration plates) 3

hǎoxiàng *to seem* 18

hē *to drink* 10

hé *and* 4

hé *box* 16

hē de *something to drink* 12

hēi(sè) (de) *black* 7

hěn *very* 1

hépíng *peace* 3

héshì *suitable* 8

hézī qǐyè *joint venture* 21

hézuò *co-operation, to co-operate* 16

hóng(sè) (de) *red* 7

hòu *later* 16

hòulái *later* 18

hòutiān *the day after tomorrow* 13

hú *lake* 14

Huá *another word for China* 19

huá bīng *to skate* 14

Huá-rén *overseas Chinese people* 19

huài *broken, not working; bad* 18

huán *to return something to* 12

huàn *to change* 9

huàn qián *to change money* 6

huáng(sè) (de) *yellow* 7

huānyíng *to welcome* 16

huì *can, be able to* 2

huì *meeting* 5

huí guó *to return to one's own country* 20

huí lái *to come back* 20

huí qù *to go back* 16

huò(zhě) *or* (used in statements) 16

huǒchē *train* 5

huódòng *activity* 14

huǒtuǐ *ham* 12

hùshi *nurse* 17

hùzhào *passport* 12

jǐ *how many?* (usually less than ten) 4

jǐ *crowded* 7

jǐ *several, a few* 17

jì *to post* 15

jǐ hào? *which number?* 3

jiā *home* 9

jiā *to add* 12

jià(qī) *holiday, vacation* 8

jiān *(measure word for rooms)* 12

jiàn *(measure word for clothes)* 7

jiàn miàn *to meet* 20

jiǎndān *simple* 19

jiānglái *in (the) future* 15

jiànkāng *health, healthy* 16

jiào *to call, to be called* 2

jiāotōng *transport traffic* 18

jiàoxǐng *to (call to) wake up* 12

jiàoxué *teaching* 21

jiǎozi *(Chinese) dumplings* 21

jiè (yān) *to give up (smoking)* 10

jié hūn *to marry* 4

jié zhàng *to have the bill* 10

jiějie *elder sister* 4

jiěmèi *sisters* 4

jièshào *to introduce; introduction* 19

jīhuì *opportunity* 14

jì(jié) *seasons* 20

-jíle *(suffix) extremely* 10

jīn *half a kilogram* 7

jìn *to enter* 1

jìn *near* 7

jǐn(yi)jǐn *to tighten* 18

jǐngchá *police officer* 18

jīngjì *economy* 19

jīngjù *Peking opera* 6

jīnglǐ *manager* 12

jīnnián *this year* 4

jīntiān *today* 1

jīròu *chicken (meat)* 12

jiǔ *alcohol* 16

jiù *just; only* 7

jiùshi *it's just that* 21

jìzhě *journalist* 19

juéde *to feel, to think* 8

juédìng *to decide* 14

júzizhī *orange juice* 10

kāfēi *coffee* 12

kāi *to drive* 13

kāi (huì) *to have (a meeting)* 5

kāi (mén) *to open (a door)* 5

kāi xué *to start a term* 20

kāishǐ *to start, start* 5

kāishuǐ *boiled water* 17

kàn *to look at, watch* 5

kàn bìng *to see a doctor* 17

kàn(yi)kàn *to have a look* 5

kàn-jiàn *to see* 16

kē *department (in a hospital)* 17

kěkǒukělè *Coca-Cola* 10

kěnéng *possible, possibly* 15

kèqi *polite* 16

kěshì *but* 7

késou *cough, to cough* 17

kètīng *sitting room* 16

kěxī *it's a pity* 5

kǒuyīn *accent* 19

kǔ *bitter* 17

kuài *(Chinese unit of money)* 7

kuài *fast* 8

kuàilè *happy* 21

kuàizi *chopsticks* 10

kuòdà *to expand* 21

là *hot, spicy* 10

lā dùzi *to have diarrhoea* 17

lái *to come* 1

lái *I'll have (colloquial)* 10

lán(sè) (de) *blue* 7

lǎo *old* 14

lǎoshī *teacher* 1

le *grammatical marker* 4

lèi *tired, tiring* 9

lěng *cold* 20

lí *distance from* 7

lǐ *inside* 18
lì *pill* 17
liǎng *two (of anything)* 4
liàng (measure word for vehicles (inc. bicycles)) 18
liáng(kuai) *cold, cool* 16
liànxí *to practise; exercise* 14
líng *zero* 3
líng (brakes) *work well* 18
lìng yí gè *another; another one* 18
línghuó *flexible* 15
línyù *shower* 12
lìshǐ *history* 19
liúlì *fluent* 19
liúxuéshēng *overseas student* 21
lóu *floor; building* 7
lóushàng *upstairs* 14
lóuxià *downstairs* 14
lù *road, street* 3
lǜ(sè) (de) *green* 7
lǚguǎn *hotel* 12
Lúndūn *London* 3
lǚxíng *to travel; travel* 14
lǚxíngtuán *tourist group* 14
lǚyóu *to travel* 21

ma (question particle) 1
máfan *(to) trouble* 12
mǎi *to buy* 6
mài *to sell* 7
mǎlù *road* 9
māma *mum, mother* 4
màn *slow* 8
mǎnyì *satisfied* 21
màn zǒu *take care (as in goodbye; lit. walk slowly)* 16
màoxiǎn *adventurous; to take the risk* 9
máoyī *woollen pullover* 7

mápó dòufu *spicy beancurd/tofu* 10
mǎshàng *at once* 18
méi *no, not, (have not)* 2
měi *every* 8
měi *beautiful* 20
méi guānxi *it's OK, it doesn't matter* 2
Měiguó *USA* 3
méi shénme *it's nothing, don't mention it* 9
měi tiān *every day* 8
méi wèntí *no problem* 6
mèimei *younger sister* 4
měiyuán *US dollar* 12
mén *door* 5
míngbai *to understand* 13
míngnián *next year* 5
míngpiàn *namecard* 3
míngtiǎn *tomorrow* 1
míngtiān jiàn *see you tomorrow* 1
míngxìnpiàn *postcard* 15
míngzi *name* 2
mínzú *nationality* 19
mō(mo) *to feel, touch* 8

ná *to take, to fetch* 17
nǎr?/nǎli? *where?* 3
nǎ/něi *which?* 7
nǎ/něi zhǒng? *which kind?* 13
nà/nèi *that* 2
nǎi *milk* 12
nǎilào *cheese* 12
nǎli nǎli *not really (response to a compliment)* 8
nàme *in that case, then* 6
nán *male* 2
nán *difficult* 6
nán *south* 9
nánfāng *the south* 20
nánkàn *ugly* 8
nánshuō *difficult to say* 21

nàr/nàli *there* 9

ne question particle 2

nèibiān *over there* 15

nèixiē *those* 17

néng *to be able to, can* 12

nǐ *you* (singular) 1

nián *year* 11

niánqīng *young* 14

nǐde *your* 2

nǐmen *you* (plural) 1

nín *you* (polite form) 2

niúròu *beef* 12

nǚ'ér *daughter* 4

nuǎn(huo) *warm* 20

Ōuzhōu (dàlù) *(continental) Europe* 18

ōuyuán *euro* 15

pà *afraid* 9

pái *row* (of seats) 14

pàng *fat* 10

péngyou *friend* 2

piàn(r) *tablets* 17

piányi *cheap* 8

piào *ticket* 3

piàoliang *beautiful* 2

píjiǔ *beer* 16

píngguǒ *apple* 7

píng(zi) *bottle* 17

pípa *a musical instrument* 19

pútao *grapes* 7

pútáojiǔ *wine* 10

pǔtōnghuà *common language, Chinese (Mandarin)* 19

qí *to ride* 9

qǐ *to get up* 14

qiān *thousand* 7

qián *money* 6

qián *front, ahead* 9

qiánbāo *purse/wallet* 18

qiānxū *modest* 19

qiānzhèng *visa* 14

qiǎokèlì *chocolate(s)* 16

qìchē *vehicle, bus* 9

qìhòu *climate* 20

qǐng *to invite; please* 1

qīngchu *clear* 8

qīng cài *vegetables* 10

qíngtiān *sunny (day)* 20

qìngzhù *to celebrate* 21

qiūtiān *autumn* 14

qìwēn *(weather) temperature* 20

qū *district, area* 3

qù *to go to* 5

qǔ qián *withdraw money* 15

qǔkuǎnjī *ATM* 15

ràng *to let, allow* 10

ránhòu *afterwards* 6

rè *hot* 10

rén *person* 3

rénmen *people (in general)* 16

rénmín *the people (of a country)* 19

rénmínbì Chinese currency 13

rènshi *to recognize, to know (people)* 2

rènwéi *to think, believe* 14

Rìběn *Japan* 3

róngyì *easy* 6

ròu *meat* 10

ruǎnwò *soft sleeper* 13

ruǎnzuò *soft seat* 13

rúguǒ *if* 12

sàn bù *to stroll* 14

sānmíngzhì *sandwich* 12

shān *mountain* 21

shāndìché *mountain bike* 18

shàng *on* 5

shàng *to board* (a vehicle) 13

shàng cì *last time* 10

shāngdiàn *shop* 6

shàng wǎng *to use the internet* 15

shàngwǔ *morning* 5

shǎo *few; less* 10

shǎoshù (mínzú) *(national) minority* 19

shéi /shuí? *who?* 2

shéide? *whose?* 18

shēnfènzhèng *identity card* 18

shēng *tone* (e.g. *dì-yī/èr shēng* the first/second tone) 19

shēngdiào *tones* 19

shēngrì *birthday* 5

shēngyi *business* 21

shénme shíhou? *when, what time?* 6

shénme yàng de? *what kind?* 12

shénme? *what?* 2

shēntǐ *health, body* 10

shì *to be* 2

shìchǎng *market* 7

shīfu *title used when addressing a craftsman* (lit. *master*) 18

shìhé *to suit* 7

shíjiān *time* 5

shìjiè (shàng) *(in the) world* 18

shìqing *matter, issue, thing* 16

shìshi *to try* 7

shōu *to accept, receive* 10

shǒu *hand* 18

shòu *thin* 14

shǒujī *mobile (phone)* 21

shōujù *receipt* 15

shū *book* 15

shūfu *comfortable* 9

shuǐ *water* 12

shuì *to sleep* 13

shuǐguǒ *fruit* 16

shuō *to speak, to say* 2

shūshu *uncle* (on father's side or someone of his father's generation) 16

sì jì *four seasons* 20

sòng lái *to send over* (to the speaker) 12

sòng qù *to send over* (away from the speaker) 12

suàn-cuò le *calculated wrongly* 10

Sūgélán *Scotland* 3

...suì ...*years old, age* 4

suíbiàn *casually* 10

suǒ (measure word for schools, houses, etc.) 21

suǒyǐ *so, therefore* 13

suǒyǒude *all* 16

tā *she, he, it* 1

tāde *his, her, its* 2

tài...le! *too...!* 7

tàitai *Mrs, wife* 1

tāmen *they, them* 21

tán *to talk, to chat* 14

tán liàn'ài *to be in love, go steady* (lit. *talk love*) 14

tán(yi)tán *to talk (a bit) about* 21

tāng *soup* 10

táng *sugar* 12

tānzi *stall* 10

tè *extremely* (colloquial) 20

tèkuài *special express (train)* 13

téng *pain; painful* **17**

tèsè *feature, characteristic* **21**

tiān *day* **9**

tiān *to add* **21**

tián *to fill* (in a form) **12**

tián (de) *sweet* **7**

tiānqi *weather* **10**

tiánshí *dessert* **16**

tiào wǔ *to dance* **14**

tiáojiàn *condition* **12**

tīng *to listen to,* (attend concert) **6**

tīng (measure word for cans (of drink)) **10**

tǐng *quite, fairly* **14**

tīngshuō *I heard, I am told* **9**

tóngshì(men) *colleague(s)* **21**

tóngxué(men) *fellow student(s)* **21**

tōngzhī *to inform* **18**

tóu téng *headache* **17**

tóuděng (piào) *first-class (ticket)* **13**

tóupán *starter* **16**

tuìxiū *to retire* **9**

wàiguó *foreign country* **16**

wàiguó-rén *foreigner* **16**

wàizī qǐyè *foreign enterprise* **21**

wǎn *bowl* **10**

wàn *ten thousand* **21**

wǎn'ān *good night* **12**

wán(r) *(Chinese medicine) ball* **17**

wǎnfàn *dinner, supper* **12**

wǎng *in the direction of* **9**

wǎnshang *evening* **5**

wèi (measure word for person (polite)) **2**

wèi *for* (formal) **16**

wèi . . . gān bēi! *to . . .* (used in a toast) **16**

Wēi'ěrshì *Wales* **3**

wèishēng *hygiene, hygienic* **10**

wèishénme? *why?* **12**

wēixiǎn *dangerous* **9**

wèizi *seat* **14**

wēn *warm* **17**

wén *language, writing* **19**

wèn *to ask* **1**

wénhuà *culture* **21**

wèntí *question, problem* **6**

wénxué *literature* **19**

wǒ *I, me* **2**

wǒde *my* **2**

wǒmen *we, us* **2**

xī *west* **9**

xià chē *to get off* (a vehicle) **9**

xià qí *to play chess* **14**

xià xuě *to snow* (lit. *descend snow*) **20**

xià yǔ *to rain* (lit. *descend rain*) **8, 20**

xià(yí)ge *next* **9**

xiān *first* **6**

xiàndàihuà (de) *modern* **16**

xiāng *fragrant* **16**

xiǎng *would like to; to think* **6**

xiǎng *to miss, long for* **20**

xiàng *to (look) like* **4**

Xiānggǎng *Hong Kong* **9**

xiāngjiāo *bananas* **7**

xiǎngyào *would like* **12**

xiànjīn *cash* **10**

xiànmu *to envy* **9**

xiānsheng *Mr; husband; gentleman* **1**

xiànzài *now* **5**

xiǎo   *little, young, small*   1
xiǎojie   *Miss, young lady*   2
xiǎoshí   *hour*   12
xiǎoxi   *news, information*
   18
xiàtiān   *summer*   14
xiàwǔ   *afternoon*   5
xiě   *to write*   19
xièxie (nǐ)   *to thank;
   thank you*   1
Xīfāng   *the West, western*   6
xíguàn   *habit, customs*   16
xǐhuan   *to like*   3
xīn   *new*   8
xìn   *letter*   15
xìnfēng   *envelope*   15
xíng   *OK*   9
xìng   *surname*   2
xīngqī   *week*   5
xìngqu   *interest*   19
xìntǒng   *postbox,
   mailbox*   15
xīnxian   *fresh*   7
xìnyòng kǎ   *credit card*   10
xiōngdì   *brothers*   4
xiū   *to repair*   12
xiūxi   *to rest*   6
xīwàng   *to hope; hope*   16
Xīyào   *Western medicine*
   17
Xīyī   *Western medical
   (doctor)*   17
xǐzǎojiān   *bathroom*   12
xuǎnzé   *to choose*   12
xuě   *snow*   20
xuésheng   *student*   19
xué(xí)   *to study, to learn*   8
xuéxiào   *school*   21

yǎn   *to act*   14
yànhuì   *banquet*   17
yánjiū   *to study,
   to research*   19
yánsè   *colour*   8

yànwō   *birds' nest*   16
yào   *it takes . . .*   9
yào   *to want, to need;
   will*   6
yào   *medicine*   17
yàofāng   *prescription*   17
yàofáng   *pharmacy*   17
yàoshi   *key*   12
yàoshi   *if*   18
yě   *also*   2
yè   *page*   15
yí ge . . . yí ge   *one . . . ,
   the other*   4
yí kè   *a quarter (time)*   5
yìbān   *usually*   12
yìbānláishuō   *generally
   speaking*   20
Yìdàlì   *Italy*   8
yìdiǎn(r)   *a little*   2
yídìng   *certainly,
   definitely*   12
yígòng   *altogether*   10
yǐhòu   *later, in future;
   after*   8
yìhuǐ(r)   *a short while*   12
yǐjīng   *already*   5
yīliáo   *medical care*   17
Yīngguó   *England*   3
Yīngwén   *English
   (language)*   2
yìngwò   *hard sleeper*   13
yíngyèbù   *branch
   (of a bank)*   15
yìngzuò   *hard seat*   13
yínháng   *bank*   6
yǐnliào   *drinks*   12
yīntiān   *cloudy (day)*   20
yīnwei/yīnwéi   *because*   20
yìnxiàng   *impression*   21
yīnyuè   *music*   6
yīnyuèhuì   *concert*   6
yìqǐ   *together*   9
yǐqián   *before, in the
   past*   8

zhè/zhèi   *this*   2

zhème (gui)   *so (expensive)*   7

zhēn   *real, really*   2

zhēn dǎoméi!   *how unfortunate! bad luck!*   18

zhēnde   *really*   4

zhèngcān   *main course*   16

zhènghǎo   *just right (amount)*   15

zhěngtiān   *all day*   14

zhèngzài   *at this moment*   12

zhēnjiǔ   *acupuncture*   17

zhěnsuǒ   *clinic (open to the general public)*   17

zhèr   *here, this place*   7

zhéxué   *philosophy*   19

zhèyàng   *like this, in this way*   17

zhī   *(measure word for cigarettes)*   10

zhǐ   *only*   10

zhǐ   *to refer to*   19

zhǐ yào   *only need/cost*   8

zhīdao   *to know*   5

zhíjiē   *direct(ly)*   17

zhíkuài   *express (train)*   13

zhìliàng   *quality*   8

zhīpiào   *cheque, check*   10

zhǐyào . . . jiù . . .   *so long as . . . then . . .*   19

zhǒng   *kind, sort (measure word)*   17

Zhōngguó   *China*   3

Zhōngguóchéng   *Chinatown*   16

Zhōngguó-rén   *Chinese*   3

Zhōngwén   *Chinese (language)*   2

zhōngwǔ   *noon*   5

Zhōngyào   *Chinese medicine*   17

Zhōngyī   *Chinese medical (doctor)*   17

zhōumò   *weekend*   5

zhù (nǐ)   *to wish (you)*   5

zhù (zài)   *to live (in/at a place)*   3

zhuǎn   *to change to (extension)*   15

zhuàng   *to collide*   18

zhuàng-huài(le)   *damage(ed)*   18

zhuānkē   *special, specialized; speciality*   17

zhǔyì   *idea*   8

zì   *(Chinese) character*   11

zìjǐ   *oneself*   14

zìxíngchē   *bicycle*   9

zìxíngchē dào   *bicycle lane*   18

zìyóu   *free, freedom*   7

zōngjiào   *religion*   21

zǒngshì   *always*   18

zǒu   *to leave*   12

zǒu (lù)   *to walk, on foot*   7

zū   *to hire, to rent*   18

zuì   *the most*   7

zuìhòu   *last*   16

zuìjìn   *recent, recently*   14

zuǒ   *left*   18

zuò   *to sit*   1

zuò   *to do*   6

zuò (fàn)   *to cook*   16

zuò chē   *to take the bus*   6

zuò kè   *to be a guest*   16

zuò qìgōng   *to do qigong*   6

zuǒshǒu   *left-hand*   16

zúqiú   *football*   8

English–Chinese

afternoon xiàwǔ
afterwards ránhòu
alcohol jiǔ
all + noun suǒyǒude +
  noun
all, both dōu
already yǐjīng
also yě
always zǒngshì
America Měiguó
apple píngguǒ
arrangement; to arrange
  ānpái
to ask wèn
assistant, housestaff
  fúwùyuán
autumn qiūtiān

bag bāo
bank yínháng
banquet yànhuì
bathroom xǐzǎojiān
to be shì
to be at/in zài
beautiful měi, piàoliang
because yīnwei
beer píjiǔ
before yǐqián
bicycle zìxíngchē
big dà
birthday shēngrì
black hēi(sè) (de)
blue lán(sè) (de)
to board (a vehicle) shàng
  (chē)
boiled water kāishuǐ
book shū
to book (a ticket) dìng
  (piào)
both dōu
bottle píngzi
breakfast zǎocān/zǎofàn

broken, not working; bad
  huài
bus gōnggòng qìchē
business shēngyi
but kěshì
to buy mǎi

to call, to be called jiào
camera zhàoxiàngjī
can, be able to néng
can, know how to huì
car qìchē
cash xiànjīn
CD guāngpán
certainly, definitely yídìng
to change huàn
to change money huàn qián
cheap piányi
cheers! gān bēi!
cheque, check zhīpiào
child/children háizi
China Zhōngguó
Chinese (language)
  Zhōngwén
Chinese characters Hànzì
chocolate(s) qiǎokèlì
to choose xuǎnzé
chopsticks kuàizi
city chéngshì
clean gānjìng
clear qīngchu
clever cōngming
to close (door) guān (mén)
coach (vehicle)
  chángtú qìchē
coffee kāfēi
cold lěng
cold, cool liáng(kuai)
colleague tóngshì
to come lái
to come back huí lái
comfortable shūfu

company gōngsī
concert yīnyuèhuì
convenient fāngbiàn
to cook zuò (fàn)
cough; to cough késou
country guójiā
credit card xìnyòng kǎ
crowded jǐ
cup(ful) bēi

dad, father bàba
dangerous wēixiǎn
daughter nǚ'ér
day tiān
to decide juédìng
delicious, tasty hǎochī (de)
difficult nán
dish cài
to do zuò
doctor yīshēng, dàifu
don't bié
door mén
double room shuāngrén
  fángjiān
downstairs lóuxià
to drink hē
to drive kāi

early zǎo
east dōng
easy róngyì
to eat chī
economy jīngjì
elder brother gēge
elder sister jiějie
e-mail diànzǐ yóujiàn
embassy dàshǐguǎn
English (language)
  Yīngwén
to enter jìn
euro ōuyuán
every měi
everyone dàjiā
everything yíqiè

excuse me duìbuqǐ
expensive; honourable guì
extremely fēicháng, tè

far yuǎn
fast kuài
fat pàng
fault cuò
fax chuánzhēn
to feel, to think juéde
few; less shǎo
to fill (in a form) tián (biǎo)
film, movie diànyǐng
first xiān
fish yú
floor/storey lóu
food, meal fàn
football zúqiú
for; to give gěi
foreign country wàiguó
foreign enterprise wàizī qǐyè
form biǎo
free; freedom zìyóu
friend péngyou
friendly yǒuhǎo
friendship yǒuyì
from cóng
fruit shuǐguǒ

to get off the bus xià chē
to go back huí qù
to go to qù, dào
good; well hǎo
goodbye zàijiàn
green lǜ(sè) (de)
guest kèren

half bàn
hand shǒu
happy gāoxìng/kuàilè
to have yǒu
to have a cold gǎnmào
to have diarrhoea lā dùzi
he/she/it tā

headache tóu téng
health, body shēntǐ
health; healthy jiànkāng
to help bāng
here, this place zhèr
to hire, to rent zū
his, her, its tāde
holiday, vacation jià(qī)
home jiā
to hope; hope xīwàng
hospital yīyuàn
hot rè
hot, spicy là
hotel fàndiàn, bīnguǎn,
    lǚguǎn
hour xiǎoshí
how far? duō yuǎn?
how is it? how about
    it? zěnmeyàng?
how much? how
    many? duōshao?
how? zěnme?
hundred bǎi
hungry è
husband xiānsheng, àiren

I, me wǒ
idea zhǔyì
identity card shēnfènzhèng
if rúguǒ, yàoshi
illness bìng
to inform tōngzhī
inside lǐ
interest xìngqu
interesting yǒu yìsi
international guójì
interpreter, translator;
    fānyì
to interpret, translate
to introduce;
    introduction jièshào
to invite; please qǐng

joint venture hézī qǐyè

key yàoshi
kilogram gōngjīn
knife and fork dāochā
to know (a fact) zhīdao
to know (people) rènshi

language yǔyán
last zuìhòu
later, after yǐhòu
to leave; to walk zǒu
left zuǒ
to let, allow ràng
letter xìn
letter box xìnxiāng
light(s) dēng
to (look) like xiàng
to like xǐhuan
to listen to tīng
a little yìdiǎn(r)
little, young, small xiǎo
to live (in/at a place)
    zhù (zài)
long cháng
to look at, watch kàn
to look for zhǎo
to lose diū
to love; love ài

male nán
many; more duō
to marry jié hūn
meaning yìsi
meat ròu
medicine yào
to meet jiàn miàn
meeting huì
menu càidān
minute fēn(zhōng)
Miss, young lady xiǎojie
mobile (phone) shǒujī
money qián
month yuè
morning shàngwǔ
morning (early) zǎoshang

most zuì
mountain shān
mountain bike shāndìchē
Mr; husband; gentleman xiānsheng
Mrs; wife tàitai
mum, mother māma
music yīnyuè

name míngzi
near jìn
to need, must; it takes děi
new xīn
news, information xiāoxi
next xià(yí)ge
nice looking hǎokàn
no, not, (have not) méi
noisy chǎo
north běi
not bù
not bad, pretty good búcuò
now xiànzài
number hào
number (telephone, telex, fax) hàomǎ
nurse hùshi

o'clock diǎn(zhōng)
of course dāngrán
often chángcháng
old lǎo
Olympic Games Àolínpǐkè Yùndònghuì
on shàng
only zhǐ
opportunity jīhuì
opposite duìmiàn
other biéde

pain; painful téng
park gōngyuán
passport hùzhào
to pay (money) fù qián
peace hépíng

person rén
pharmacy yàofáng
place dìfang
to plan dǎsuàn
plane fēijī
platform zhàntái
pleasant, happy yúkuài
police officer jǐngchá
polite kèqi
possible; possibly kěnéng
to post jì
post office yóujú
postcard míngxìnpiàn
to practise; exercise liànxí
prescription yàofāng
pretty good búcuò
pound (money) (Yīng)bàng
purse/wallet qiánbāo
to put fàng

question, problem wèntí
quiet ānjìng

rain yǔ
to rain xià yǔ
real; really zhēn
really zhēnde
receipt shōujù
recent; recently zuìjìn
to recognize, to know (people) rènshi
red hóng(sè) (de)
to rest xiūxi
to return something (to) huán (gěi)
right (the opposite of left) yòu
road, street lù
room fángjiān

safe ānquán
same yíyàng
sandwich sānmíngzhì
satisfied mǎnyì

seat wèizi
to see kàn-jiàn
to see a doctor kàn bìng,
  kàn yīshēng
to seem hǎoxiàng
to sell mài
service fúwù
she, he, it tā
ship, boat chuán
a short while, after a
  moment yìhuǐ(r)
sightseeing yóulǎn
simple jiǎndān
to sing (a song) chàng (gē)
single room dānrén fángjiān
to sit zuò
size dàxiǎo
to sleep shuì
slow màn
to smoke (a cigarette)
  chōu (yān)
to snow xià xuě
so, therefore suǒyǐ
some yìxiē, yǒude
sometimes yǒu shíhou
son érzi
soup tāng
south nán
to speak, to say shuō
sports; to take exercise
  yùndòng
spring chūntiān
stamp yóupiào
to start kāishǐ
station, (bus) stop
  (chē) zhàn
still hái
to stroll sàn bù
student xuésheng
to study, to learn xué(xí)
success; successful
  chénggōng
sugar táng
summer xiàtiān

sunny (day) qíngtiān
surname xìng
sweet tián (de)
to swim yóuyǒng

to take a holiday dù jià
to take the bus zuò chē
to take, to fetch ná
to talk, chat tán
taxi chūzū (qì)chē
tea chá
teacher lǎoshī
telephone diànhuà
to telephone dǎ diànhuà
television diànshì
to tell gàosu
to thank; thank you
  xièxie (nǐ)
that nà/nèi
there nàr/nàli
they, them tāmen
thin shòu
thing, matter, issue shìqing
thing, object dōngxi
to think, believe rènwéi
to think, to assume yǐwéi
this zhè/zhèi
this year jīnnián
those nèixiē
thousand qiān
ticket piào
time shíjiān
time, occasion cì
tired, tiring lèi
to; to arrive, to go to dào
today jīntiān
together yìqǐ
toilet cèsuǒ
tomorrow míngtiān
too . . . ! tài . . . le!
train huǒchē
transport, traffic jiāotōng
to travel; travel lǚxíng,
  lǚyóu

to *try* shìshi
to *turn* guǎi
TV diànshì
two (of anything) liǎng

underground, subway dìtiě
to *understand* dǒng, míngbai
university dàxué
upstairs lóushàng
to *use* yòng
US dollar měiyuán
usually yìbān

vegetables qīng cài
vehicle (bus, bike, car) chē
very hěn
video (tape) lùxiàngdài
visa qiānzhèng
visit; to visit (formal) fǎngwèn

to *wait* děng
to *walk, on foot* zǒu lù
to *want (to), need, will* yào
to *want to, would like to;* xiǎng
miss
warm nuǎn(huo)
water shuǐ
we, us wǒmen
weather tiānqi
week xīngqī
weekend zhōumò

to *welcome; welcome* huānyíng
west xī
what kind? shénme yàng de?
what? shénme?
when, what time? shénme shíhou?
where? nǎr?/nǎli?
which number? jǐ hào?
which? nǎ/něi?
white bái(sè) (de)
who? shéi/shuí?
whose? shéide?/shuíde?
why? wèishénme?
wife tàitai, àiren
wife (formal); madam fūren
wind fēng
wine pútáojiǔ
winter dōngtiān
to *work; work* gōngzuò
to *write* xiě

year nián
. . . year (of age) . . . suì
yellow huáng(sè) (de)
yes, correct duì
you (singular) nǐ
you (polite form) nín
you (plural) nǐmen
young niánqīng
younger brother dìdi
younger sister mèimei
your (singular) nǐde
your (plural) nǐmende

第一课　你好！你好吗？
01　hello! how are you?

Dialogue 1

格林太太：　你好，小王！
格林先生：　小王，你好!
小王：　　　格林先生，格林太太，你们好！
格林太太：　你太太好吗？
小王：　　　她很好，谢谢。

Dialogue 2

格林先生：　小王，谢谢你。
格林太太：　谢谢你，小王。
小王：　　　不用谢。
格林先生：　再见。
小王：　　　再见。
格林太太：　再见。

Dialogue 3

李先生：　　请进。
格林先生：　*(enters the room)*
李先生：　　格林先生，你好！
格林先生：　你好，李先生。

李先生： 请坐。
格林先生： 谢谢。
李先生： 格林太太好吗？
格林先生： 她很好。谢谢。

Dialogue 4

Frank： 请问，张老师在吗？
李老师： 对不起，她不在。
Frank： 她今天来吗？
李老师： 不来。她明天来。
Frank： 谢谢你。
李老师： 不用谢。明天见。
Frank： 明天见。

第二课　你叫什么？
02　what's your name?

Dialogue 1

Jane： 您贵姓？
陈： 我姓陈。您呢？
Jane： 我姓 Lord。这是您的孩子吗？
陈： 不是。我没有孩子。这是李太太的孩子。
Jane： (to the child) 你叫什么名字？
孩子： 我叫盼盼。

Dialogue 2

White： 郑先生，你好！
常： 我姓常，不姓郑。 我叫常正。
White： 对不起，常先生。
常： 没关系。White先生，你有没有中文
　　　　 名字？
White： 有。我叫白彼德。

常： 白先生，你会不会说英文？
White： 当然会。常先生，你也会说英文吗？
常： 会一点儿。

Dialogue 3

白： 那是谁？你认识不认识她？
吴： 认识。她是郭小姐。
白： 她真漂亮。
......
白： 你好！我叫白比德。你呢？
郭： 你好，我叫郭玉婕。
......
郭： 这是我的男朋友。他叫刘文光。这是白先生。
刘： 白先生，你好！
白： 哦，你好！

第三课　你是哪国人？
03　where are you from?

Dialogue 1

林： 您是哪国人？
白： 我是英国人。这是我的名片。
林： 谢谢。哦，白先生，你住在伦敦？
白： 对。你是中国人吧？
林： 是，我是广东人。

Dialogue 2

营业员*： 这是您的飞机票。
白： 谢谢。我住在什么饭店？
营业员： 你住在和平饭店。
白： 和平是什么意思？

营业员：　和平是 peace 的意思。
白：　　　很好。我喜欢和平。
*营业员　　yíngyèyuán　assistant

Dialogue 3

林：　你住在哪儿？
白：　我住在和平饭店。
林：　几号房间？
白：　五零八号房间。你住在哪儿？
林：　我住在平安路七号。
白：　平安路在哪儿？
林：　平安路在西城区。
白：　和平饭店也在西城区，是不是？
林：　不在。在东城区。
白：　你的电话号码是多少？
林：　六五五二 九三二四。你的呢？
白：　我的是六六七三 八八三零。

第四课　你有兄弟、姐妹吗？
04　do you have brothers and sisters?

Dialogue 1

丁：　您叫什么名字？
刘：　我叫刘富贵。
丁：　刘先生结婚了吗？
刘：　结婚了。
丁：　有没有孩子？
刘：　有两个，一个儿子，一个女儿。
丁：　他们几岁？
刘：　儿子两岁，女儿五岁。

Dialogue 2

丁： 您有兄弟、姐妹吗？

刘： 有两个弟弟、一个妹妹。没有哥哥和姐姐。

丁： 您弟弟、妹妹多大？

刘： 大弟弟二十六，小弟弟二十四。

丁： 妹妹呢？

刘： 妹妹二十八。

丁： 很好，谢谢您。

刘： 不客气。

丁： 再见！

刘： 再见！

Dialogue 3

吴： 你爸爸、妈妈多大年纪？

陆： 爸爸五十三，妈妈四十九。

吴： 不象、不象。这是你妹妹吧。她真漂亮。

陆： 她今年二十二。

吴： 真的？她结婚了吗？

陆： 没有。可是有男朋友了。

吴： 哦。

第五课　几点了？
05　what time is it now?

Dialogue 1

顾客*： 请问，你们几点开门？

营业员： 上午八点到下午五点半。

顾客： 中午关门吗？

营业员： 不关。

顾客： 周末开不开？

营业员： 星期六开，星期天不开。

*顾客　　gùkè　*customer*

Dialogue 2

小许：　现在几点了？
老万：　两点一刻了。
小许：　噢，会已经开始了。
老万：　什么会？你不是明天开会吗？
小许：　今天星期几？
老万：　星期三。
小许：　噢，我还以为是星期四呢。

Dialogue 3

Jane：　　您去哪儿？
中国人：　我去利物浦。
Jane：　　几点的火车？
中国人：　我不知道。票上没有时间。
Jane：　　我帮你看看。(Looks at the notice board)
　　　　　啊，三点一刻，在第六站台。
中国人：　现在三点差五分，还有二十分钟。
Jane：　　祝你一路顺风。
中国人：　谢谢你。再见。

Dialogue 4

Ann：　明年春节是几月几号？
朋友：　二月十二号。
Ann：　真可惜。我的生日是二月十一号。
朋友：　没关系。英国十一号的晚上就是中国十二号
　　　　的早上。

第六课　你今天想做什么？
06　what do you want to do today?

Dialogue 1

小吴：　　今天休息。你想做什么？

Frank：　　我想去买东西。可是我要先换钱。

小吴：　　好。我们先坐车去中国银行换钱，然后去商店买东西。

Frank：　　好。下午我想去北海公园。

小吴：　　没问题。晚上呢？

Frank：　　晚上我们去看杂技好不好？

小吴：　　太好了。我请服务员给我们订票。

Dialogue 2

小吴：　　今天晚上你想看电影还是看京剧？

Frank：　　我不喜欢京剧。

小吴：　　那么我们看电影吧。电影比京剧有意思。

Frank：　　有没有音乐会？

小吴：　　你想听中国音乐还是听西方音乐？

Frank：　　在中国当然听中国音乐。

Dialogue 3

Passer-by：　早上好！

Frank：　　早上好！(*Pointing to somebody doing Tai Chi*) 他在做什么？

Passer-by：　他在打太极拳。

Frank：　　那个人也在打太极拳吗？

Passer-by：　不。他在做气功。

Frank：　　气功跟太极拳一样吗？

Passer-by：　不一样。

Frank：　　气功比太极拳难吗？

Passer-by：　不一定。我说气功比太极拳容易。

第七课 多少钱？
07 how much is it?

Dialogue 1

顾客：	请问，在哪儿买毛衣？
营业员：	在二搂。
	········
营业员：	您买什么？
顾客：	我想买一件毛衣。
营业员：	要哪件？您喜欢什么颜色的？
顾客：	那件红色的给我看看行吗？
营业员：	这件很好。
顾客：	哦，太大了。那件黄色的我试试可以吗？
营业员：	这件也不错。
顾客：	哦，太小了。
营业员：	这件蓝色的很适合你。
顾客：	太好了。多少钱？
营业员：	五百块。
顾客：	嗯，太贵了。对不起，谢谢你。
营业员：	········

Dialogue 2

小芳：	我们去自由市场看看吧。
Ann：	好。自由市场离这儿多远？
小芳：	很近。坐车两、三站就到了。
Ann：	车太挤了。咱们走路去吧。
小芳：	可是走路太远了。
Ann：	走路要多长时间？
小芳：	走路要二、三十分钟才能到。
Ann：	好吧。那么咱们坐车去吧。

Dialogue 3

顾客：	苹果怎么卖？
摊贩：	四块一斤。
顾客：	真贵！他们的苹果三块八一斤。
摊贩：	可是我的苹果比他们的大一点儿。
顾客：	葡萄多少钱一斤？
摊贩：	四块两毛五一斤。
顾客：	这么贵！他们的四块一斤。
摊贩：	可是我的葡萄比他们的甜多了。
顾客：	草莓一斤多少钱？
摊贩：	八块二。
顾客：	太贵了！
摊贩：	可是我的草莓比他们的新鲜得多！
顾客：	你的东西最贵。
摊贩：	可是我的东西最好！

第八课　怎么样？
08　what's it like?

Dialogue 1

素兰：	这是我新买的毛衣。你看怎么样？
Colin：	不错，不错。
素兰：	大小合适吗？
Colin：	嗯，有点儿大。
素兰：	颜色好看吗？
Colin：	嗯，不难看。
素兰：	你摸模……你觉得质量怎么样？
Colin：	嗯，还可以。多少钱？
素兰：	不贵，只要一百五十块。
Colin：	什么？！一百五十块我可以买三张足球票！

Dialogue 2

罗太太： 假期过得好吗？

李先生： 非常好，就是东西不便宜。

罗太太： 我早就知道了。

李先生： 我以前觉得英国的东西贵，现在才知道法国的东西更贵。

罗太太： 意大利的东西也很贵是不是？

李先生： 意大利的东西也不比法国的便宜。你的假期过得怎么样？

罗太太： 不怎么样。

李先生： 怎么了？

罗太太： 每天都下雨。

Dialogue 3

宝婕： 你的中文说得真好。

Martin： 哪里，哪里。我的中文没有你的英文好。

宝婕： 不。你的中文比我的英文好得多。

Martin： 以后我帮你学英文，你帮我学中文，怎么样？

宝婕： 好主意。可是我学得不快。

Martin： 没关系，我学得也很慢。

第九课 去……怎么走？
09 how do I get to . . . ?

Dialogue 1

乔： 听说你快要去渡假了。

冯： 对，我有三个星期的假，从六月二十七号到七月十八号。

乔： 你打算去哪儿？

冯： 香港和澳门。这两个地方我都没去过。

乔： 你怎么去？

冯： 我先坐飞机到香港，在那儿住五天。再从香港坐船到澳门。

乔： 我真羡慕你。

冯： 你什么时候渡假？

乔： 我？噢，十二月。

冯： 多长时间？

乔： 不知道。

冯： 怎么会不知道？

乔： 今年十二月我就要退休了。

冯： 我真羡慕你。

Dialogue 2

Ann： 请问，去天坛怎么走？

Passer-by： 天坛在西南边。坐车四站就到了。

Ann： 坐几路车？

Passer-by： 你先从这儿往东走。再坐往南开的车，十五路、二十三路都行。车站在银行对面儿。

Ann： 用换车吗？

Passer-by： 不用。下车以后往前走一点儿。天坛就在马路西边儿。

Ann： 谢谢您。

Passer-by： 没什么。

Dialogue 3

James： 你去过天津吗？

黄： 没去过。

James： 下个周末咱们一起去吧。

黄： 好啊。你打算怎么去？坐汽车还是坐火车？

James： 咱们骑车去，怎么样？

黄： 什么？你发疯了！骑车去天津要两、三天，又累又危险。

James：　我不怕累，也喜欢冒险！
黄：　　反正我不跟你一起去。我在家看电视，又
　　　　舒服又安全。

第十课　您想吃什么？
10　what would you like to eat?

Dialogue 1

服务员：　你们预订了吗？
Brown：　预订了。我叫John Brown.
服务员：　我看一看。……Mr Brown, 七点半，两个
　　　　　人。
Brown：　对，对。
服务员：　好，请跟我来。
　　　　　… …
服务员：　这是菜单。你们先喝点儿什么？
余乔：　　我要一杯桔子汁。
Brown：　你们有什么葡萄酒？
服务员：　我们有长城白葡萄酒和中国红葡萄酒。
Brown：　来一杯白葡萄酒吧。
　　　　　… …
服务员：　酒来了。你们要什么菜？
余乔：　　我不吃肉。
Brown：　你吃不吃鱼？
余乔：　　不吃。我只要青菜和豆腐。
Brown：　什么？你现在吃素了？
余乔：　　是啊。我已经很胖了。
服务员：　你们喜欢吃辣的吗？
余乔：　　喜欢。可是别太辣了。
服务员：　来一个麻婆豆腐吧。
Brown：　好啊。先来两个酸辣汤。
余乔：　　今天已经很热了，我们应该少吃辣的。

服务员：　没关系。吃完饭以后，你们多吃一点儿冰
　　　　　淇淋。我们的冰淇淋非常好吃。

Dialogue 2

Brown：　抽支烟吧。

余乔：　　我不抽烟了。

Brown：　为什么？

余乔：　　我爱人不让我抽了。她说抽烟对我的身体
　　　　　不好，对她的身体也不好。

Brown：　我也不想抽了。可是我有一个朋友，戒烟
　　　　　以前不胖，戒烟以后就胖了。我怕胖。

余乔：　　我也怕胖，可是今天的菜太好吃了。

Brown：　你吃饱了吗？

余乔：　　吃饱了。

Brown：　我们结账吧。　服务员，请结账。

服务员：　你们吃好了吗？

余乔：　　吃好了，谢谢。

Brown：　你们收不收信用卡和支票？

服务员：　对不起，我们只收现金。

Dialogue 3

Ann：　　我饿了，我们随便吃点儿吧。

方：　　　那儿有个小摊子，他们的炒面好吃极了。

Ann：　　(*At the food stall*) (*whispering*) 我看这儿
　　　　　不太干净。

方：　　　没关系，他们会给我们卫生筷子。

　　　　　…… ……

方：　　　请来两碗儿炒面、两听可口可乐。

服务员：　请先付钱。两碗儿炒面十二块，两听可口
　　　　　可乐十四块，一共二十六块。

方：　　　什么？你算错了吧。上次炒面五块
　　　　　一碗儿。

服务员：　没算错。上次是上次，现在一碗儿
　　　　　六块了。

第十二课　在旅馆
12　at the hotel

选择旅馆

Hotel 这个词的中文可以是宾馆、饭店、旅馆和旅店。饭店和宾馆一般很大，旅馆和旅店一般不大。"馆"和"店"都是 house 的意思。"宾"的意思是 guest，"旅"的意思是 travel。"饭"是 food 的意思。

大饭店、宾馆的条件比旅馆、旅店的条件好多了。当然他们也比旅馆、旅店也贵多了。

Dialogue 1

服务员：	您好！
Frank：	你好！我想要一间单人房间。
服务员：	您预订了吗？
Frank：	没有。
服务员：	您要住几天？
Frank：	三、四天。我明天告诉你我什么时候走，可以吗？
服务员：	可以。
Frank：	一天多少钱？
服务员：	单人房间每天五十美元。
Frank：	包早餐吗？
服务员：	当然包。
Frank：	有洗澡间吗？
服务员：	有。不过只有淋浴和厕所。
Frank：	好吧。
服务员：	请先填一下儿这张表。……请给我您的护照。您走的时候还给您。
Frank：	这是我的护照。
服务员：	您的房间是二零一，在二楼。这是钥匙。
Frank：	谢谢。

服务员： 如果您有问题，请给服务台打电话。

Frank： 不会有问题吧。

Dialogue 2

服务员： 您好。服务台。

Frank： 我是住二零一房间的Frank。我的房间太吵了。能不能换一间安静一点儿的？

服务员： 对不起，没有别的单人房间了。只有双人房间。

Frank： 双人房间一晚上多少钱？

服务员： 比单人房间贵二十美元。

Frank： 太贵了。

服务员： 如果明天我们有别的单人房间，一定给您换。

Frank： 好吧。哦，还有，我的淋浴怎么没有热水？

服务员： 对不起，现在正在修。五个小时以后就有了。

Frank： 五个小时以后？不行。我要找你们的经理。

Dialogue 3

服务员： 您好。服务台。

Frank： 我是二零一房间的Frank。能不能麻烦你们给我送来一点儿吃的？我饿了。

服务员： 对不起，餐厅现在关门了。我们只有三明治和饮料。

Frank： 可以。你们有什么样的三明治？

服务员： 我们有奶酪的、火腿的、鸡肉和牛肉的。

Frank： 我要一个奶酪的、一个牛肉的和一杯咖啡。

服务员：	好的。咖啡要加奶、加糖吗？
Frank：	要加奶，不加糖。
服务员：	行。我们一会儿就送去。
Frank：	还有。明天早上我要起得很早。你们能不能打电话叫醒我？
服务员：	可以。几点？
Frank：	七点半。
服务员：	没问题。
Frank：	谢谢你。晚安。
服务员：	晚安。

第十三课　火车、票和出租车
13　trains, tickets and taxis

Dialogue 1

Frank：	我想买一张去上海的火车票。
售票员*：	哪天的？
Frank：	后天的。
售票员：	要哪次车的？
Frank：	我不明白你的意思。
售票员：	去上海的火车有十三次、二十一次和一六一次。
Frank：	它们有什么不一样？
售票员：	十三次和二十一次是特快，一百六十一次是直快。
Frank：	什么是特快和直快？
售票员：	特快就是非常快的意思。十三次特快比一六一次直快快四、五个小时。
Frank：	是不是特快的票也比直快的票贵？
售票员：	那当然了。

*售票员　　shòupiàoyuán　*ticketseller, assistant*

Dialogue 2

Ann：	请问，还有十八号二十一次的票吗？
售票员：	有。您要哪种票？
Ann：	我要三张硬卧。
售票员：	对不起。硬卧只有一张了。我们还有软卧和硬座。
Ann：	软卧比硬卧贵多少？
售票员：	一百八十块。
Ann：	那么十八号一六一次还有硬卧吗？
售票员：	有。
Ann：	太好了！我买三张十八号一六一次的硬卧票。
售票员：	一六一次比二十一次慢四个小时。
Ann：	没关系。我们可以在火车上多睡四个小时。

Dialogue 3

司机：	您去哪儿？
乘客：	我想先去雍和宫，再去天坛。
司机：	请上车吧。
乘客：	你能不能先告诉我去这两个地方大概得多少钱？
司机：	去雍和宫四十五块，再去天坛也是四十五块。
乘客：	是人民币还是美元？
司机：	人民币。
乘客：	好吧。
	(*Getting off at Tiāntán Park*)
乘客：	谢谢你。这是一百块。别找（钱）了。
司机：	对不起。一共一百九十块。
乘客：	怎么是一百九十块？
司机：	你去雍和宫的时候，我等了你两个小时。等一个小时五十块。所以 一共一百九十块。

乘客： 你怎么没先告诉我？

司机： 你没问呀。

第十四课　娱乐活动

14　free time and entertainment

在公园

很多中国人起得很早。他们认为早睡早起对身体好。早上他们做什么？很多人去公园。

在公园里，他们打太极拳、作气功、唱歌、跳舞，等等。有的老人在公园里散步、下棋、打牌、唱京剧。

很多公园都有湖。在北方夏天可以在湖里游泳，冬天可以在湖上滑冰。

Dialogue 1

Edward： 你喜欢什么运动？

小付： 我最喜欢网球和游泳。

Edward： 我也喜欢网球，可是更喜欢足球。

小付： 你喜欢踢足球还是看足球？

Edward： 都喜欢。

小付： 我只喜欢看，不喜欢踢。

Dialogue 2

明力： 听说今年秋天你要去中国旅行。

Ann： 对。可是我还没决定怎么去。

明力： 怎么去？当然坐飞机去。坐火车又慢又不舒服。

Ann： 我不是那个意思。我还没决定跟旅行团去还是自己去。

明力： 跟旅行团去很方便，可是又贵又不自由。

Ann:	自己去又便宜又自由，可是真不方便。
明力:	怎么不方便？
Ann:	我要自己去办签证、订飞机票，找旅馆、等等。
明力:	可是自己去可以有更多的机会练习中文。
Ann:	对，我一定要学好中文，二零零八年去北京看奥林匹克运动会。

Dialogue 3

小赵:	老钱，好久不见。
老钱:	小赵，是你呀！
小赵:	您现在在做什么？
老钱:	跟以前一样。每天打打牌、下下棋、打打太极拳，挺有意思。
小赵:	你比以前年轻多了。
老钱:	哪里、哪里。老多了。小赵，你最近在做什么？
小赵:	我正在谈恋爱。整天买东西、看电影、跳舞，真没意思。
老钱:	你比以前瘦多了。
小赵:	谈恋爱又累又不自由。
老钱:	你的女朋友呢？
小赵:	她还没来呢。我在等她。

Dialogue 4

Edward:	你坐哪儿？
小付:	五排四号。
Edward:	你的位子真好。
小付:	你在哪儿？
Edward:	我在楼上十排三十号。
小付:	你觉得今天的表演怎么样？
Edward:	他们唱得挺好。你觉得呢？
小付:	我觉得他们唱得还不错。可是演得不怎么样。

Edward： 听说后面的表演很棒。

小付： 但愿如此。

第十五课　在邮局和换钱

15　at a post office and changing money

邮局

中国的邮局跟英国的邮局差不多。在邮局你可以
寄信、寄钱、寄包裹，也可以买邮票、信封和明信
片，还可以存钱、取钱和付账。在中国的邮局你还
可以打长途电话和国际电话。

邮局的开门时间常常不一样，有的上午八点开门，
有的八点半开门。有的下午五点半关门，有的晚上
七点关门。星期六、星期天都开门。

顺便说一下，中国的信筒是绿色的，英国的信筒
是红色的。

Dialogue 1

Ann： 请问，这封信寄到英国多少钱？

营业员： 请放在秤上。……超重了。三块九。

Ann： 几天能到？

营业员： 不一定。一般五、六天。这是您的邮票。

Ann： 这张邮票真好看，我能买一套吗？

营业员： 当然可以。一套六块七。

Ann： 我还想寄一个包裹。

营业员： 是什么东西？

Ann： 都是书和光盘。

营业员： 也请放在秤上。……两公斤。您寄航空
还是海运？

Ann： 航空。

Dialogue 2

Colin：	小姐，请问，可以在这儿发（一）个传真吗？
营业员：	可以。发到哪儿？
Colin：	德国。
营业员：	一共几页？
Colin：	两页。
营业员：	好的。请给我传真号码。
Colin：	这是传真号码。
营业员：	请等一等。……发完了。这是收据。
Colin：	多少钱？
营业员：	四十块。请到那边付钱。
Colin：	谢谢你。顺便问一下，可以在这儿上网和发电子邮件吗？
营业员：	当然可以。

Dialogue 3

总机：	您好。南方大学。
谢：	请转四二七分机。
总机：	对不起，四二七占线。您愿意等一等还是一会儿再打来？
谢：	我这是国际电话。您能不能叫四二七的王葆平给我打个电话？
总机：	您的号码是多少？
谢：	英国伦敦是四四二零七。我的电话是二一六七七九二。
总机：	您贵姓？
谢：	我叫谢群毅。
总机：	没问题。
谢：	谢谢您。

换钱

中国换钱一般只能在大银行的分行换，兑换率都差不多。有的大饭店和大商店也有换钱的地方。银行

的开门时间跟普通的商店不一样，比商店开门时间
晚一点，关门时间早一点。可是在大饭店里的换钱
的地方开门时间比较灵活，可能会开到很晚。

将来，取款机多了，取钱更方便了，就不用去银行
换钱了。

Dialogue 4

顾客：　　请问，今天美元和人民币的对换率是多
　　　　　少？
营业员：　一比八点九。
顾客：　　一美元换八块九，对吗？
营业员：　对。
顾客：　　我想换两百美元的人民币。
营业员：　请先填这张兑换单。
顾客：　　……填好了。这是两百美元。
营业员：　请等一等。……这是一千七百八十块。
　　　　　请点一点。
顾客：　　正好。谢谢你。
营业员：　不客气。

第十六课　作客
16　being a guest

吃中国饭

中国人常常为客人做很多菜。他们希望客人多喝
酒、多吃菜。

中国人和西方人吃饭的习惯不一样。中国人吃饭用
碗和筷子；西方人吃饭用盘子和刀叉。大部分中国
人一般先吃饭，后喝汤。在西方，人们一般先喝
汤，后吃饭。中国人常常先喝酒，吃凉菜，然后吃
热饭、热菜，最后吃水果。西方人先吃头盘，然后
吃正餐，最后吃甜食或水果。

中国人在家里吃饭和在饭馆吃饭差不多，大家一起吃所有的菜。西方人在饭馆自己吃自己的菜。在家吃饭的时候，不同的菜先放在自己的盘里，然后才吃。

Dialogue 1

袁先生： 老白，欢迎，欢迎。

白先生： 老袁，你好。我知道你爱喝酒。这是给你的酒。

袁先生： 法国葡萄酒！你太客气了。

白先生： 这盒巧克力是给你们女儿的。

袁先生： 珍珍，快谢谢白叔叔。

珍珍： 谢谢白叔叔。

白先生： 不用谢。......真香啊！袁太太，做什么好吃的呢？

袁太太： 没什么好吃的。都是家常便饭。

白先生： 你们的厨房挺现代化的。

袁太太： 可惜太小了。

袁先生： 老白，客厅里坐吧。

白先生： 好，好。你们的客厅真漂亮。

袁先生： 哪里，哪里。老白，你想喝点儿什么？

白先生： 喝点儿茶吧。

Dialogue 2

袁先生： 老白，咱们先喝一杯。

白先生： 好啊。

袁先生： 你喝啤酒，葡萄酒还是来点儿白酒？

白先生： 白酒我喝不了。喝点儿葡萄酒吧。

袁先生： 白的还是红的？

白先生： 红的吧。

袁先生： 这种酒不甜。我知道外国人一般不喜欢喝甜的酒。

白先生： 是，我不喜欢喝甜的酒。

袁先生： 咱们先干一杯！祝你工作顺利，生活愉快！

白先生： 祝你们全家幸福，万事如意！

袁先生： 干杯！

白先生： 干杯！

袁太太： 别客气，多吃点儿。

白先生： 好，好，我自己来。

　　　　　..........

白先生： 菜都非常好吃。

袁先生： 再多吃一点儿。

白先生： 我已经吃饱了。

袁太太： 你吃得太少了。

白先生： 我真的吃不下了。

袁先生： 你太客气了。

白先生： 我没客气。

Dialogue 3

白先生： 我可以用一下你们的厕所吗？

袁先生： 左手第二间就是。

　　　　　........

白先生： 喔，已经九点多了。我该回去了。

袁先生： 还早呢。再坐一会儿吧。

白先生： 不坐了。明天早上我还有事情。

袁先生： 好吧。那就不留你了。

白先生： 给你们添麻烦了。

袁先生： 没什么。欢迎你再来。

白先生： 一定，一定。

袁先生： 我送送你。

白先生： 不用了。请回去吧。

袁先生： 慢走。

袁太太： 路上小心。

白先生： 没问题。再见！

袁先生 & 袁太太： 再见！

Dialogue 4

董事长： 白先生，您筷子用得真好。
白先生： 我常常吃中国饭。
夫人： 您自己做饭吗？
白先生： 我做得不好。我常去中国城的饭馆儿吃饭。

董事长： 来，先喝一杯。这是茅台酒。您喝过吗？
白先生： 喝过两次。
董事长： 为我们两个公司的成功合作干杯！
白先生： 为董事长和董事长夫人的健康干杯！
夫人： 这是燕窝汤，非常有营养。
白先生： 我听说过，可是没喝过。
董事长： 这是凤爪，不知道你吃过吗？
白先生： 看见过，还没吃过。
夫人： 正好，请尝尝吧。

          ‥‥‥‥‥

夫人： 多吃点儿菜。
董事长： 再喝一杯。
白先生： 我吃不下了，也喝不下了。
董事长： 再喝最后一杯。为中英两国人民的友谊干杯！
白先生： 干杯！希望你们有机会去英国访问。

第十七课　看医生
17　seeing a doctor

中国的医疗

在中国，很多单位有自己的医务所。小的医务所只有一个医生，大的可以有几个医生和护士。如果你有病，你可以去单位的医务所，也可以直接去医院。

中国的医院一般分成不同的科。有的医院是专科医院，只看一、两种病。大的医院一般又有中医，又有西医。你可以看中医，也可以看西医。

Dialogue 1

医生：	你哪儿不舒服？
白先生：	我肚子不舒服。
医生：	拉肚子吗？
白先生：	有一点儿。
医生：	你昨天吃什么了？
白先生：	我参加了一个宴会，吃了凤爪，喝了燕窝汤。
医生：	那些都是好东西，对你身体好。
白先生：	我可能吃得太多了。
医生：	你喝了很多酒，是不是？
白先生：	不多。只喝了八杯。
医生：	我明白了。我给你一些药。你愿意试试中药吗？
白先生：	我没吃过中药。听说中药很苦，是吗？
医生：	有的苦，有的不苦。我给你的药不苦。
白先生：	那我试试吧。
医生：	这是药方。请到药房去拿药。
白先生：	医生，谢谢您。
医生：	不用谢。

Dialogue 2

药济师*：	这是您的药。
白先生：	怎么吃呀？
药济师：	瓶子上有服用方法。
白先生：	对不起，我还不认识汉字。
药济师：	哦，对不起。我告诉你。一天吃三次，一次吃二十粒。

白先生：	什么？一天吃六十粒？！
药济师：	对。
白先生：	我的天啊！
药济师：	吃药的时候不要喝咖啡、茶和酒。应该喝温开水。
白先生：	为什么？
药济师：	吃药都应该这样。
白先生：	我的药饭前吃还是饭后吃？
药济师：	都可以。
白先生：	谢谢您。
药济师：	不谢。

*药济师　　yàojìshī　*pharmacist*

Dialogue 3

参观者*：	你们诊所病人多吗？
医生：	不少。
参观者：	你们都看什么病？
医生：	各种各样的病。你看，这个病人常常头疼。她看过西医，吃过西药，可是还不好。我们给她扎了针灸，现在她好多了。
参观者：	真的？我也有时候头疼。她扎了几次了？
医生：	四次了。
参观者：	针灸是不是很疼？
医生：	针灸是不舒服，可是常常很有效。
参观者：	真的吗？
医生：	你有什么病？我可以给你扎。
参观者：	不用、不用。我没病。我的身体很好。谢谢您。

*参观者　　cānguānzhe　*visitor*

第十八课　对付问题

18　coping with problems

中国的交通

在中国，开车和骑自行车都走路的右边。这跟在美国和欧洲大陆一样，跟在英国不一样。

中国是世界上自行车最多的国家。在大城市有很多自行车道。现在在中国租汽车还很难，可是租自行车比较方便。骑自行车又便宜又有意思。

在中国有地铁的城市很少。不少城市有电车。

因为中国人太多，所以路上总是很挤常常堵车。公共汽车也非常挤。当然你可以坐出租车。出租车不挤，可是不便宜。

要是你从一个城市去另一个城市，你可以坐飞机、火车，也可以坐长途汽车。长途汽车有时候不太舒服。

Dialogue 1

Ann：	我想租两辆自行车。
店主*：	有身份证吗？
Ann：	有。这是我的护照。
店主：	好。您租哪种车？
Ann：	我要一辆小的。我的朋友要一辆大的。
店主：	你们租几天？
Ann：	一天。
店主：	那两辆山地车不错。你们试试吧。
Ann：	这辆车的闸好象不太灵。
店主：	是吗？我给你紧一紧。
Ann：	这些车怎么都没有灯？
店主：	在城里用不着灯。
Ann：	好吧。我租这两辆。多少钱？

店主：	这辆大的一天十八块。那辆小的一天十五块。一共三十三块。
Ann：	给您四十块。
店主：	找您七块。

*店主　　diànzhǔ　*shopkeeper*

Dialogue 2

Ann：	师傅，我的车带坏了，您能帮我修修吗？
师傅：	没问题。
Ann：	得多长时间？
师傅：	一会儿就行。
Ann：	师傅，抽支烟吧。
师傅：	好、好。谢谢、谢谢。
Ann：	师傅，去香山还有多远？
师傅：	往北骑二十分钟，再往西拐就到了。……修好了。
Ann：	真快。谢谢您。这辆车的闸不太灵，您能看看吗？
师傅：	可以。我给你紧紧。……行了。
Ann：	谢谢您。一共多少钱？
师傅：	补车带两块五。紧闸就不收你钱了。
Ann：	谢谢师傅。您再抽支烟吧。

Dialogue 3

安音：	你好象有点儿不高兴。
Ben：	没什么。
安音：	你的手怎么了？
Ben：	哦，我摔了一跤。
安音：	怎么回事？
Ben：	真倒霉！我跟别人撞车了。
安音：	是谁的错？
Ben：	我说是他的错，他说是我的错。
安音：	车撞坏了吗？

Ben： 撞坏了。

安音： 你们找警察了吗？

Ben： 找了。警察说我们都有错。

安音： 后来呢？

Ben： 后来，我们都去修自己的车了。

Dialogue 4

警察： 您有什么事？

Ben： 我的包丢了。

警察： 包里面有什么？

Ben： 有我的护照和钱包。钱包里有我的信用卡、四百多人民币和两百美元。哦，还有一个小照相机。

警察： 您丢了护照，应该通知你们国家的大使馆。

Ben： 我给大使馆打电话了。

警察： 您现在住在哪儿？

Ben： 玉龙饭店三零一房间。

警察： 请您先回去。我们一有消息就马上通知您。

第十九课　学中文

19　learning Chinese

中文还是汉语

中文一般指汉语。中文的"中"是中国的中。文是 writing 或者 language 的意思。汉语的"汉"是汉族的汉。"语"是语言的语，也是 language 的意思。汉语就是汉族人的语言。中国的很多少数民族都有自己的语言。

汉语有很多种方言。上海话是一种方言。上海人说上海话。广东话也是一种方言。广东人和香港人说广东话。

我们学习的中文是普通话。普通话不是方言，是官方语言。台湾人叫它国语，东南亚的华人叫它华语。国语和华语就是普通话。普通话不是北京话。北京话和普通话差不多。很多北京人说的普通话有北京口音。

Dialogue 1

华岩：　你的中文真棒，说得真流利。

兰音：　哪里、哪里，说得不好。

华岩：　你的语音、声调都非常好。

兰音：　不行，不行，还差得很远。

华岩：　你学了几年了？

兰音：　三年了。

华岩：　什么？只有三年？！你太聪明了。

兰音：　你过奖了。

华岩：　我学了六年英语了，可是说得还很差。

兰音：　你真谦虚。

华岩：　你一定要告诉我你的学习方法。

兰音：　很简单。我先生是中国人。

Dialogue 2

老师：　你们好。我姓唐，是你们的老师。你们可以叫我唐老师。我还不认识你们。先请大家介绍一下儿自己。

为民：　我是俄国人。我叫白为民。白是李白的白。我很喜欢中国文学。将来我想当翻译。

安芳：　我姓崔，叫崔安芳。我是韩国人。我对中国音乐很有兴趣。我现在在学习二胡和琵琶。

文哲：　我是美国人。我的中文名字叫史文哲。史是历史的史，文是文学的文，哲是哲学的哲。我也喜欢中国文学。我更喜欢中国哲学。我要研究孔子、老子和庄子。

兰音：　我是英国人。我对中国的少数民族很有兴趣。我将来想研究他们的历史和语言。

老师：	你叫什么名字？
兰音：	哦，对不起。我叫兰音，我还不知道将来做什么，可能当记者。
山本：	我叫山本，是日本人。我现在在研究中国经济。
老师：	谢谢大家的介绍。

Dialogue 3

老师：	你们觉得中文难不难？
山本：	汉字不难，语音很难。
兰音：	因为你是日本人，会写汉字，所以你觉得汉字不难。我觉得汉字太难了。
兰音：	汉字不容易，可是语法更难。我总是不知道什么时候用‘了’，什么时候不用‘了’。
为民：	汉语语法不太难，声调真不容易。我常常说不好第二声和第四声。
安芳：	我觉得第三声最难。
老师：	中文不容易，可是只要我们多听、多说、多读、多写，我们就一定可以学好。

第二十课　旅行和天气
20　travel and weather

气候和天气

中国很大，东、西、南、北的气候常常很不一样。
一般来说，南方的夏天比北方的热，北方的冬天比南方的冷。

在中国，大部分地方有四个季节：春、夏、秋、冬。春天从三月到五月。六月、七月、八月是夏天。秋天是九、十和十一月。十二月到二月是冬天。一般七、八月最热；一、二月最冷。

中国人比较喜欢春天和秋天，因为春天和秋天不冷
也不热。

Dialogue 1

Colin：　这几天天津特冷，可是风景真美。昨天下
　　　　雪了。

素兰：　雪大吗？

Colin：　不小。天气预报说，明天还要下雪。

素兰：　昆明从来不下雪。我真想去天津看雪。

Colin：　你那儿天气怎么样？

素兰：　不暖和。今天的气温是十五度。

Colin：　什么？十五度？跟天津的春天一样暖和。

素兰：　可是我觉得冷。今天上午下了小雨。

Colin：　我最喜欢小雨。可是天津冬天很少下雨。

素兰：　你来昆明看雨，我去天津看雪，怎么样？

Colin：　真是个好主意！我来安排吧。

素兰：　等一等，那么我们在哪儿见面呢？

Dialogue 2

老师：　假期你们打算去哪儿？

山本：　我喜欢大城市。我想去上海，然后去广州。
　　　　上海和广州的经济最发达。

兰音：　我不喜欢大城市。我要去云南和贵州。那儿
　　　　有很多少数民族。

文哲：　云南和贵州都在中国的南方，夏天一定很
　　　　热。我去山西的五台山。那儿一定很凉快。

为民：　这个假期我有工作。我去天津给一个代表团
　　　　当翻译。

老师：　安芳，你呢？

安芳：　我真羡慕你们。可是我要回韩国。我太想我
　　　　爸爸、妈妈了。开学的时候我再回来。

Dialogue 3

老师： 你们怎么去？

为民： 天津不远。我坐火车去。两、三个小时就到了。

兰音： 云南离北京很远。我可以坐火车，也可以坐飞机。我还没有决定。

老师： 飞机比火车快多了，可是也贵多了。

文哲： 五台山不远也不近。我想先坐火车，再坐长途汽车。

老师： 山本，你要去两个地方。你怎么去？

山本： 我想坐飞机到上海，再坐火车去广州。

安芳： 我不喜欢坐飞机，可是我只能坐飞机回国。

老师： 好。祝大家假期愉快。

第二十一课　谈感想
21　experiences, feelings and reflections

去中国学习

每年有很多外国人去中国学习。他们学习中国的语言、文学、文化、历史、宗教，等等。在中国的一百多所大学里，有几万个外国留学生。

去中国旅游的外国人越来越多。他们很多人对中国的文化和历史感兴趣。很多人去过中国很多次。

这几年去中国工作的外国人也越来越多。在中国的外资企业和合资企业也越来越多。很多公司都想在中国扩大生意。

Dialogue 1

老师： 同学们，你们假期过得好吗？

学生们： 很好。不太好。非常好。还可以。

老师： 请每个人都谈一谈，好吗？

文哲：	我去了五台山。那里一切都好，就是饭不好。
老师：	饭怎么不好？
文哲：	他们不吃肉。可是我最爱吃肉，所以我常常觉得饿。
为民：	你应该跟我一起去天津。我们的代表团每天都有宴会。
老师：	兰音，少数民族的饭你吃得惯吗？
兰音：	开始的时候吃不惯，后来就吃得惯了。那些少数民族的人真友好。
老师：	那儿是不是很热？
兰音：	我去的地方是山区，所以不太热。那儿的风景美极了。
老师：	山本，你对上海和广州有什么印象？
山本：	这两个城市的经济都发展得很快。可惜我听不懂上海话和广东话。
老师：	这两种方言都不容易懂。安芳，你爸爸，妈妈都好吗？
安芳：	他们都很好，谢谢您。 我爸爸、妈妈说下个假期他们要来中国。我们一起在中国旅游。
大家：	那太好了！

Dialogue 2

记者：	福特先生，祝您生日快乐！
福特：	谢谢，谢谢。
记者：	您在中国几年了？
福特：	差不多十二年了。
记者：	您一直在大学工作吗？
福特：	对。我非常喜欢当老师。
记者：	在中国您对什么最满意？
福特：	当然是我的工作。我们学校的教学越来越好。
记者：	那么您对什么最不满意？

福特： 我对很多事情不满意。可是很难说对什么最
不满意。

记者： 您打算怎么庆祝您的生日？

福特： 早上我太太给我做了中国的长寿面。晚上同
事们来我家包饺子。

记者： 您的生日过得真有中国特色。

福特： 我现在已经是半个中国人了。

teach yourself

mandarin chinese conversation
elizabeth scurfield & song lianyi

- Do you want to talk with confidence?
- Are you looking for basic conversation skills?
- Do you want to understand what people say to you?

Mandarin Chinese Conversation is a 3-hour, all-audio course to use at any time, whether you want a quick refresher before a trip or you are a complete beginner. The 20 dialogues on CDs 1 and 2 will teach you the Chinese you will need to speak and understand, without getting bogged down with grammar. CD 3, uniquely, teache skills for listening and understanding. The perfect accompaniment t Beginner's Chinese and Chinese in the teach yourself range.